D1487165

IRELAND

Hotels and Restaurants – Town Plans

1997

Northern Ireland
& the Republic of Ireland

Dear Reader

*This Guide is an extract
from the Michelin Guide
« Great Britain and Ireland » 1997
and has been created
specially for your visits
to Ireland.*

*Independently compiled by our inspectors,
the Guide provides travellers
with a wide choice of establishments
at all levels of comfort and price.*

*We are committed to providing readers
with the most up to date information
and this edition has been produced
with the greatest care.*

*That is why only this year's guide
merits your complete confidence.*

*Thank you for your comments,
which are always appreciated.*

Bon voyage

Contents

How to use this guide

This guide offers a selection of hotels and restaurants to help the motorist on his travels. In each category establishments are listed in order of preference according to the degree of comfort they offer.

CATEGORIES

Luxury in the traditional style	
Top class comfort	
Very comfortable	
Comfortable	
Quite comfortable	
Simple comfort	
Other recommended accommodation, at moderate prices	

without rest.   The hotel has no restaurant

The restaurant also offers accommodation   with rm

PEACEFUL ATMOSPHERE AND SETTING

Certain establishments are distinguished in the guide by the red symbols shown below.

Your stay in such hotels will be particularly pleasant or restful, owing to the character of the building, its decor, the setting, the welcome and services offered, or simply the peace and quiet to be enjoyed there.

to ⋔	Pleasant hotels
XXXXX to X	Pleasant restaurants
« Park »	Particularly attractive feature
⑤	Very quiet or quiet, secluded hotel
⑤	Quiet hotel
⩽ sea	Exceptional view
⩽	Interesting or extensive view

The maps located at the beginning of each regional section in the guide indicate places with such peaceful, pleasant hotels and restaurants.

By consulting them before setting out and sending us your comments on your return you can help us with our enquiries.

HOTEL FACILITIES

In general the hotels we recommend have full bathroom and toilet facilities in each room. This may not be the case, however for certain rooms in categories 🏨, 🏠, ✿ and 🏠.

30 rm	Number of rooms
🛗	Lift (elevator)
▤	Air conditioning
📺	Television in room
⇥	Establishment either partly or wholly reserved for non-smokers
☎	Telephone in room: outside calls connected by the operator
☏	Telephone in room: direct dialling for outside calls
⚹	Rooms accessible to disabled people
🏠	Meals served in garden or on terrace
🖫 🔲	Outdoor or indoor swimming pool
🏋 ⚐s	Exercise room – Sauna
⚘	Garden
✗ 🏌18	Hotel tennis court – Golf course and number of holes
🎣	Fishing available to hotel guests. A charge may be made
👥 150	Equipped conference hall: maximum capacity
🚗	Hotel garage (additional charge in most cases)
Ⓟ	Car park for customers only
🐕✗	Dogs are excluded from all or part of the hotel
Fax	Telephone document transmission
May-October	Dates when open, as indicated by the hotelier
season	Probably open for the season – precise dates not available Where no date or season is shown, establishments are open all year round
BT42 3LZ	Postal code
(Forte)	Hotel Group

Animals

It is illegal to bring domestic animals (dogs, cats...) into the North and in the Republic of Ireland.

STARS

Certain establishments deserve to be brought to your attention for the particularly fine quality of their cooking. **Michelin stars** are awarded for the standard of meals served.

For such restaurants we list three culinary specialities typical of their style of cooking to assist you in your choice.

✿✿✿	**Exceptional cuisine, worth a special journey**
	One always eats here extremely well, sometimes superbly.
	Fine wines, faultless service, elegant surroundings. One will pay accordingly !
✿✿	**Excellent cooking, worth a detour**
	Specialities and wines of first class quality. This will be reflected in the price.
✿	**A very good restaurant in its category**
	The star indicates a good place to stop on your journey.
	But beware of comparing the star given to an expensive « de luxe » establishment to that of a simple restaurant where you can appreciate fine cuisine at a reasonable price.

☺ GOOD FOOD AT MODERATE PRICES

| ☺ | You may also like to know of other restaurants with less elaborate, moderately priced menus that offer good value for money and serve carefully prepared meals. We bring them to your attention by marking them with a red ☺ and **Meals** in the text of the Guide, e.g. **Meals** 19.00/25.00. |
| | Please refer to the map of stars and ☺ **Meals** rated restaurants located at the beginning of each regional section in the guide. |

Alcoholic beverages-conditions of sale

The sale of alcoholic drinks is governed in the North and in the Republic of Ireland by licensing laws which vary greatly from country to country.

Allowing for local variations, restaurants may stay open and serve alcohol with a bona fide meal during the afternoon. Hotel bars and public houses are generally open between 11am and 11pm at the discretion of the licensee. Hotel residents, however, may buy drinks outside the permitted hours at the discretion of the hotelier.

Children under the age of 14 are not allowed in bars.

PRICES

Prices quoted are valid for autumn 1996. Changes may arise if goods and service costs are revised.

Your recommendation is self-evident if you always walk into a hotel guide in hand.

Hotels and restaurants in bold type have supplied details of all their rates and have assumed responsibility for maintaining them for all travellers in possession of this guide.

Prices are given in £ sterling in Northern Ireland and Irish pounds (punt) in the Republic of Ireland.

Where no mention **s., t.,** or **st.** is shown, prices may be subject to the addition of service charge, V.A.T., or both.

Meals

Meals 13.00/28.00	**Set meals** – Lunch 13.00, dinner 28.00 – including cover charge, where applicable
Meals 19.00/25.00	See page 12
s. – t.	Service only included – V.A.T. only included
st.	Service and V.A.T. included
🍷 6.00	Price of 1/2 bottle or carafe of house wine
Meals a la carte 20.00/35.00	**A la carte meals** – The prices represent the range of charges from a simple to an elaborate 3 course meal and include a cover charge where applicable
🍵 8.50	Charge for full cooked breakfast (i.e. not included in the room rate) Continental breakfast may be available at a lower rate

↑ : Dinner in this category of establishment will generally be offered from a fixed price menu of limited choice, served at a set time to residents only. Lunch is rarely offered. Many will not be licensed to sell alcohol.

Rooms

rm 50.00/80.00	Lowest price 50.00 per room for a comfortable single and highest price 80.00 per room for the best double or twin
rm 🍵 55.00/ 85.00	Full cooked breakfast (whether taken or not) is included in the price of the room

Short breaks (SB)

Many hotels offer a special rate for a stay of two or more nights which comprises dinner, room and breakfast usually for a minimum of two people. Please enquire at hotel for rates.

Deposits – Credit cards

Some hotels will require a deposit, which confirms the commitment of customer and hotelier alike. Make sure the terms of the agreement are clear.

🔵 AE ⑩ VISA JCB	Credit cards accepted by the establishment: MasterCard (Eurocard, Access) – American Express – Diners Club – Visa – Japan Credit Bureau

TOWNS

✉ Kilkenny	Postal address
✆ 071 Sligo	STD dialling code (name of exchange indicated only when different from name of the town). Omit 0 when dialling from abroad
405 N 3, ④	Michelin map and co-ordinates or fold
pop. 1057	Population
BX **A**	Letters giving the location of a place on the town plan
⛳₁₈	Golf course and number of holes (handicap usually required, telephone reservation strongly advised)
✳, ≼	Panoramic view, viewpoint
✈	Airport
⛴	Shipping line
⛴	Passenger transport only
🛈	Tourist Information Centre

Standard Time

In winter standard time throughout the British Isles is Greenwich Mean Time (G.M.T.). In summer British clocks are advanced by one hour to give British Summer Time (B.S.T.). The actual dates are announced annually but always occur over weekends in March and October.

SIGHTS

Star rating

★★★	Worth a journey
★★	Worth a detour
★	Interesting
AC	Admission charge

Location

See	Sights in town
Envir.	On the outskirts
Exc.	In the surrounding area
N, S, E, W	The sight lies north, south, east or west of the town
A 22	Take road A 22, indicated by the same symbol on the Guide map
2 m.	Mileage

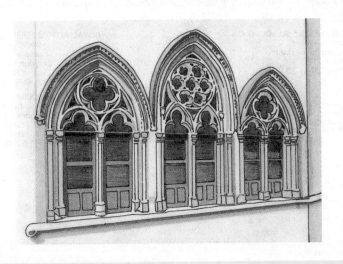

CAR, TYRES

The wearing of seat belts in Great Britain is obligatory for drivers, front seat passengers and rear seat passengers where seat belts are fitted. It is illegal for front seat passengers to carry children on their lap.

In the Republic of Ireland seat belts are compulsory, if fitted, for drivers and front seat passengers. Children under 12 are not allowed in front seats unless in a suitable safety restraint.

MICHELIN TYRE SUPPLIERS

The address of the nearest ATS tyre dealer can be obtained by contacting the address below between 9am and 5pm.

ATS NORTHERN IRELAND LTD
8 Donegall Square North,
Belfast, BT1 5GB
℘ (01232) 241037

MOTORING ORGANISATIONS

The major motoring organisations in Great Britain and Ireland are the Automobile Association and the Royal Automobile Club. Each provides services in varying degrees for non-resident members of affiliated clubs.

AUTOMOBILE ASSOCIATION
Fanum House
Basingstoke, Hants
RG21 2EA
℘ (01256) 20123

ROYAL AUTOMOBILE CLUB
RAC House
Lansdowne Rd
Croydon, Surrey
CR9 2JA
℘ (0181) 686 2525

AUTOMOBILE ASSOCIATION
23 Rock Hill
Blackrock
Co-Dublin
℘ (01) 283-3555

ROYAL AUTOMOBILE CLUB
RAC IRELAND
New Mount House
22-24 Lower Mount St.
Dublin 2
℘ (01) 6760113

TOWN PLANS

ⓐ ●a	**Hotels – Restaurants**
	Sights
	Place of interest and its main entrance
	Interesting place of worship
	Roads
M 1	Motorway
④ ④	Junctions : complete, limited
	Dual carriageway with motorway characteristics
	Main traffic artery
A2 N4	Primary route (network currently being reclassified)
◄ ⊏=====⊐	One-way street – Unsuitable for traffic, street subject to restrictions
⊏==⊐ ==	Pedestrian street
Patrick St. 🅿	Shopping street – Car park
╬ ╪╞ ╪╞	Gateway – Street passing under arch – Tunnel
15.5	Low headroom (16'6" max.) on major through routes
	Station and railway
o+++++o o-■-■-o	Funicular – Cable-car
△ 🅱	Lever bridge – Car ferry
	Various signs
🛈	Tourist Information Centre
☩ ✡	Mosque – Synagogue
⸸ ∴	Communications tower or mast – Ruins
▨ ᵗⁱᵗ	Garden, park, wood – Cemetery
◯ 🏇 ⌐	Stadium – Racecourse – Golf course
⚑	Golf course (with restrictions for visitors)
≼ �	View – Panorama
■ ◎ ⊞	Monument – Fountain – Hospital
⚓ ⛯	Pleasure boat harbour – Lighthouse
✈	Airport
⛴	Ferry services : passengers and cars
⊠	Main post office with poste restante, telephone
▭	Public buildings located by letter :
C H	County Council Offices – Town Hall
M T U	Museum – Theatre – University, College
POL.	Police (in large towns police headquarters)

North is at the top on all town plans.

Ami lecteur

Cette publication,
réalisée d'après le guide Michelin
« Great Britain and Ireland » 1997,
a été conçue spécialement
pour vos voyages en Irlande.

Réalisée en toute indépendance
par nos Inspecteurs,
elle offre au voyageur de passage
un large choix d'adresses
à tous les niveaux de confort et de prix.

Toujours soucieux d'apporter
à nos lecteurs l'information
la plus récente, nous avons mis à jour
cette édition avec le plus grand soin.

C'est pourquoi, seul,
le Guide de l'année en cours
mérite votre confiance.

Merci de vos commentaires toujours
appréciés.

MICHELIN vous souhaite « Bon voyage ! »

Sommaire

Comprendre

Ce guide vous propose une sélection d'hôtels et restaurants établie à l'usage de l'automobiliste de passage. Les établissements, classés selon leur confort, sont cités par ordre de préférence dans chaque catégorie.

CATÉGORIES

🏨	Grand luxe et tradition	XXXXX
🏨	Grand confort	XXXX
🏨	Très confortable	XXX
🏨	De bon confort	XX
🏨	Assez confortable	X
🏨	Simple mais convenable	
🏠	Autre ressource hôtelière conseillée, à prix modérés	
Without rest.	L'hôtel n'a pas de restaurant	
	Le restaurant possède des chambres	with rm

AGRÉMENT ET TRANQUILLITÉ

Certains établissements se distinguent dans le guide par les symboles rouges indiqués ci-après. Le séjour dans ces hôtels se révèle particulièrement agréable ou reposant.

Cela peut tenir d'une part au caractère de l'édifice, au décor original, au site, à l'accueil et aux services qui sont proposés, d'autre part à la tranquillité des lieux.

🏨 à 🏠	Hôtels agréables
XXXXX à X	Restaurants agréables
« Park »	Élément particulièrement agréable
🕭	Hôtel très tranquille ou isolé et tranquille
🕭	Hôtel tranquille
⩽ sea	Vue exceptionnelle
⩽	Vue intéressante ou étendue.

Les localités possédant des établissements agréables ou tranquilles sont repérées sur les cartes placées au début de chacune des régions traitées dans ce guide.

Consultez-les pour la préparation de vos voyages et donnez-nous vos appréciations à votre retour, vous faciliterez ainsi nos enquêtes.

L'INSTALLATION

Les chambres des hôtels que nous recommandons possèdent, en général, des installations sanitaires complètes. Il est toutefois possible que dans les catégories 🏠, 🏠, 🏡 et 🏠, certaines chambres en soient dépourvues.

30 ch	Nombre de chambres
⬆	Ascenseur
▤	Air conditionné
📺	Télévision dans la chambre
↢✗	Établissement entièrement ou en partie réservé aux non-fumeurs
☏	Téléphone dans la chambre relié par standard
☎	Téléphone dans la chambre, direct avec l'extérieur
♿	Chambres accessibles aux handicapés physiques
⛱	Repas servis au jardin ou en terrasse
⚓ ⬛	Piscine : de plein air ou couverte
⅃⭕ ⬛	Salle de remise en forme – Sauna
⚘	Jardin de repos
✗ ⛳	Tennis à l'hôtel – Golf et nombre de trous
⚓	Pêche ouverte aux clients de l'hôtel (éventuellement payant)
🏛 150	Salles de conférences : capacité maximum
🚗	Garage dans l'hôtel (généralement payant)
P	Parking réservé à la clientèle
🐕⃠	Accès interdit aux chiens (dans tout ou partie de l'établissement)
Fax	Transmission de documents par télécopie
May-October	Période d'ouverture, communiquée par l'hôtelier
season	Ouverture probable en saison mais dates non précisées. En l'absence de mention, l'établissement est ouvert toute l'année.
BT42 3LZ	Code postal de l'établissement
(Forte)	Chaîne hôtelière

Animaux
L'introduction d'animaux domestiques (chiens, chats...) est interdite en Irlande.

LES ÉTOILES

Certains établissements méritent d'être signalés à votre attention pour la qualité de leur cuisine. Nous les distinguons par **les étoiles de bonne table**.

Nous indiquons, pour ces établissements, trois spécialités culinaires qui pourront orienter votre choix.

❀❀❀ | **Une des meilleures tables, vaut le voyage**
On y mange toujours très bien, parfois merveilleusement, grands vins, service impeccable, cadre élégant... Prix en conséquence.

❀❀ | **Table excellente, mérite un détour**
Spécialités et vins de choix... Attendez-vous à une dépense en rapport.

❀ | **Une très bonne table dans sa catégorie**
L'étoile marque une bonne étape sur votre itinéraire.
Mais ne comparez pas l'étoile d'un établissement de luxe à prix élevés avec celle d'une petite maison où à prix raisonnables, on sert également une cuisine de qualité.

🐧 REPAS SOIGNÉS À PRIX MODÉRÉS

🐧 | Vous souhaitez parfois trouver des tables plus simples, à prix modérés ; c'est pourquoi nous avons sélectionné des restaurants proposant, pour un rapport qualité-prix particulièrement favorable, un repas soigné.
Ces restaurants sont signalés par 🐧 Meals. Ex. 🐧 Meals 19.00/25.00.
Consultez les cartes des localités (étoiles de bonne table et 🐧 Meals) placées au début de chacune des régions traitées dans ce guide.

La vente de boissons alcoolisées

En Irlande, la vente de boissons alcoolisées est soumise à des lois pouvant varier d'une région à l'autre.

D'une façon générale, les hôtels, les restaurants et les pubs peuvent demeurer ouverts l'après-midi et servir des boissons alcoolisées dans la mesure où elles accompagnent un repas suffisamment consistant. Les bars ferment après 23 heures.

Néanmoins, l'hôtelier a toujours la possibilité de servir, à sa clientèle, des boissons alcoolisées en dehors des heures légales.

Les enfants au-dessous de 14 ans n'ont pas accès aux bars.

LES PRIX

Les prix que nous indiquons dans ce guide ont été établis en automne 1996. Ils sont susceptibles de modifications, notamment en cas de variations des prix des biens et services.

Entrez à l'hôtel le guide à la main, vous montrerez ainsi qu'il vous conduit là en confiance.

Les hôtels et restaurants figurent en gros caractères lorsque les hôteliers nous ont donné tous leurs prix et se sont engagés, sous leur propre responsabilité, à les appliquer aux touristes de passage porteurs de notre guide. Les prix sont indiqués en livres sterling (1 L = 100 pence) en Irlande du Nord et en livres irlandaises (punt) pour la République d'Irlande. Lorsque les mentions **s., t.**, ou **st.** ne figurent pas, les prix indiqués peuvent être majorés d'un pourcentage pour le service, la T.V.A., ou les deux.

Repas

Meals 13.00/28.00	**Repas à prix fixe** – Déjeuner 13.00, diner 28.00. Ces prix s'entendent couvert compris
Meals 19.00/25.00	Voir page 24
s. – t.	Service compris – T.V.A. comprise
st.	Service et T.V.A. compris (prix nets)
⌅ 6.00	Prix de la 1/2 bouteille ou carafe de vin ordinaire
Meals à la carte 20.00/35.00	**Repas à la carte** – Le 1er prix correspond à un repas simple mais soigné, comprenant : petite entrée, plat du jour garni, dessert. Le 2e prix concerne un repas plus complet, comprenant : hors-d'œuvre, plat principal, fromage ou dessert. Ces prix s'entendent couvert compris
⊇ 8.50	Prix du petit déjeuner à l'anglaise, s'il n'est pas compris dans celui de la chambre. Un petit déjeuner continental peut être obtenu à moindre prix

✿: Dans les établissements de cette catégorie, le dîner est servi à heure fixe exclusivement aux personnes ayant une chambre. Le menu, à prix unique, offre un choix limité de plats. Le déjeuner est rarement proposé. Beaucoup de ces établissements ne sont pas autorisés à vendre des boissons alcoolisées.

Chambres

rm 50.00/80.00	Prix minimum 50.00 d'une chambre pour une personne et prix maximum 80.00 de la plus belle chambre occupée par deux personnes
rm ⊇ 55.00/ 85.00	Le prix du petit déjeuner à l'anglaise est inclus dans le prix de la chambre, même s'il n'est pas consommé

Short Breaks (SB)

Certains hôtels proposent des conditions avantageuses ou « Short Break » pour un séjour minimum de 2 nuits. Ce forfait, calculé par personne pour 2 personnes au minimum, comprend la chambre, le dîner et le petit déjeuner. Se renseigner auprès de l'hôtelier.

Les arrhes – Cartes de crédit

Certains hôteliers demandent le versement d'arrhes. Il s'agit d'un dépôt-garantie qui engage l'hôtelier comme le client. Bien faire préciser les dispositions de cette garantie.

🅼🅾 🄰🄴 🅾 **VISA** 🅹🅲🅱	Cartes de crédit acceptées par l'établissement : MasterCard (Eurocard, Access) – American Express – Diners Club – Visa – Japan Credit Bureau

LES VILLES

⊠ Kilkenny	Bureau de poste desservant la localité
☻ 071 Sligo	Indicatif téléphonique interurbain suivi, si nécessaire, de la localité de rattachement (de l'étranger, ne pas composer le 0)
405 N 3, ④	Numéro des cartes Michelin et carroyage ou numéro du pli
pop. 1057	Population
BX A	Lettres repérant un emplacement sur le plan
⛳18	Golf et nombre de trous (Handicap généralement demandé, réservation par téléphone vivement recommandée)
☀, ≤	Panorama, point de vue
✈	Aéroport
⛴	Transports maritimes
⛵	Transports maritimes (pour passagers seulement)
🛈	Information touristique

Heure légale

Les visiteurs devront tenir compte de l'heure officielle en Irlande : une heure de retard sur l'heure française.

LES CURIOSITÉS

Intérêts

★★★	Vaut le voyage
★★	Mérite un détour
★	Intéressant
AC	Entrée payante

Situation

See	Dans la ville
Envir.	Aux environs de la ville
Exc.	Excursions dans la région
N, S, E, W	La curiosité est située : au Nord, au Sud, à l'Est, à l'Ouest
A 22	On s'y rend par la route A 22, repérée par le même signe sur le plan du Guide
2 m.	Distance en miles

LA VOITURE, LES PNEUS

En Irlande du Nord, le port de la ceinture de sécurité est obligatoire pour le conducteur et le passager avant ainsi qu'à l'arrière, si le véhicule en est équipé. La loi interdit au passager avant de prendre un enfant sur ses genoux.

En République d'Irlande, le port de la ceinture de sécurité est obligatoire pour le conducteur et le passager avant, si le véhicule en est équipé. Les enfants de moins de 12 ans ne sont pas autorisés à s'asseoir à l'avant, sauf si le véhicule est muni d'un système d'attache approprié.

FOURNISSEURS DE PNEUS MICHELIN

Des renseignements sur le plus proche point de vente de pneus ATS pourront être obtenus en s'informant entre 9 h et 17 h à l'adresse indiquée ci-dessous.

ATS NORTHERN IRELAND LTD
8 Donegall Square North,
Belfast, BT1 5GB
☎ (01232) 241 037

Dans nos agences, nous nous faisons un plaisir de donner à nos clients tous conseils pour la meilleure utilisation de leurs pneus.

AUTOMOBILE CLUBS

Les principales organisations de secours automobile dans le pays sont l'Automobile Association et le Royal Automobile Club, toutes deux offrant certains de leurs services aux membres de clubs affiliés.

AUTOMOBILE ASSOCIATION
Fanum House
Basingstoke, Hants
RG21 2EA
☎ (01256) 20123

AUTOMOBILE ASSOCIATION
23 Rock Hill
Blackrock
Co-Dublin
☎ (01) 283-3555

ROYAL AUTOMOBILE CLUB
RAC House
Lansdowne Rd
Croydon, Surrey
CR9 2JA
☎ (0181) 686 2525

ROYAL AUTOMOBILE CLUB
RAC IRELAND
22-24 Lower Mount St.
Dublin 2
New Mount House
☎ (01) 6760113

LES PLANS

⊕ ●a	**Hôtels – Restaurants**

Curiosités
Bâtiment intéressant et entrée principale
Édifice religieux intéressant

Voirie
Autoroute
échangeurs : complet, partiel
Route à chaussées séparées de type autoroutier
Grand axe de circulation
Itinéraire principal (Primary route) réseau en cours de révision
Sens unique – Rue impraticable, réglementée
Rue piétonne
Patrick St. Rue commerçante – Parc de stationnement
Porte – Passage sous voûte – Tunnel
Passage bas (inférieur à 16'6") sur les grandes voies de circulation
Gare et voie ferrée
Funiculaire – Téléphérique, télécabine
Pont mobile – Bac pour autos

Signes divers
Information touristique
Mosquée – Synagogue
Tour ou pylône de télécommunication – Ruines
Jardin, parc, bois – Cimetière
Stade – Hippodrome – Golf
Golf (réservé)
Vue – Panorama
Monument – Fontaine – Hôpital
Port de plaisance – Phare
Airport
Transport par bateau : passagers et voitures
Bureau principal de poste restante, téléphone
Bâtiment public repéré par une lettre :
C H   Bureau de l'Administration du Comté – Hôtel de ville
M T U   Musée – Théâtre – Université, grande école
POL.   Police (commissariat central)

Les plans de villes sont disposés le Nord en haut.

Amico Lettore

*Questa pubblicazione ricavata
dalla « Guida Michelin
Great Britain and Ireland » 1997,
è stata realizzata appositamente
per i vostri viaggi in Irlanda.*

*Realizzata dai nostri ispettori
in piena autonomia offre al viaggiatore
di passaggio un'ampia scelta
a tutti i livelli di comfort e prezzo.*

*Con l'intento di fornire
ai nostri lettori l'informazione più recente,
abbiamo aggiornato questa edizione
con la massima cura.*

*Per questo solo la Guida dell'anno
in corso merita pienamente
la vostra fiducia.*

Grazie delle vostre segnalazioni sempre gradite.

Michelin vi augura "Buon Viaggio!"

Sommario

Come servirsi della Guida

Questa guida Vi propone una selezione di alberghi e ristoranti stabilita ad uso dell'automobilista di passaggio. Gli esercizi, classificati in base al confort che offrono, vengono citati in ordine di preferenza per ogni categoria.

CATEGORIE

🏰	Gran lusso e tradizione	XXXXX
🏨	Gran confort	XXXX
🏨	Molto confortevole	XXX
🏨	Di buon confort	XX
🏠	Abbastanza confortevole	X
🏡	Semplice, ma conveniente	
🏠	Altra risorsa, consigliata per prezzi contenuti	
without rest.	L'albergo non ha ristorante	
	Il ristorante dispone di camere	with rm

AMENITÀ E TRANQUILLITÀ

Alcuni esercizi sono evidenziati nella guida dai simboli rossi indicati qui di seguito. Il soggiorno in questi alberghi dovrebbe rivelarsi particolarmente ameno o riposante.

Ciò può dipendere sia dalle caratteristiche dell'edifico, dalle decorazioni non comuni, dalla sua posizione e dal servizio offerto, sia dalla tranquillità dei luoghi.

🏰 a 🏠	Alberghi ameni
XXXXX a X	Ristoranti ameni
« Park »	Un particolare piacevole
⅁	Albergo molto tranquillo o isolato e tranquillo
⅁	Albergo tranquillo
≤ sea	Vista eccezionale
≤	Vista interessante o estesa

Le località che possiedono degli esercizi ameni o tranquilli sono riportate sulle carte che precedono ciascuna delle regioni trattate nella guida.

Consultatele per la preparazione dei Vostri viaggi e, al ritorno, inviateci i Vostri pareri ; in tal modo agevolerete le nostre inchieste.

INSTALLAZIONI

Le camere degli alberghi che raccomandiamo possiedono, generalmente, delle installazioni sanitarie complete. È possibile tuttavia che nelle categorie 🏠, 🏠, ⚘ e ⚘ alcune camere ne siano sprovviste.

30 rm	Numero di camere
🛗	Ascensore
▦	Aria condizionata
TV	Televisione in camera
⚛	Esercizio riservato completamente o in parte ai non fumatori
☏	Telefono in camera collegato con il centralino
☎	Telefono in camera comunicante direttamente con l'esterno
🚹	Camere di agevole accesso per i minorati fisici
🏡	Pasti serviti in giardino o in terrazza
🏊 🏊	Piscina : all'aperto, coperta
🏋 🧖	Palestra – Sauna
🌳	Giardino da riposo
🎾 ⛳	Tennis appartenente all'albergo – Golf e numero di buche
🎣	Pesca aperta ai clienti dell' albergo (eventualmente a pagamento)
🏛 150	Sale per conferenze : capienza massima
🚗	Garage nell'albergo (generalmente a pagamento)
Ⓟ	Parcheggio riservato alla clientela
🐕	Accesso vietato ai cani (in tutto o in parte dell'esercizio)
Fax	Trasmissione telefonica di documenti
May-October	Periodo di apertura, comunicato dall'albergatore
season	Probabile apertura in stagione, ma periodo non precisato. Gli esercizi senza tali menzioni sono aperti tutto l'anno.
BT42 3LZ	Codice postale dell' esercizio
(Forte)	Catena alberghiera

Animali

L'introduzione di animali domestici (cani, gatti...),
in Irlanda, è vietata.

LE STELLE

Alcuni esercizi meritano di essere segnalati alla Vostra attenzione per la qualità tutta particolare della loro cucina. Noi li evidenziamo con le « **stelle di ottima tavola** ».

Per questi ristoranti indichiamo tre specialità culinarie e alcuni vini locali che potranno aiutarVi nella scelta.

✿✿✿	**Una delle migliori tavole, vale il viaggio** Vi si mangia sempre molto bene, a volte meravigliosamente, grandi vini, servizio impeccabile, ambientazione accurata... Prezzi conformi.
✿✿	**Tavola eccellente, merita una deviazione** Specialità e vini scelti... AspettateVi una spesa in proporzione.
✿	**Un'ottima tavola nella sua categoria** La stella indica una tappa gastronomica sul Vostro itinerario. Non mettete però a confronto la stella di un esercizio di lusso, dai prezzi elevati, con quella di un piccolo esercizio dove, a prezzi ragionevoli, viene offerta una cucina di qualità.

🙂 PASTI ACCURATI
A PREZZI CONTENUTI

🙂	Per quando desiderate trovare delle tavole più semplici a prezzi contenuti abbiamo selezionato dei ristoranti che, per un rapporto qualità-prezzo particolarmente favorevole, offrono un pasto accurato. Questi ristoranti sono evidenziati nel testo con la sigla 🙂 Meals evidenziata in rosso, davanti ai prezzi. Ex. 🙂 Meals 19.00/25.00. Consultate le carte delle località con stelle e con 🙂 Meals che precedono ciascuna delle regioni trattate nella guida.

La vendita di bevande alcoliche

Nell'Irlanda del Nord e in Repubblica d'Irlanda la vendita di bevande alcoliche è soggetta a leggi che possono variare da una regione all'altra.

In generale gli alberghi, i ristoranti e i pubs possono restare aperti il pomeriggio e servire bevande alcoliche nella misura in cui queste accompagnano un pasto abbastanza consistente. I bar chiudono dopo le ore 23.00.

L'albergatore ha tuttavia la possibilità di servire alla clientela bevande alcoliche anche oltre le ore legali.

Ai ragazzi inferiori ai 14 anni è vietato l'accesso ai bar.

I PREZZI

I prezzi che indichiamo in questa guida sono stati stabiliti nell'autunno 1996. Potranno pertanto subire delle variazioni in relazione ai cambiamenti dei prezzi di beni e servizi.

Entrate nell'albergo o nel ristorante con la guida in mano, dimostrando in tal modo la fiducia in chi vi ha indirizzato.

Gli alberghi e i ristoranti vengono menzionati in carattere grassetto quando gli albergatori ci hanno comunicato tutti i loro prezzi e si sono impegnati, sotto la propria responsabilità, ad applicarli ai turisti di passaggio, in possesso della nostra guida.

I prezzi sono indicati in lire sterline (1 £ = 100 pence) nell'Irlanda del Nord e in lire irlandesi (punt) nella Repubblica d'Irlanda.

Quando non figurano le lettere **s.**, **t.**, o **st.** i prezzi indicati possono essere maggiorati per il servizio o per l'I.V.A. o per entrambi.

Pasti

Meals 13.00/28.00	**Prezzo fisso** – Pranzo 13.00, cena 28.00.
Meals 19.00/25.00	Vedere p. 36
s. - t. - st.	Servizio compreso – I.V.A. compresa – Servizio ed I.V.A. compresi
🍶 6.00	Prezzo della mezza bottiglia o di una caraffa di vino
Meals a la carte 20.00/35.00	**Alla carta** – Il 1° prezzo corrisponde ad un pasto semplice comprendente : primo piatto, piatto del giorno con contorno, dessert. Il 2° prezzo corrisponde ad un pasto più completo comprendente : antipasto, piatto principale, formaggio e dessert
☕ 8.50	Prezzo della prima colazione inglese se non è compreso nel prezzo della camera. Una prima colazione continentale può essere ottenuta a minor prezzo

↑ : Negli alberghi di questa categoria, la cena viene servita, ad un'ora stabilita, esclusivamente a chi vi alloggia. Il menu, a prezzo fisso, offre una scelta limitata di piatti. Raramente viene servito anche il pranzo. Molti di questi esercizi non hanno l'autorizzazione a vendere alcolici.

Camere

rm 50.00/80.00	Prezzo minimo 50.00 per una camera singola e prezzo massimo 80.00 per la camera più bella per due persone
rm ☕ 55.00/ 85.00	Il prezzo della prima colazione inglese è compreso nel prezzo della camera anche se non viene consumata

« Short Breaks » (SB)

Alcuni alberghi propongono delle condizioni particolarmente vantaggiose o short break per un soggiorno minimo di due notti. Questo prezzo, calcolato per persona e per un minimo di due persone, comprende: camera, cena e prima colazione. Informarsi presso l'albergatore.

La caparra – Carte di credito:

Alcuni albergatori chiedono il versamento di una caparra. Si tratta di un deposito-garanzia che impegna tanto l'albergatore che il cliente. Vi raccomandiamo di farVi precisare le norme riguardanti la reciproca garanzia.

🅼🅲 AE ① VISA JCB	Carte di credito accettate dall'esercizio : MasterCard (Eurocard, Access) – American Express – Diners Club – Visa – Japan Credit Bureau

LE CITTÀ

✉ Kilkenny	Sede dell'ufficio postale
✆ 071 Sligo	Prefisso telefonico interurbano (nome del distretto indicato solo quando differisce dal nome della località). Dall'estero non formare lo 0
405 N 3, ④	Numero della carta Michelin e del riquadro o numero della piega
pop. 1057	Popolazione
BX **A**	Lettere indicanti l'ubicazione sulla pianta
⌁18	Golf e numero di buche (handicap generalmente richiesto, prenotazione telefonica vivamente consigliata)
✳, ≤	Panorama, punto di vista
✈	Aeroporto
⛴	Trasporti marittimi
⛴	Trasporti marittimi (solo passeggeri)
🛈	Ufficio informazioni turistiche

Ora legale

I visitatori dovranno tenere in considerazione l'ora ufficiale in Irlanda : un'ora di ritardo sull'ora italiana.

LE CURIOSITÀ

Grado di interesse

★★★	Vale il viaggio
★★	Merita una deviazione
★	Interessante
AC	Entrata a pagamento

Ubicazione

See	Nella città
Envir.	Nei dintorni della città
Exc.	Nella regione
N, S, E, W	La curiosità è situata : a Nord, a Sud, a Est, a Ovest
A 22	Ci si va per la strada A 22 indicata con lo stesso segno sulla pianta
2 m.	Distanza in miglia

L'AUTOMOBILE, I PNEUMATICI

Nell'Irlanda del Nord, l'uso delle cinture di sicurezza è obbligatorio per il conducente e il passeggero del sedile anteriore, nonchè per i sedili posteriori, se ne sono equipaggiati. La legge non consente al passeggero seduto davanti di tenere un bambino sulle ginocchia.

Nella Repubblica d'Irlanda, l'uso delle cinture di sicurezza è obligatorio per il conducente e il passeggero d'avanti, se il veicolo ne è equipaggiato. I bambini di meno di 12 anni non sono autorizzati a viaggiare sul sedile anteriore, a meno che questo non sia fornito di un sistema di ritenuta espressamente concepito per loro.

RIVENDITORI DI PNEUMATICI MICHELIN

Potrete avere delle informazioni sul più vicino punto vendita di pneumatici ATS, rivolgendovi, tra le 9 e le 17, all'indirizzo indicato qui di seguito :

ATS NORTHERN IRELAND LTD
8 Donegall Square North,
Belfast, BT1 5GB
℘ (01232) 241 037

Le nostre Succursali sono in grado di dare ai nostri clienti tutti i consigli relativi alla migliore utilizzazione dei pneumatici.

AUTOMOBILE CLUBS

Le principali organizzazioni di soccorso automobilistico sono l'Automobile Association ed il Royal Automobile Club : entrambe offrono alcuni loro servizi ai membri dei club affiliati.

AUTOMOBILE ASSOCIATION
Fanum House
Basingstoke, Hants
RG21 2EA
℘ (01256) 20123

ROYAL AUTOMOBILE CLUB
RAC House
Lansdowne Rd
Croydon, Surrey
CR9 2JA
℘ (0181) 686 2525

AUTOMOBILE ASSOCIATION
23 Rock Hill
Blackrock
Co-Dublin
℘ (01) 283-3555

ROYAL AUTOMOBILE CLUB
RAC IRELAND
New Mount House
22-24 Lower Mount St.
Dublin 2
℘ (01) 6760113

LE PIANTE

⊜ ●a		**Alberghi – Ristoranti**

Curiosità

Edificio interessante ed entrata principale
Costruzione religiosa interessante

Viabilità

Autostrada
   svincoli : completo, parziale,
Strada a carregiate separate di tipo autostradale
Asse principale di circolazione
Itinerario principale
   (« Primary route », rete stradale in corso di revisione)
Senso unico – Via impraticabile, a circolazione regolamentata
Via pedonale
Via commerciale – Parcheggio
Porta – Sottopassaggio – Galleria
Sottopassaggio (altezza inferiore a 16′6″) sulle grandi vie di
circolazione
Stazione e ferrovia
Funicolare – Funivia, Cabinovia
Ponte mobile – Battello per auto

Simboli vari

Ufficio informazioni turistiche
Moschea – Sinagoga
Torre o pilone per telecomunicazione – Ruderi
Giardino, parco, bosco – Cimitero
Stadio – Ippodromo – Golf
Golf riservato
Vista – Panorama
Monumento – Fontana – Ospedale
Porto per imbarcazioni da diporto – Faro
Aeroporto
Trasporto con traghetto : passeggeri ed autovetture
Ufficio centrale di fermo posta, telefono
Edificio pubblico indicato con lettera :
   Sede dell'Amministrazione di Contea – Municipio
   Museo – Teatro – Università, grande scuola
   Polizia (Questura, nelle grandi città)

Le piante topografiche sono orientate col Nord in alto

Lieber Leser

*Dieser Führer wurde als Auszug
aus dem Roten Michelin-Führer
« Great Britain and Ireland » 1997
für Ihre Reisen in Irland entwickelt.*

*Von unseren unabhängigen
Hotelinspektoren ausgearbeitet,
bietet der Hotelführer dem
Reisenden eine große Auswahl
an Hotels und Restaurants
in jeder Kategorie
sowohl was den Preis als
auch den Komfort anbelangt.*

*Stets bemüht, unseren Lesern
die neueste Information anzubieten,
wurde diese Ausgabe
mit größter Sorgfalt erstellt.*

*Deshalb sollten Sie immer
nur dem aktuellen Hotelführer
Ihr Vertrauen schenken.*

*Ihre Kommentare
sind uns immer willkommen.*

Gute Reise mit Michelin !

Inhaltsverzeichnis

Zum Gebrauch des Führers

Die Auswahl der in diesem Führer aufgeführten Hotels und Restaurants ist für Durchreisende gedacht. In jeder Kategorie drückt die Reihenfolge der Betriebe (sie sind nach ihrem Komfort klassifiziert) eine weitere Rangordnung aus.

KATEGORIEN

🏨	Großer Luxus und Tradition	XXXXX
🏛	Großer Komfort	XXXX
🏠	Sehr komfortabel	XXX
🏦	Mit gutem Komfort	XX
🏚	Mit standard Komfort	X
🕏	Bürgerlich	
🏠	Preiswerte, empfehlenswerte Gasthäuser und Pensionen	
without rest.	Hotel ohne Restaurant	
	Restaurant vermietet auch Zimmer	with rm

ANNEHMLICHKEITEN

Manche Häuser sind im Führer durch rote Symbole gekennzeichnet (s. unten). Der Aufenthalt in diesen ist wegen der schönen, ruhigen Lage, der nicht alltäglichen Einrichtung und Atmosphäre sowie dem gebotenen Service besonders angenehm und erholsam.

🏨 bis 🏠	Angenehme Hotels
XXXXX bis X	Angenehme Restaurants
« Park »	Besondere Annehmlichkeit
🕉	Sehr ruhiges, oder abgelegenes und ruhiges Hotel
🕉	Ruhiges Hotel
≤ sea	Reizvolle Aussicht
≤	Interessante oder weite Sicht

Die den einzelnen Regionen vorangestellten Übersichtskarten, auf denen die Orte mit besonders angenehmen oder ruhigen Häusern eingezeichnet sind, helfen Ihnen bei der Reisevorbereitung. Teilen Sie uns bitte nach der Reise Ihre Erfahrungen und Meinungen mit. Sie helfen uns damit, den Führer weiter zu verbessern.

Die meisten der empfohlenen Hotels verfügen über Zimmer, die alle oder doch zum größten Teil mit einer Naßzelle ausgestattet sind. In den Häusern der Kategorien 🏨, 🏠, 🛎 und 🛏 kann diese jedoch in einigen Zimmern fehlen.

30 rm	Anzahl der Zimmer
🛗	Fahrstuhl
▤	Klimaanlage
📺	Fernsehen im Zimmer
🚭	Hotel ganz oder teilweise reserviert für Nichtraucher
☏	Zimmertelefon mit Außenverbindung über Telefonzentrale
☎	Zimmertelefon mit direkter Außenverbindung
♿	Für Körperbehinderte leicht zugängliche Zimmer
☂	Garten-, Terrassenrestaurant
🛝 🛏	Freibad, Hallenbad
🏋 ⌘	Fitneßraum – Sauna
🛋	Liegewiese, Garten
✗ 🏌	Hoteleigener Tennisplatz – Golfplatz und Lochzahl
⌐	Angelmöglichkeit für Hotelgäste, evtl. gegen Gebühr
👥 150	Konferenzräume : Höchstkapazität
🚗	Hotelgarage (wird gewöhnlich berechnet)
Ⓟ	Parkplatz reserviert für Gäste
🐕	Hunde sind unerwünscht (im ganzen Haus bzw. in den Zimmern oder im Restaurant)
Fax	Telefonische Dokumentenübermittlung
May-October	Öffnungszeit, vom Hotelier mitgeteilt
season	Unbestimmte Öffnungszeit eines Saisonhotels. Die Häuser, für die wir keine Schließungszeiten angeben, sind im allgemeinen ganzjährig geöffnet
BT42 3LZ	Angabe des Postbezirks (hinter der Hoteladresse)
(Forte)	Hotelkette

Tiere

Das Mitführen von Haustieren (Hunde, Katzen u. dgl.) ist bei der Einreise in Irland untersagt.

DIE STERNE

Einige Häuser verdienen wegen ihrer überdurchschnittlich guten Küche Ihre besondere Beachtung. Auf diese Häuser weisen die Sterne hin.

Bei den mit « **Stern** » ausgezeichneten Betrieben nennen wir drei kulinarische Spezialitäten, die Sie probieren sollten.

❀❀❀ | **Eine der besten Küchen : eine Reise wert**
Mar ißt hier immer sehr gut, öfters auch hervorragend, edle Weine, tadelloser Service, gepflegte Atmosphäre ... entsprechende Preise.

❀❀ | **Eine hervorragende Küche : verdient einen Umweg**
Ausgesuchte Menus und Weine ... angemessene Preise.

❀ | **Eine sehr gute Küche : verdient Ihre besondere Beachtung**
Der Stern bedeutet eine angenehme Unterbrechung Ihrer Reise.
Vergleichen Sie aber bitte nicht den Stern eines sehr teuren Luxusrestaurants mit dem Stern eines kleineren oder mittleren Hauses, wo man Ihnen zu einem annehmbaren Preis eine ebenfalls vorzügliche Mahlzeit reicht.

🐧 SORGFÄLTIG ZUBEREITETE, PREISWERTE MAHLZEITEN

🐧 | Für Sie wird es interessant sein, auch solche Häuser kennenzulernen, die eine sehr gute, Küche zu einem besonders günstigen Preis/Leistungs-Verhältnis bieten. Im Text sind die betreffenden Restaurants durch die rote Angabe 🐧 **Meals** kenntlich gemacht, z. B Meals 19.00/25.00.
Siehe Karten der Orte mit Stern und 🐧 **Meals**, die den einzelnen im Führer behandelten Regionen vorangestellt sind.

Ausschank alkoholischer Getränke

In Großbritannien und Irland unterliegt der Ausschank alkoholischer Getränke gesetzlichen Bestimmungen, die in den einzelnen Gegenden verschieden sind.

Generell können Hotels, Restaurants und Pubs nachmittags geöffnet sein und alkoholische Getränke ausschenken, wenn diese zu einer entsprechend gehaltvollen Mahlzeit genossen werden. Die Bars schließen nach 23 Uhr.

Hotelgästen können alkoholische Getränke jedoch auch außerhalb der Ausschankzeiten serviert werden.

Kindern unter 14 Jahren ist der Zutritt zu den Bars untersagt.

PREISE

Die in diesem Führer genannten Preise wurden uns im Herbst 1996 angegeben. Sie können sich mit den Preisen von Waren und Dienstleistungen ändern.

Halten Sie beim Betreten des Hotels den Führer in der Hand. Sie zeigen damit, daß Sie aufgrund dieser Empfehlung gekommen sind.

Die Preise sind in Nordirland in Pfund Sterling und in der Republik Irland in Irischem Pfund (punt) angegeben.

Wenn die Buchstaben **s., t.,** oder **st.** nicht hinter den angegebenen Preisen aufgeführt sind, können sich diese um den Zuschlag für Bedienung und/oder MWSt erhöhen. Die Namen der Hotels und Restaurants, die ihre Preise genannt haben, sind fett gedruckt. Gleichzeitig haben sich diese Häuser verpflichtet, die von den Hoteliers selbst angegebenen Preise den Benutzern des Michelin-Führers zu berechnen.

Mahlzeiten

Meals 13.00/28.00	**Feste Menupreise** – Mittagessen 13.00, Abendessen 28.00
Meals 19.00/25.00	Siehe Seite 48
s. - t. - st.	Bedienung inkl. – MWSt inkl. – Bedienung und MWSt inkl.
₰ 6.00	Preis für 1/2 Flasche oder eine Karaffe Tafelwein
Meals a la carte	**Mahlzeiten « à la carte »** – Der erste Preis entspricht einer
20.00/35.00	einfachen aber sorgfältig zubereiteten Mahlzeit, bestehend aus kleiner Vorspeise, Tagesgericht mit Beilage und Nachtisch. Der zweite Preis entspricht einer reichlicheren Mahlzeit mit Vorspeise, Hauptgericht, Käse oder Nachtisch (inkl. Couvert)
☕ 8.50	Preis des englischen Frühstücks, wenn dieser nicht im Übernachtungspreis enthalten ist. Einfaches, billigeres Frühstück (Continental breakfast) erhältlich

⋔ : In dieser Hotelkategorie wird ein Abendessen normalerweise nur zu bestimmten Zeiten für Hotelgäste angeboten. Es besteht aus einem Menu mit begrenzter Auswahl zu festgesetztem Preis. Mittagessen wird selten angeboten. Viele dieser Hotels sind nicht berechtigt, alkoholische Getränke auszuschenken.

Zimmer (SB)

rm 50.00/80.00	Mindestpreis 50.00 für ein Einzelzimmer und Höchstpreis 80.00 für das schönste Doppelzimmer
rm ☕ 55.00/	Übernachtung mit englischem Frühstück, selbst wenn dieses
85.00	nicht eingenommen wird

« Short Breaks » (SB)

Einige Hotels bieten Vorzugskonditionen für einen Mindestaufenthalt von zwei Nächten (Short Break). Der Preis ist pro Person kalkuliert, bei einer Mindestbeteiligung von zwei Personen und schließt das Zimmer, das Abendessen und das Frühstück ein.

Anzahlung – Kreditkarten

Einige Hoteliers verlangen eine Anzahlung. Diese ist als Garantie sowohl für den Hotelier als auch für den Gast anzusehen.

🅼🅲 🅰🅴 🅾 *VISA* 🅹🅲🅱	Vom Haus akzeptierte Kreditkarten : MasterCard (Eurocard, Access) – American Express – Diners Club – Visa (Carte Bleue) – Japan Credit Bureau

STÄDTE

✉ Kilkenny	Zuständiges Postamt
✆ 071 Sligo	Vorwahlnummer und evtl. zuständiges Fernsprechamt (bei Gesprächen vom Ausland aus wird die erste Null weggelassen)
405 N 3, ④	Nummer der Michelin-Karte und Koordinaten des Planfeldes oder Faltseite
pop. 1057	Einwohnerzahl
BX A	Markierung auf dem Stadtplan
⛳18	Öffentlicher Golfplatz und Lochzahl (Handicap erforderlich, telefonische Reservierung empfehlenswert)
※, ≤	Rundblick, Aussichtspunkt
✈	Flughafen
⛴	Autofähre
⛴	Personenfähre
🛈	Informationsstelle

Uhrzeit

In Nordirland und in der Republik Irland ist eine Zeitverschiebung zu beachten und die Uhr gegenüber der deutschen Zeit um 1 Stunde zurückzustellen.

SEHENSWÜRDIGKEITEN

Bewertung

★★★	Eine Reise wert
★★	Verdient einen Umweg
★	Sehenswert
AC	Eintritt (gegen Gebühr)

Lage

See	In der Stadt
Envir.	In der Umgebung der Stadt
Exc.	Ausflugsziele
N, S, E, W	Im Norden (N), Süden (S), Osten (E), Westen (W) der Stadt
A 22	Zu erreichen über die Straße A 22
2 m.	Entfernung in Meilen

DAS AUTO, DIE REIFEN

In Nordirland herrscht Anschnallpflicht für Fahrer, Beifahrer und auf dem Rücksitz, wenn Gurte vorhanden sind. Es ist verboten, Kinder auf den Vordersitzen auf dem Schoß zu befördern. In der Republik Irland besteht für den Fahrer und den Beifahrer Anschnallpflicht, wenn Gurte vorhanden sind. Kinder unter 12 Jahren dürfen allerdings nicht auf den Vordersitzen befördert werden, es sei denn es existiert ein entsprechender Kindersitz.

LIEFERANTEN VON MICHELIN-REIFEN

Die Anschrift der nächstgelegenen ATS-Verkaufsstelle erhalten Sie auf Anfrage (9-17 Uhr) bei

ATS NORTHERN IRELAND LTD
8 Donegall Square North,
Belfast, BT1 5GB
☎ (01232) 241037

AUTOMOBILCLUBS

Die wichtigsten Automobilclubs des Landes sind die Automobile Association und der Royal Automobile Club, die den Mitgliedern der der FIA angeschlossenen Automobilclubs Pannenhilfe leisten und einige ihrer Dienstleistungen anbieten.

AUTOMOBILE ASSOCIATION
Fanum House
Basingstoke, Hants
RG21 2EA
☎ (01256) 20123

ROYAL AUTOMOBILE CLUB
RAC House
Lansdowne Rd
Croydon, Surrey
CR9 2JA
☎ (0181) 686 2525

AUTOMOBILE ASSOCIATION
23 Rock Hill
Blackrock
Co-Dublin
☎ (01) 283-3555

ROYAL AUTOMOBILE CLUB
RAC IRELAND
New Mount House
22-24 Lower Mount St.
Dublin 2
☎ (01) 6760113

STADTPLÄNE

⊜ ●a	**Hotels – Restaurants**	

Sehenswürdigkeiten

Sehenswertes Gebäude mit Haupteingang

Sehenswerter Sakralbau

Straßen

M 1 Autobahn

⓪ ⓪ Anschlußstellen : Autobahneinfahrt und/oder-ausfahrt,
Schnellstraße mit getrennten Fahrbahnen

Hauptverkehrsstraße

A 2 N 4 Fernverkehrsstraße (Primary route) Netz wird z.z. neu eingestuft

◄ ːːːːːː Einbahnstraße – Gesperrte Straße, mit Verkehrsbeschränkungen

Fußgängerzone

Patrick St. P Einkaufsstraße – Parkplatz

╬ ╬ ╬ Tor – Passage – Tunnel

15.5 Unterführung (Höhe angegeben bis 16'6") auf Hauptverkehrsstraßen

Bahnhof und Bahnlinie

Standseilbahn – Seilschwebebahn

⚠ B Bewegliche Brücke – Autofähre

Sonstige Zeichen

Informationsstelle

ᵈ ⊠ Moschee – Synagoge

Funk-, Fernsehturm – Ruine

Garten, Park, Wäldchen – Friedhof

⃝ 🐎 ⌐ Stadion – Pferderennbahn – Golfplatz

Golfplatz (Zutritt bedingt erlaubt)

Aussicht – Rundblick

▪ ◎ ⊞ Denkmal – Brunnen – Krankenhaus

Jachthafen – Leuchtturm

Flughafen

Schiffsverbindungen : Autofähre

⊗ Hauptpostamt (postlagernde Sendungen), Telefon

Öffentliches Gebäude, durch einen Buchstaben gekennzeichnet :

C H Sitz der Grafschaftsverwaltung – Rathaus

M T U Museum – Theater – Universität, Hochschule

POL. Polizei (in größeren Städten Polizeipräsidium)

Die Stadtpläne sind eingenordet (Norden = oben).

Starred establishments

Les établissements à étoiles
Gli esercizi con stelle
Die Stern-Restaurants

Republic of Ireland

Dublin	Patrick Guilbaud

Northern Ireland		**Republic of Ireland**	
Bangor	Shanks	Ahakista	Shiro
Belfast	Roscoff	Dublin	The Commons
Helen's Bay	Deanes on the Square	Dublin	Thornton's
		Kenmare	Park
		Kenmare	Sheen Falls Lodge

Good food at moderate prices

Repas soignés à prix modérés
Pasti accurati a prezzi contenuti
Sorgfältig zubereitete, preiswerte Mahzeiten

Meals

Northern Ireland		Dublin	Chapter One
Portrush	Ramore	Dublin	L'Ecrivain
		Dublin	Ernie's
Republic of Ireland		Dublin	Roly's Bistro
Castlebaldwin	Cromleach Lodge	Dun Laoghaire	Morels Bistro
Dingle	Doyle's Seafood Bar	Kenmare	d'Arcy's
		Kenmare	Lime Tree

Particularly pleasant hotels and restaurants

Hôtels et restaurants agréables
Alberghi e ristoranti ameni
Angenehme Hotels und Restaurants

Northern Ireland			Ballingarry	Mustard Seed	🏨
Holywood	Rayanne House	🏛		at Echo Lodge	
Belfast	Cottage (without rest)	🏠	Cashel Bay	Cashel House	🏨
Coleraine	Greenhill House	🏠	Castlebaldwin	Cromleach Lodge	🏨
			Donegal	St Ernan's House	🏨
			Kanturk	Assolas Country House	🏨
			Shanagarry	Ballymaloe House	🏨
			Skibbereen	Liss Ard Lake Lodge	🏨
Republic of Ireland			Ahakista	Shiro	🏛
Straffan	Kildare H	🏨	Bagenalstown	Kilgraney	🏛
	& Country Club			Country House	
Kenmare	Park	🏨	Kenmare	Sallyport House	🏛
Kenmare	Sheen Falls Lodge	🏨		(without rest)	
Cashel	Cashel Palace	🏛	Leenane	Delphi Lodge	🏛
Dublin	The Clarence	🏛	Wicklow	Old Rectory	🏛
Gorey	Marlfield House	🏛	Kenmare	Lime Tree	🍴
Mallow	Longueville House	🏛	Inistioge	Berryhill	🏠
Wicklow	Tinakilly House	🏛	Kilkenny	Blanchville House	🏠

Northern
Ireland

Place with at least :

a hotel or restaurant .... ● Londonderry
a pleasant hotel or restaurant .. 🏨🏨, 🛏, ✗
a quiet, secluded hotel .... 🍃
a restaurant with .. 🕸, 🕸🕸, 🕸🕸🕸, 🍴 **Meals**
See this town for establishments
  located in its vicinity .... BELFAST

Localité offrant au moins :

une ressource hôtelière ...... ● Londonderry
un hôtel ou restaurant agréable 🏨🏨, 🛏, ✗
un hôtel très tranquille, isolé .... 🍃
une bonne table à .. 🕸, 🕸🕸, 🕸🕸🕸, 🍴 **Meals**
Localité groupant dans le texte
  les ressources de ses environs .... BELFAST

La località possiede come minimo :

una risorsa alberghiera ...... ● Londonderry
Albergo o ristorante ameno .... 🏨🏨, 🛏, ✗
un albergo molto tranquillo, isolato ...... 🍃
un'ottima tavola con .. 🕸, 🕸🕸, 🕸🕸🕸, 🍴 **Meals**
La località raggruppa nel suo testo
  le risorse dei dintorni .... BELFAST

Ort mit mindestens :

einem Hotel oder Restaurant ● Londonderry
ein angenehmes Hotel oder Restaurant . 🏨🏨, 🛏, ✗
einem sehr ruhigen und abgelegenen Hotel 🍃
einem Restaurant mit . 🕸, 🕸🕸, 🕸🕸🕸, 🍴 **Meals**
Ort mit Angaben über Hotels und Restaurants
  in der Umgebung .... BELFAST

ANNALONG (Áth na Long) Down **405** O 5 Ireland G. – pop. 1 937 – ✪ 0139 67.

Exc. : W : Mourne Mountains★★ ·:– Bryansford, Tollymore Forest Park★★ *AC*, Annalong Marine Park and Cornmill★ *AC* – Silent Valley Reservoir★ (≼★) – Spelga Pass
and Dam★ – Drumena Cashel and Souterrain★ – Kilbroney Forest Park (view-
point★).

Belfast 37 – Dundalk 36.

   🏠   Glassdrumman Lodge
        85 Mill Rd BT34 4RH 𝒫 68451, Fax 67041
        🐦, ≼ Irish Sea and Mourne mountains, 🎾, park – 📺 ☎ 🅿. 🆖 🅰🅴 🅾 💳. 🎿
        Meals (booking essential) (communal dining) (dinner only) 27.50/35.00 **t.**
        🍷 6.00 – **8 rm** 🖙 85.00/110.00 **t.**, 2 suites – SB.

BALLYCASTLE (Baile an Chaistil) Antrim **405** N 2 – ✪ 01265 7.

🏌 Cushendall Rd 𝒫 62536.

🏛 7 Mary St. BT54 6QH 𝒫 62024.

Belfast 55 – Ballymena 27 – Coleraine 22.

   🏠   Marine
        North St. BT64 6BN 𝒫 62222, Fax 69507
        ≼ Fair Head and Rathlin Island, 🛠, ⛉, ▣ – ▮ 🍴 rm 📺 ☎ 🅿 – 🏋 150. 🆖 🅰🅴
        🅾 💳. 🎿
        Meals (bar lunch)/dinner 13.50 **t.** and a la carte 🍷 3.95 – **32 rm** 🖙 50.00/
        70.00 **t.** – SB.

BALLYCLARE (Bealach Cláir) Antrim **405** N/O 3 – ✪ 01232.

🏌 25 Springvale Rd 𝒫 (019603) 42352/24542.

Belfast 10 – Ballymena 14 – Larne 10.

   ✗✗   Ginger Tree
        29 Ballyrobert Rd BT39 9RY, S : 3 ¼ m. by A 57 on B 56 𝒫 848176
        🅿. 🆖 🅰🅴 🅾 💳 🇯🇨🇧
        closed Sunday, 12-13 July and 25-26 December – **Meals** - Japanese - 10.75/
        26.75 and a la carte 🍷 5.25.

BALLYMENA (An Baile Meánach) Antrim **405** N 3 Ireland G. – pop. 28 717 –
✪ 01266.

Exc. : Antrim Glens★★★ ·:– Murlough Bay★★★ (Fair Head ≼★★★) Glengariff Forest
Park★★ *AC* (Waterfall★★) Glengariff★, Glendun★, Rathlin Island★ – Antrim (Shane's
Castle Railway★ *AC*, Round Tower★) S : 9 ½m. by A 26.

🏌 128 Raceview Rd 𝒫 861207/861487.

🏛 Ardeevin, Council Offices, 80 Galgorm Rd, BT42 1AB 𝒫 44111 – Morrows Shop,
13-15 Bridge St., BT43 5EJ 𝒫 653663 (summer only).

Belfast 28 – Dundalk 78 – Larne 21 – Londonderry 51 – Omagh 53.

   🏠🏠   Galgorm Manor
        BT42 1EA, W : 3 ¾ m. by A 42 on Cullybackey rd 𝒫 881001, Fax 880080
        🐦, ≼, « Part 19C country house on banks of River Main », 🐾, 🎾, park –
        ▤ rest 📺 ☎ 🅿 – 🏋 400. 🆖 🅰🅴 🅾 💳. 🎿
        closed 24 to 27 December – **Meals** 15.00/25.00 **st.** – 🖙 9.50 – **23 rm** 95.00/
        120.00 – SB.

   🏠   Country House
        20 Doagh Rd BT42 3LZ, SE : 6 m. by A 36 on B 59 𝒫 891663, Fax 891477
        🐦, 🛠, ⛉, 🎾 – 📺 ☎ 🅿 – 🏋 150. 🆖 🅰🅴 🅾 💳
        closed 25 and 26 December – **Meals** *(closed Saturday lunch and Sunday
        dinner)* 11.95/17.95 **t.** and dinner a la carte 🍷 5.95 – **39 rm** 🖙 70.00/100.00 **t.**
        – SB.

🅿 ATS Antrim Rd 𝒫 652888

BANGOR (Beannchar) Down 405 O/P 4 – ☎ 01247.

ℹ 34 Quay St. BT20 5ED ✆ 270069.

Belfast 14 – Newtownards 5.

Marine Court
18-20 Quay St. BT20 5ED ✆ 451100, Fax 451200
Fa, ▭ – ▯ TV ☎ ♿ – ⛹ 300. MC AE ⊙ VISA. ✗
Meals *(closed lunch Monday and Tuesday)* a la carte 10.00/25.00 **t.** 🍷 4.00 – **51 rm** ☐ 75.00/90.00 **st.** – SB.

Clandeboye Lodge
Crawfordsburn Rd, Clandeboye BT19 1UR, SW : 3 m. by A 2 and B 170 following signs for Blackwood Golf Centre ✆ 852500, Fax 852772
18 – ▯ ✗ rm TV ☎ ♿ P – ⛹ 300. MC AE ⊙ VISA
closed 24 to 27 December – **Meals** (bar lunch)/dinner 17.50 **st.** 🍷 4.75 – ☐ 7.75 – **43 rm** 85.00/95.00 – SB.

Royal
26 Quay St. BT20 5ED ✆ 271866, Fax 467810
▯ TV ☎ – ⛹ 60. MC AE ⊙ VISA. ✗
closed 25 December – **Meals** 16.50 **t.** (dinner) and a la carte 8.20/22.75 **t.** 🍷 4.25 – **34 rm** ☐ 65.00/85.00 **t.** – SB.

Shelleven
61 Princetown Rd BT20 3TA ✆ 271777, Fax 271777
✗ TV ☎ P. MC VISA. ✗
Meals (by arrangement) 12.50 **st.** – **12 rm** ☐ 27.50/50.00 **st.**

Shanks
✿ The Blackwood, Crawfordsburn Rd, Clandeboye BT19 1GB, SW : 3 ¼ m. by A 2 and B 170 following signs for Blackwood Golf Centre ✆ 853313, Fax 853785
18 – P. MC AE VISA
closed Saturday lunch, Sunday, Monday and 24 to 26 December – **Meals** 14.95/28.50 **t.** 🍷 7.00
Spec. Duck confit and shiitake mushroom tart, Chinese five spice, Seared local scallops, baby leeks, porcini and white truffle aïoli, Caramelised banana tart with coconut ice cream.

ATS 161 Clandeboye Rd ✆ 271736

When visiting Ireland,
use the Michelin Green Guide **"Ireland"**.
– *Detailed descriptions of places of interest*
– *Touring programmes*
– *Maps and street plans*
– *The history of the country*
– *Photographs and drawings of monuments, beauty spots, houses...*

BELFAST (Béal Feirste) Antrim 🄰🄾🄴 O 4 Ireland G. – pop. 279 237 – ☎ 01232.

See : City★ - Ulster Museum★★ (Spanish Armada Treasure★★, Shrine of St. Patrick's Hand★) AZ **M1** – City Hall★ BZ – Donegall Square★ BZ **20** – Botanic Gardens (Palm House★) AZ – St Anne's Cathedral★ BY – Crown Liquor Saloon★ BZ – Sinclair Seamen's Church★ BY – St Malachy's Church★ BZ.

Env : Belfast Zoological Gardens★★ *AC*, N : 5 m. by A 6 AY.

Exc. : Carrickfergus (Castle★★ *AC*, St. Nicholas' Church★) NE : 9½m. by A 2 – Talnotry Cottage Bird Garden, Crumlin★ *AC*, W : 13½m. by A 52.

🄸🄸 Balmoral, 518 Lisburn Rd ✆ 381514, AZ – 🄸🄸 Belvoir Park, Newtownbreda ✆ 491693 AZ – 🄸🄸 Fortwilliam, Downview Av. ✆ 370770, AY – 🄸🄸 The Knock, Summerfield, Dundonald ✆ 482249, AZ – 🄸🄸 Shandon Park, 73 Shandon Park ✆ 793730, AZ – 🄹 Cliftonville, Westland Rd ✆ 744158/746595, AY – 🄹 Ormeau, 50 Park Rd ✆ 641069, AZ.

✈ Belfast International Airport, Aldergrove : ✆ (01849) 422888, W : 15½ m. by A 52 AY – Belfast City Airport : ✆ 457745 – **Terminal :** Coach service (Ulsterbus Ltd.) from Great Victoria Street Station (40 mn).

🚢 to Isle of Man (Douglas) (Isle of Man Steam Packet Co. Ltd) (summer only) (4 h 30 mn) – to Stranraer (Stena Line) 2-4 daily (3 h), (Sea Containers Ferries Scotland Ltd and Stena Line) (1 h 30 mn) – to Liverpool (Norse Irish Ferries Ltd) (11 h).

🄱 St. Annes Court, 59 North St., BT1 1NB ✆ 246609 – Belfast International Airport, BT29 4AB ✆ 422888 – Belfast City Airport, Sydenham Bypass, BT3 9JH ✆ 457745.

Dublin 103 – Londonderry 70.

Plans on following pages

🏨 **Europa**   BZ **e**
  Great Victoria St. BT2 7AP ✆ 327000, Fax 327800
  🛗 ⇎ rm ▤ rest 📺 ☎ & – 🛎 1000. 🄼🄾 🄰🄴 🄾 *VISA* . ⌘
  closed 24 and 25 December – **Gallery : Meals** *(closed Saturday lunch and Sunday dinner)* 13.95/22.95 **t.** and a la carte
  Brasserie : Meals a la carte 10.00/18.00 – ⌷ 10.00 – **179 rm** ⌷ 105.00/185.00 **st.**, 5 suites.

🏨 **Stormont**
  587 Upper Newtownards Rd BT4 3LP, E : 4 ½ m. by A 2 on A 20 ✆ 658621, Fax 480240
  🛗 ⇎ rm ▤ rest 📺 ☎ & 🄿 – 🛎 400. 🄼🄾 🄰🄴 🄾 *VISA*. ⌘
  closed 25 December – **McMaster's : Meals** *(closed Sunday dinner)* a la carte 12.50/22.50
  La Scala : Meals *(closed Sunday lunch)* a la carte approx. 14.00 – ⌷ 10.00 – **109 rm** 95.00/170.00 **st.** – SB.

🏨 **Dukes**   AZ **a**
  65 University St. BT7 1HL ✆ 236666, Fax 237177
  🕭, ⇆s – 🛗 ⇎ rm ▤ rest 📺 ☎ – 🛎 130. 🄼🄾 🄰🄴 🄾 *VISA*. ⌘
  Meals 10.50/15.00 **t.** – ⌷ 5.25 – **21 rm** 87.50/105.00 **st.** – SB.

🏨 **Holiday Inn Garden Court**   BZ **a**
  15 Brunswick St. BT2 7GE ✆ 333555, Fax 232999
  🛗 ⇎ rm 📺 ☎ & – 🛎 70
  76 rm.

🏨 **Holiday Inn Express**   AZ **z**
  106 University St. BT7 1HP ✆ 311909, Fax 311910
  🛗 ⇎ rm 📺 ☎ & 🄿 – 🛎 300. 🄼🄾 🄰🄴 🄾 *VISA* 🄹🄲🄱. ⌘
  Meals (buffet only) 6.95/12.95 **st.** – ⌷ 5.95 – **114 rm** 49.95 **st.**

🏨 **Stranmillis Lodge**   AZ **x**
  14 Chlorine Gdns. BT9 5DJ ✆ 682009, Fax 682009
  without rest. – ⇎ 📺 ☎ 🄿. 🄼🄾 🄰🄴 *VISA* 🄹🄲🄱. ⌘
  6 rm ⌷ 40.00/56.00 **t.**

⌂ **Ash Rowan**   AZ **c**
12 Windsor Av. BT9 6EE ℰ 661758, Fax 663227
🍴 – 📺 ☎ 🅿 ⓂⓈ *VISA* ⚗
closed 23 December-6 January – **Meals** (by arrangement) 25.00 **st.** – **4 rm**
� 46.00/72.00 **t.**

⌂ **Malone**   AZ **n**
79 Malone Rd BT9 6SH ℰ 669565
without rest. – 📺 🅿 ⚗
closed Christmas and New Year – **8 rm** ⊏ 33.00/48.00 **st.**

✕✕ **Roscoff** (Rankin)   AZ **r**
✿ 7 Lesley House, Shaftesbury Sq. BT2 7DB ℰ 331532, Fax 312093
▤. ⓂⓈ 🆎 ⓪ *VISA*
closed Saturday lunch, Sunday, 1 January, 12-13 July and 25 December –
Meals 16.95/28.95 **t.**

✕ **Nick's Warehouse**   BY **a**
37-39 Hill St. (1st Floor) BT1 2LB ℰ 439690, Fax 230514
▤. ⓂⓈ 🆎 ⓪ *VISA*
*closed Saturday lunch, Monday dinner, Sunday, 12-13 July, 25-26 December
and Bank Holidays* – **Meals** 19.95 **t.** (dinner) and lunch a la carte 15.85/22.80 **t.**
⌗ 4.00.

✕ **La Belle Epoque**   AZ **o**
61-63 Dublin Rd BT2 7HE ℰ 323244, Fax 323244
ⓂⓈ 🆎 ⓪ *VISA*
closed Saturday lunch, Sunday, 7-14 July and 25-26 December – **Meals** 15.00 **t.**
(dinner) and a la carte 14.25/20.00 **t.** ⌗ 5.00.

✕ **Strand**   AZ **e**
12 Stranmillis Rd BT9 5AA ℰ 682266, Fax 663189
ⓂⓈ 🆎 ⓪ *VISA*
Meals a la carte 12.85/17.80 **t.** ⌗ 4.25.

✕ **Saints and Scholars**   AZ **s**
3 University St. BT7 1FY ℰ 325137, Fax 323240
ⓂⓈ 🆎 ⓪ *VISA*
closed Saturday lunch, 12 July and 25 December – **Meals** 11.95 **t.** (lunch)
and a la carte 12.30/17.50 **t.** ⌗ 5.85.

✕ **Manor House**   AZ **u**
43-47 Donegall Pass BT7 1DQ ℰ 238755, Fax 238755
▤. ⓂⓈ ⓪ *VISA*
closed 25 and 26 December – **Meals** - Chinese (Canton) - 5.50/14.50 **t.**
and a la carte ⌗ 4.50.

at Dundonald E : 5 ½ m. on A 20 – AZ – ✉ Belfast – ✆ 01247 :

⌂ **Cottage**
377 Comber Rd BT16 0XB, SE : 1 ¾ m. on Comber Rd (A 22) ℰ 878189
without rest., 🍴 – ⤢ 🅿 ⚗
3 rm ⊏ 20.00/38.00.

at Dunmurry SW : 5 ½ m. on A 1 – AZ – ✉ Belfast – ✆ 01232 :

🏨 **Forte Posthouse Belfast**
300 Kingsway BT17 9ES ℰ 612101, Fax 626546
🍴, park – 📶 ⤢ rm ▤ rest 📺 ☎ 🅿 – 🔬 400. ⓂⓈ 🆎 ⓪ *VISA*
Meals *(closed Saturday lunch)* a la carte 15.85/21.65 **t.** ⌗ 6.95 – ⊏ 9.95 –
82 rm 85.00 **st.** – SB.

🔧 ATS **4** Duncrue St. ℰ 749531   🔧 ATS **37** Boucher Rd ℰ 663623

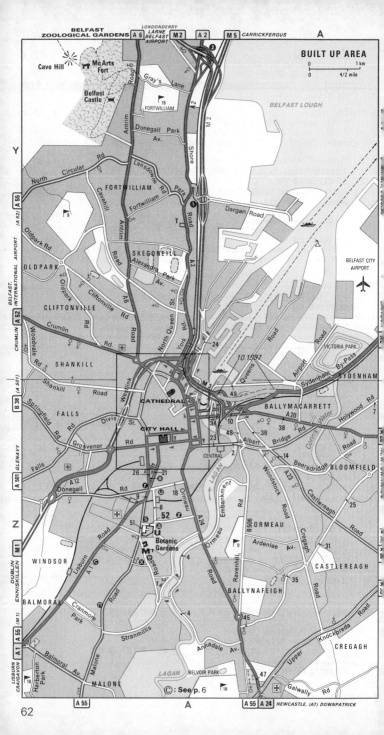

BELFAST

CENTRE

In Northern Ireland traffic and parking are controlled in the town centres. No vehicle may be left unattended in a Control Zone.

Your recommendation is self-evident if you always walk into a hotel Guide in hand.

BELFAST INTERNATIONAL AIRPORT (Aerphort Béal Feirste) Antrim 405 N 4 – ⊠ Aldergrove – ✪ 01849.

✈ Belfast International Airport, Aldergrove : ✆ 422888.

Belfast 15 – Ballymena 20 – Larne 23.

🏨 **Aldergrove**
Aldergrove BT29 4AB ✆ 422033, Fax 423500
ß, ⇌, – 🗘 ¾ rm ▤ 📺 ☎ 👌 👄 – 🔏 230. 🅼🅾 🅰🅴 🅾 𝘝𝘐𝘚𝘈. ✨
Meals 8.50/14.95 **st.** and dinner a la carte ⅄ 5.00 – ☲ 7.50 – **108 rm** 85.00 **st.**
– SB.

BELLEEK (Béal Leice) Fermanagh 405 H 4 – ✪ 0136 56.

Belfast 117 – Londonderry 56.

⌂ **Moohan's Fiddlestone**
Main St. BT93 3FY ✆ 58008
without rest. – 🅼🅾 𝘝𝘐𝘚𝘈
5 rm ☲ 18.00/36.00 **st.**

BUSHMILLS (Muileann na Buaise) Antrim 405 M 2 Ireland G. – pop. 1 348 – ⊠
Bushmills – ✪ 0126 57.

Exc. : Causeway Coast★★ : Giant's Causeway★★★ (Hamilton's Seat ≤★★), Carrick-a-rede Rope Bridge★★★, Dunluce Castle★★ AC, Gortmore Viewpoint★★ – Magilligan
Strand★★, Downhill★ (Mussenden Temple★).

🏌 Bushfoot, Portballintrae ✆ 31317.

Belfast 57 – Ballycastle 12 – Coleraine 10.

🏨 **Bushmills Inn**
25 Main St. BT57 8QA ✆ 32339, Fax 32048
« Part 18C » – 📺 ☎ 👄 – 🔏 100. 🅼🅾 𝘝𝘐𝘚𝘈
Meals 15.00 **t.** (dinner) and a la carte 15.00/19.00 **t.** ⅄ 6.15 – **11 rm** ☲ 55.00/
88.00 **st.** – SB.

CASTLEROCK (Carraig Ceasail) Londonderry – see Coleraine.

COLERAINE (Cúil Raithin) Londonderry 405 L 2 Ireland G. – pop. 20 721 –
✪ 01265.

Exc. : Antrim Glens★★★ :– Murlough Bay★★★ (Fair Head ≤★★★), Glenariff Forest
Park★★ AC (Waterfall★★) – Glenariff★, Glendun★, Rathlin Island★ – Causeway
Coast★★ : Giant's Causeway★★★ (Hamilton's Seat ≤★★) – Carrick-a-rede Rope
Bridge★★★ – Dunluce Castle★★ AC – Gortmore Viewpoint★★ – Magilligan Strand★★
– Downhill★ (Mussenden Temple★).

🏌, 🏌 Castlerock, Circular Rd ✆ 848314 – 🏌 Brown Trout, 209 Agivey Rd ✆ 868209.

🚉 Railway Rd, BT52 1PE ✆ 44723.

Belfast 53 – Ballymena 25 – Londonderry 31 – Omagh 65.

🏨 **Bushtown House**
283 Drumcroone Rd BT51 3QT, S : 2 ½ m. on A 29 ✆ 58367, Fax 320909
ß, ⇌, 🏊 – rm 📺 ☎ 👌 👄 – 🔏 250. 🅼🅾 🅰🅴 𝘝𝘐𝘚𝘈. ✨
closed 25 and 26 December – **Meals** 9.25/16.50 **t.** and dinner a la carte ⅄ 4.95
– **40 rm** ☲ 48.00/75.00 **t.** – SB.

⌂ **Greenhill House**
24 Greenhill Rd, Aghadowey BT51 4EU, S : 9 m. by A 29 on B 66 ✆ 868241,
Fax 868365
⊱, � – ¾ rest 📺 👄. 🅼🅾 🅰🅴 𝘝𝘐𝘚𝘈. ✨
March-October – **Meals** (by arrangement) 15.00 – **6 rm** ☲ 29.00/48.00 – SB.

⌂ **Camus House**
27 Curragh Rd BT51 3RY, SE : 3 ¾ m. on A 54 ✆ 42982
⊱ without rest., 🌣, �, park – ¾ 📺 👄. ✨
3 rm ☲ 25.00/45.00 **t.**

at Castlerock NW : 6 m. by A 2 on B 119 – ✉ Castlerock – ☎ 01265 :

Maritima House
43 Main St. BT51 4RA ☎ 848388
without rest., ≤, 🌳 – Ⓟ. ✗
3 rm ☕ 23.50/39.00 **s.**

ATS Loguestown Ind. Est., Bushmills Rd
☎ 42329

COOKSTOWN (An Chorr Chráochach) Tyrone 405 L 4 – ☎ 01648 7.

⛳18 Killymoon, 200 Killymoon Rd ☎ 63762/62254.

🅘 48 Molesworth St. BT80 8TA ☎ 66727.

Belfast 45 – Ballymena 27 – Londonderry 49.

Tullylagan Country House
40B Tullylagan Rd, Sandholes BT80 8UP, S : 4 m. by A 29 ☎ 65100, Fax 61715
🐎, 🎣, 🌳, park – TV ☎ ♿ Ⓟ. MC VISA. ✗
closed 24 to 26 December – **Meals** (bar lunch)/dinner a la carte 15.00/20.75 **st.** 🍷 4.95 – **15 rm** ☕ 45.00/90.00 **st.** – SB.

CRAWFORDSBURN (Sruth Chráfard) Down 405 O 4 **Ireland G.** – pop. 572 – ☎ 01247.

Env : Heritage Centre, Bangor★, E : 3 m. by B 20.

Exc. : – Priory (Cross Slabs★) – Mount Stewart★★★ *AC*, SE : 12 m. by A 2, A 21 and A 20 – Scrabo Tower (≤ ★★★), SW : 8 m. – Ballycopeland Windmill★ *AC*, E : 13 m. by A 2, A 21 and B 172 – Strangford Lough★ (Castle Espie Centre★ *AC* - Nendrum Monastery★) – Grey Abbey★ *AC*, SE : 14 m. by A 2, A 21 and A 20.

Belfast 10 – Bangor 3.

Old Inn
15 Main St. BT19 1JH ☎ 853255, Fax 852775
🌳 – TV ☎ Ⓟ – 🧑‍🏫 25. MC AE ◑ VISA. ✗
Meals 15.00/20.00 **t.** and a la carte 18.00/25.00 **t.** 🍷 4.75 – **33 rm** ☕ 70.00/135.00 **st.** – SB.

DUNADRY (Dún Eadradh) Antrim 405 N 3 **Ireland G.** – ☎ 01849.

Env : Antrim (Round tower★, Shane's Castle Railway★ *AC*) NW : 4 m. by A 6.

Exc. : Crumlin : Talnotry Cottage Bird Garden★ *AC*, SW : 10 ½m. by A 5, A 26 and A 52.

Belfast 15 – Larne 18 – Londonderry 56.

Dunadry
2 Islandreagh Drive BT41 2HA ☎ 432474, Fax 433389
🏋, 🏊, 🎣, 🌳 – ⇔ rm TV ☎ Ⓟ – 🧑‍🏫 300. MC AE ◑ VISA. ✗
closed 24 to 26 December – **Meals** (buffet lunch Saturday) 15.00/20.00 **st.** and a la carte – ☕ 6.00 – **67 rm** 92.50/115.00 **st.** – SB.

DUNDONALD (Dún Dónaill) Antrim 405 O 4 – see Belfast.

DUNGANNON (Dún Geanainn) Tyrone 405 L 4 – ☎ 01868.

Belfast 42 – Ballymena 37 – Dundalk 47 – Londonderry 60.

Cohannon Inn & Auto Lodge
212 Ballynakelly Rd BT71 6HJ, E : 6 ¼ m. by A 29 and M 1 on A 45 ☎ 724488, Fax 724488
🌳 – TV ♿ Ⓟ – 🧑‍🏫 30. MC AE ◑ VISA. ✗
Meals (carving lunch)/dinner a la carte 8.05/15.05 **st.** 🍷 3.95 – ☕ 3.95 – **50 rm** 31.95 **st.**

ATS 51 Oaks Rd ☎ 723772

DUNMURRY (Dún Muirígh) Antrim 405 N 4 – see Belfast.

ENNISKILLEN (Inis Ceithleann) Fermanagh 405 J 4 Ireland G. – pop. 11 436 – ✪ 01365.

Env : Castle Coole★★★ *AC*, SE : 1 m.

Exc. : NW : Lough Erne★★ : Cliffs of Magho Viewpoint★★★ *AC* – Devenish Island★ *AC* – Castle Archdale Country Park★ – White Island★ – Janus Figure★ – Tully Castle★ *AC* – Florence Court★★ *AC*, SW : 8 m. by A 4 and A 32 – Marble Arch Caves and Forest Nature Reserve★★ *AC*, SW : 10 m. by A 4 and A 32.

🔟 Castlecoole ℰ 325250.

🖪 Fermanagh Tourist Information Centre, Wellington Rd, BT74 7EF ℰ 323110.

Belfast 87 – Londonderry 59.

🏛 Manor House Country
   Killadeas BT94 1NY, N : 7 ½ m. by A 32 on B 82 ℰ (01365 6) 21561,
   Fax 21545
   ⅏, 𝄢, ≘s, 🖾 – 📳 ✎⃰ rm 📺 ☎ ᕤ 🅿 – 🔬 300. ✪◉ 🅰🅴 𝘝𝘐𝘚𝘈. ✎⃰
   Meals 9.90/20.50 **st.** and a la carte ⍟ 5.25 – **46 rm** 🖙 65.00/125.00 **t.** – SB.

   To visit a town or region : use the Michelin Green Guides.

HELEN'S BAY (Cuan Héilin) Down 405 O 3 – ✪ 01247.

Belfast 10 – Newtownards 9.

XX Deanes on the Square (Deane)
❀ 7 Station Sq. BT19 1TN, (possibly moving during 1997 to Howard St.,
   Belfast) ℰ 852841
   « Converted 19C railway station » – ✪◉ 🅰🅴 𝘝𝘐𝘚𝘈
   *closed Sunday dinner, Monday, 25-26 December, 1 week January and 1 week
   July* – **Meals** (dinner only and Sunday lunch) 25.95 **t.**
   Spec. Risotto of pearl barley and apple, seared foie gras and roast pigeon, Fillet of beef,
   remoulade of horseradish, truffle oil mash, Roulade of chocolate.

HILLSBOROUGH (Cromghlinn) Down 405 N 4 Ireland G. – ✪ 01846.

See : Town★ – Fort★.

Exc. : – The Argory★, W : 25 m. by A 1 and M 1.

Belfast 13.

🏛 White Gables
   14 Dromore Rd BT26 6HS, SW : ½ m. ℰ 682755, Fax 689532
   ✎⃰ rm 📺 rest 📺 ☎ 🅿 – 🔬 120. ✪◉ 🅰🅴 ① 𝘝𝘐𝘚𝘈. ✎⃰
   closed 24 and 25 December – **Meals** *(closed lunch Saturday, Sunday and Bank
   Holidays)* 16.50/22.50 **t.** and a la carte ⍟ 5.10 – 🖙 9.75 – **31 rm** 71.50/
   115.00 **t.**

X Hillside
   21 Main St. BT26 6AE ℰ 682765, Fax 682557
   ✪◉ 🅰🅴 ① 𝘝𝘐𝘚𝘈
   closed Sunday – **Meals** (dinner only) 22.00 **t.** and a la carte ⍟ 5.15.

HOLYWOOD (Ard Mhic Nasca) Down 405 O 4 Ireland G. – pop. 9 252 – ✪ 01232.

Env : Cultra : Ulster Folk and Transport Museum★★ *AC*, NE : 1 m. by A 2.

Belfast 5 – Bangor 6.

🏛 Culloden
   142 Bangor Rd BT18 0EX, E : 1 ½ m. on A 2 ℰ 425223, Fax 426777
   ≤, 𝄢, 🖾, ☞, park, ✎⃰ – 📳 ✎⃰ rm 📺 ☎ 🅿 – 🔬 500. ✪◉ 🅰🅴 ① 𝘝𝘐𝘚𝘈. ✎⃰
   closed 24 and 25 December – **Mitre : Meals** *(closed Saturday lunch)*
   22.50 **st.** and a la carte
   Cultra Inn : Meals *(closed Saturday lunch)* (grill rest.) 18.50/22.50 – 🖙 13.00 –
   80 rm 120.00/145.00 **st.**, 7 suites – SB.

🏠 **Rayanne House**
60 Demesne Rd BT18 9EX, by High St. and Downshire Rd ✆ 425859, Fax 425859
≼, ≈, ✉ – ✖ 🖵 🅿. 🅬🅢 🅐🅔 VISA. ✄
Meals *(closed Sunday)* (booking essential) (dinner only) (unlicensed) a la carte 20.90/27.00 **t.** – **6 rm** ⊐ 60.00/85.00 **t.** – SB.

✗ **Sullivans**
Unit 5, Sullivan Pl. BT18 9JF ✆ 421000, Fax 421000
🅬🅢 VISA
closed Sunday, 12 to 19 July and 25-26 December – **Meals** (restricted lunch) (unlicensed) 8.95/19.95 **t.** and a la carte.

IRVINESTOWN **(Baile an Irbhinigh)** Fermanagh 405 J 4 Ireland G. – pop. 1 906 – ✆ 0136 56.

Exc. : NW : Lough Erne★★ : Cliffs of Magho Viewpoint★★★ *AC* – Devenish Island★ *AC* – Castle Archdale Country Park★ – White Island★ – Janus Figure★ – Tully Castle★ *AC*.

Belfast 78 – Dublin 132 – Donegal 27.

🏠 **Mahon's**
2-10 Mill St. BT94 1GS ✆ 21656, Fax 28344
🖵 ☎ 🅿 – 🛆 300. 🅬🅢 🅐🅔 VISA. ✄
closed 25 December – **Meals** 8.95/11.50 **st.** and a la carte 🍷 3.75 – **18 rm** ⊐ 31.00/60.00 **st.** – SB.

LARNE **(Latharna)** Antrim 405 O 3 Ireland G. – pop. 17 575 – ✆ 01574.

Env : Glenoe Waterfall★, S : 5 m. by A 2 and B 99 – SE : Island Magee (Ballylumford Dolmen★).

Exc. : NW : Antrim Glens★★★ – Murlough Bay★★★ (Fair Head≼ ★★★), Glenariff Forest Park★★ *AC* (Waterfall★★), Glenariff★, Glendun★, Rathlin Island★.

🏌 Cairndhu, 192 Coast Rd, Ballygally ✆ 583248.

⛴ – to Cairnryan (P & O European Ferries Ltd) 4-6 daily (2 h 15 mn).

🛈 Narrow Gauge Rd, BT40 1XB ✆ 260088 – Carnfunnock Country Park, Coast Road, BT40 2QZ ✆ 270541.

Belfast 23 – Ballymena 20.

🏨 **Magheramorne House**
59 Shore Rd, Magheramorne BT40 3HW, S : 3 ½ m. on A 2 ✆ 279444, Fax 260138
≋, ≼, ≈, park – 🖪 🖵 ☎ 🅿 – 🛆 200. 🅬🅢 🅐🅔 🅞 VISA. ✄
Meals (bar lunch)/dinner 14.00 **st.** and a la carte 🍷 4.95 – **22 rm** ⊐ 48.50/66.00 **st.** – SB.

⌂ **Derrin House**
2 Prince's Gdns BT40 1RQ, off Glenarm Rd (A 2) ✆ 273269, Fax 273269
without rest. – 🖵 🅿. 🅬🅢 🅐🅔 VISA
closed 25 and 26 December – **7 rm** ⊐ 21.00/36.00 **st.**

◍ ATS Narrow Gauge Rd ✆ 274491

LIMAVADY **(Léim an Mhadaidh)** Derry 405 L 2 – ✆ 0150 47.

Belfast 62 – Ballymena 39 – Coleraine 13 – Londonderry 17 – Omagh 50.

🏨 **Radisson Roe Park H. & Golf Resort**
Roe Park BT49 9LB, W : ½ m. on A 2 ✆ 22212, Fax 22313
🛋, ≘s, 🖾, 🏌, ⚲, park – 🖪 🖵 ☎ 🅿 – 🛆 440. 🅬🅢 🅐🅔 🅞 VISA. ✄
Meals (bar lunch)/dinner 23.50 **st.** and a la carte 🍷 6.95 – **63 rm** ⊐ 85.00/150.00 **st.**, 1 suite – SB.

LONDONDERRY (Doire) Londonderry 🔢 K 2-3 Ireland G. – pop. 72 334 – ✱ 01504.

See : Town★ – City Walls and Gates★★ – Guildhall★ – St. Columb's Cathedral★ AC – Long Tower Church★ – Tower Museum★.

Env : Grianan of Aileach★★ (≤ ★) (Republic of Ireland) NW : 5 m. by A 2 and N 13.

Exc. : SE : by A 6 – Sperrin Mountains★ : Ulster-American Folk Park★★ – Glenshane Pass★★ (※★★) – Sawel Mountain Drive★ (≤★★) – Roe Valley Country Park★ – Ness Wood Country Park★ – Sperrin Heritage Centre★ AC – Beaghmore Stone Circles★ – Ulster History Park★ – Oak Lough Scenic Road★ – Eglinton★ – Gortin Glen Forest Park★ AC.

🇹₈, 🇹₉ City of Derry, 49 Victoria Rd ✆ 311610/46369.

✈ Eglinton Airport : ✆ 810784, E : 6 m. by A 2.

🅱 8 Bishop St., BT48 6PW ✆ 267284.

Belfast 70 – Dublin 146.

🏰 **Everglades**
   Prehen Rd BT47 2PA, S : 1 ½ m. by A 5 ✆ 46722, Fax 49200
   📞 TV ☎ 🅿 – 🖼 300. 🆗 ⚏ ⓪ 𝘝𝘐𝘚𝘈. ❄
   closed 25 December – **Meals** (closed Saturday lunch) 12.95/17.95 **st.** and dinner a la carte ⓘ 5.00 – **51 rm** ⊇ 75.00/95.00 **st.**, 1 suite – SB.

🏰 **Beech Hill House**
   32 Ardmore Rd BT47 3QP, SE : 3 ½ m. by A 6 ✆ 49279, Fax 45366
   🌿, 🌸, 🌾, park, ❤ – ❄ rest TV ☎ 🅿 – 🖼 100. 🆗 ⚏ 𝘝𝘐𝘚𝘈. ❄
   closed 24 and 25 December – **Meals** 15.95/21.95 **t.** and dinner a la carte ⓘ 5.95 – **17 rm** ⊇ 67.50/120.00 **t.** – SB.

🏰 **Waterfoot H. & Country Club**
   14 Clooney Rd, Caw Roundabout BT47 1TB, NE : 3 ¾ m. at junction of A 39 with A 5 and A 2 ✆ 45500, Fax 311006
   𝑓₆, 🛁, 🖼 – TV ☎ & 🅿 – 🖼 100. 🆗 ⚏ ⓪ 𝘝𝘐𝘚𝘈. ❄
   closed 25 and 26 December – **Meals** (grill rest.) a la carte 9.80/21.05 **st.** ⓘ 4.85 – ⊇ 6.00 – **48 rm** 57.50/67.50 **st.** – SB.

🏰 **White Horse**
   68 Clooney Rd BT47 3PA, NE : 6 ½ m. on A 2 (Coleraine rd) ✆ 860606, Fax 860371
   TV ☎ 🅿 – 🖼 350. 🆗 ⚏ ⓪ 𝘝𝘐𝘚𝘈. ❄
   Meals (grill rest.) a la carte 10.00/21.95 **t.** ⓘ 5.00 – ⊇ 5.25 – **43 rm** 50.00/65.00 **t.** – SB.

MAGHERA (Machaire Rátha) Londonderry 🔢 L 3 – ✱ 01648.

Belfast 40 – Ballymena 19 – Coleraine 21 – Londonderry 32.

🏰 **Ardtara Country House**
   8 Gorteade Rd, Upperlands BT46 5SA, N : 3 ¼ m. by A 29 off B 75 ✆ 44490, Fax 45080
   🌿, ≤, « 19C », 🌾, ❤ – TV ☎ 🅿. 🆗 ⚏ 𝘝𝘐𝘚𝘈. ❄
   closed 25 and 26 December – **Meals** (booking essential) 13.50 **t.** (lunch) and dinner a la carte 23.45/26.50 **t.** ⓘ 6.00 – **8 rm** ⊇ 75.00/100.00 **t.** – SB.

NEWCASTLE (An Caisleán Nua) Down 🔢 O 5 Ireland G. – pop. 7 214 – ✱ 01396 7.

Env : Castlewellan Forest Park★★ AC, NW : 4 m. by A 50 – Dundrum Castle★ AC NE : 4 m. by A 2.

Exc. : SW : Mourne Mountains★★ : Bryansford, Tollymore Forest Park★★ AC – Annalong Marine Park and Cornmill★ AC – Silent Valley Reservoir★ (≤★) – Spelga Pass and Dam★ – Drumena Cashel and Souterrain★ – Kilbroney Forest Park (view point★) – Loughinisland Churches★, NE : 10 m. by A 2 and A 24.

🅱 The Newcastle Centre, 10-14 Central Promenade, BT30 6LZ ✆ 22222.

Belfast 30 – Londonderry 101.

🏨 **Burrendale H. & Country Club**
51 Castlewellan Rd BT33 0JY, N : 1 m. on A 50 ℘ 22599, Fax 22328
↥, ⇌, ⬚, ☞ – 🛗 📺 ☎ ⅄ 🅿 – 🕍 150. 🐵 🆀 ⑩ *VISA*
Meals 9.50/18.00 **st.** and a la carte – **50 rm** � 55.00/80.00 **st.** – SB.

🏨 **Briars Country House**
39 Middle Tollymore Rd BT33 0JJ, N : 1 ½ m. by Bryansford Rd (B 180) and
Tollymore Rd ℘ 24347, Fax 24347
🐾, ≤, ☞ – ⇥ rm 📺 ☎ ⅄ 🅿. 🐵 🆀 *VISA*. ⌘
Meals (unlicensed) 10.00/16.00 **st.** – **9 rm** ⊻ 35.00/50.00 **st.** – SB.

PORTAFERRY (Port an Pheire) Down 🄳🄾🄵 P 4 **Ireland G.** – pop. 2 324 – ✆ 0124 77.

See : Aquarium★.

Env : Castle Ward★★ *AC*, SW : 4 m. by boat and A 25.

Exc. : SE : Lecale Peninsula★★ – Struell Wells★, Quoile Pondage★, Ardglass★,
Strangford★, Audley's Castle★.

🛈 Shore St., Nr Strangford Ferry Departure Point (summer only).

Belfast 29 – Bangor 24.

🏨 Portaferry
10 The Strand BT22 1PE ℘ 28231, Fax 28999
≤, « 18C, loughside setting » – 📺 ☎. 🐵 🆀 ⑩ *VISA*. ⌘
closed 24 and 25 December – **Meals** (bar lunch Monday to Friday October-
April) 14.00/22.50 **t.** and dinner a la carte ≬ 5.75 – **13 rm** ⊻ 55.00/90.00 **t.** –
SB.

PORT BALLINTRAE (Port Bhaile an Trá) Antrim 🄳🄾🄵 M 2 **Ireland G.** – pop. 756 –
✉ Bushmills – ✆ 0126 57.

Exc. : Causeway Coast★★ : Giant's Causeway★★★ (Hamilton's Seat ≤★★) – Carrick-
a-rede Rope Bridge★★★ – Dunluce Castle★★ *AC* – Gortmore Viewpoint★★ – Magilligan Strand★★ – Downhill★ (Mussenden Temple★).

Belfast 68 – Coleraine 15.

🏨 Bayview
2 Bayhead Rd BT57 8RZ ℘ 31453, Fax 32360
≤, ⇌, ⬚ – 📺 ☎ 🅿 – 🕍 100. 🐵 *VISA*
Meals (bar lunch)/dinner 15.00 **st.** and a la carte ≬ 3.50 – **16 rm** ⊻ 47.50/
85.00 **st.** – SB.

PORTRUSH (Port Rois) Antrim 🄳🄾🄵 L 2 **Ireland G.** – pop. 5 703 – ✆ 01265.

Exc. : Causeway Coast★★ : Giant's Causeway★★★ (Hamilton's Seat ≤★★) – Carrick-
a-rede Rope Bridge★★★ – Dunluce Castle★★ *AC* – Gortmore Viewpoint★★ – Magilligan Strand★★ – Downhill★ (Mussenden Temple★).

🛅, 🛅, 🛅 Royal Portrush, Dunluce Rd ℘ 822311.

🛈 Dunluce Centre, Sandhill Dr., BT56 8BT ℘ 823333 (summer only).

Belfast 58 – Coleraine 4 – Londonderry 35.

🏨 Magherabuoy House
41 Magheraboy Rd BT56 8NX, SW : 1 m. by A 29 ℘ 823507, Fax 824687
≤, ⇌, ☞ – ⇥ rest 📺 ☎ 🅿 – 🕍 300. 🐵 🆀 ⑩ *VISA*. ⌘
Meals (bar lunch)/dinner 15.00 **st.** ≬ 4.00 – **38 rm** ⊻ 50.00/80.00 **st.** – SB.

🏨 O'Neill's Causeway Coast
36 Ballyreagh Rd BT56 8LR, NW : 1 ¼ m. on A 2 (Portstewart rd) ℘ 822435,
Fax 824495
≤ – 📺 ☎ 🅿 – 🕍 500. 🐵 🆀 ⑩ *VISA*. ⌘
Meals (bar lunch)/dinner 14.00 **st.** and a la carte ≬ 4.95 – **21 rm** ⊻ 53.00/
99.00 **st.** – SB.

PORTRUSH

⚓ Glencroft
95 Coleraine Rd BT56 8HN ✆ 822902
🏡 – ⇔ TV P . ✀
closed 2 weeks November and 2 weeks Christmas – **Meals** (by arrangement) 14.00 **st.** – **5 rm** ⊃ 25.00/40.00 **st.**

XX Ramore
⚓ The Harbour BT56 8BN ✆ 824313
≼ – ▤ P . 🆚🆚 VISA
closed Sunday, Monday, 24 to 26 December and 1 January – **Meals** (booking
essential) (dinner only) a la carte 15.00/28.60 **t.** 🍷 5.25.

PORTSTEWART (Port Stíobhaird) Londonderry 🄰🄾🄵 L 2 Ireland G. – pop. 6 459 –
❀ 01265.

Exc. : Causeway Coast★★ : Giant's Causeway★★★ (Hamilton's Seat ≼★★) – Carrick-
a-rede Rope Bridge★★★ – Dunluce Castle★★ AC – Gortmore Viewpoint★★ – Magilligan Strand★★ – Downhill★ (Mussenden Temple★).

🎫 Town Hall, The Crescent, BT55 7AB ✆ 832286 (summer only).

Belfast 67 – Coleraine 6.

🏨 Edgewater
88 Strand Rd BT55 7LZ ✆ 833314, Fax 832224
≼, 🛁, ⫧ – TV ☎ P – 🏋 100. 🆚🆚 🄰🄴 🄾 VISA . ✀
Meals 8.50/15.00 **t.** and dinner a la carte 🍷 3.95 – **30 rm** ⊃ 35.00/84.00 **t.** –
SB.

SAINTFIELD (Tamhnaigh Naomh) Down 🄰🄾🄵 O 4 – pop. 2 780 – ❀ 01238.

Belfast 11 – Downpatrick 11.

X The Barn
120 Monlough Rd BT24 7EU, NW : 1 ¾ m. by A 7 ✆ 510396
🏡 – P . 🆚🆚 VISA
closed Sunday dinner, Monday and 25-26 December – **Meals** (dinner only and
Sunday lunch)/dinner 22.50 **t.** 🍷 4.50.

STRABANE (An Srath Bán) Tyrone 🄰🄾🄵 J 3 Ireland G. – pop. 11 981 – ❀ 01504.

Exc. : Sperrin Mountains★ : Ulster-American Folk Park★★ – Glenshane Pass★★
(🌲★★) – Sawel Mountain Drive★ (≼★★) – Roe Valley Country Park★ – Ness Wood
Country Park★ – Sperrin Heritage Centre★ AC – E : Beaghmore Stone Circles★ –
Ulster History Park★ – Oak Lough Scenic Road★ – Eglinton★ – Gortin Glen Forest
Park★ AC.

🏌 Ballycolman ✆ 382271/382007.

🎫 Abercorn Square, BT82 8DY ✆ 883735 (summer only) – Council Offices, 47 Derry
Rd, BT82 8DY ✆ 382204.

Belfast 87 – Donegal 34 – Dundalk 98 – Londonderry 14.

🏨 Fir Trees
Melmount Rd BT82 9JT, S : 1 ¼ m. on A 5 ✆ 382382, Fax 383116
TV ☎ P . 🆚🆚 🄰🄴 VISA . ✀
Meals (dinner only) 12.95 **t.** and a la carte 🍷 4.25 – **26 rm** ⊃ 33.00/50.00 **t.** –
SB.

TEMPLEPATRICK (Teampall Phádraig) Antrim 🄰🄾🄵 N 3 – pop. 1 414 – ✉ Bally-
clare – ❀ 0184 94.

Belfast 12 – Ballymena 16 – Dundalk 65 – Larne 16.

🏨 Templeton
882 Antrim Rd BT39 0AH ✆ 432984, Fax 433406
🏡 – TV ☎ P – 🏋 300. 🆚🆚 🄰🄴 🄾 VISA JCB . ✀
closed 24 to 27 December – **Templeton : Meals** (dinner only and Sunday
lunch)/dinner 16.95 **t.** and a la carte
Upton Grill : Meals (grill rest.) a la carte 6.35/17.40 – **24 rm** ⊃ 85.00/
125.00 **st.** – SB.

Republic
of
Ireland

Place with at least :

a hotel or restaurant .... ● Adare
a pleasant hotel .... 🏨🏨, ↑, X with rm
a quiet, secluded hotel .... ℬ
a restaurant with ..... ❀, ❀❀, ❀❀❀, 🍽 **Meals**
See this town for establishments
  located in its vicinity .... DUBLIN

Localité offrant au moins :

une ressource hôtelière .... ● Adare
un hôtel agréable .... 🏨🏨, ↑, X with rm
un hôtel très tranquille, isolé .... ℬ
une bonne table à .... ❀, ❀❀, ❀❀❀, 🍽 **Meals**
Localité groupant dans le texte
  les ressources de ses environs .... DUBLIN

La località possiede come minimo :

una risorsa alberghiera .... ● Adare
un albergo ameno .... 🏨🏨, ↑, X with rm
un albergo molto tranquillo, isolato .... ℬ
un'ottima tavola con .. ❀, ❀❀, ❀❀❀, 🍽 **Meals**
La località raggruppa nel suo testo
  le risorse dei dintorni .... DUBLIN

Ort mit mindestens :

einem Hotel oder Restaurant .... ● Adare
einem angenehmen Hotel . 🏨🏨, ↑, X with rm
einem sehr ruhigen und abgelegenen Hotel ℬ
einem Restaurant mit . ❀, ❀❀, ❀❀❀, 🍽 **Meals**
Ort mit Angaben über Hotels und Restaurants
  in der Umgebung .... DUBLIN

73

ACHILL ISLAND (Acaill) Mayo 405 B 5/6 Ireland G..

See : Island★.

🛈 Achill Sound ℘ 45384 (1 July-31 August).

Doogort (Dumha Goirt) – ✉ Achill Island – ☎ 098.

🏌9 Keel ℘ 43202.

⋔ Gray's
℘ 43244
🏊, 🚗 – ⍻ rest ℗
Meals (by arrangement) 15.00 t. – 15 rm ⛌ 24.00/40.00 t.

ADARE (Áth Dara) Limerick 405 F 10 Ireland G. – pop. 899 – ☎ 061.

See : Town★ – Adare Friary★.

Exc. : Rathkeale (Castle Matrix★ AC) W : 7 ½ m. by N 21 – Newcastle West★, W : 16 m. by N 21 – Glin Castle★ AC, W : 29 m. by N 21, R 518 and N 69.

🛈 ℘ 396255 (1 June-30 October).

Dublin 131 – Killarney 59 – Limerick 10.

🏰 Adare Manor
℘ 396566, Fax 396124
🏊, ≼, « 19C Gothic mansion in extensive parkland », 𝐼𝑏, ⛋, 🎿, 🏌8, ⚲, 🚗 – ❖ 🔟 ☎ ℗ – 🕍 180. 🆎 🅰🅴 ⓪ 𝑽𝑰𝑺𝑨. 🞉
Meals 21.50/32.50 t. and dinner a la carte – ⛌ 10.50 – 64 rm 195.00/ 315.00 st. – SB.

🏯 Dunraven Arms
Main St. ℘ 396633, Fax 396541
« Attractively furnished, antiques », 𝐼𝑏, 🎿, 🚗 – ❖ 🔟 ☎ ℗ – 🕍 150. 🆎 🅰🅴 𝑽𝑰𝑺𝑨. 🞉
Meals – (see Maigue below) – ⛌ 9.95 – 66 rm 80.00/160.00 t. – SB.

🏯 Woodlands House
Knockanes, SE : 2 m. by N 21 on Croom rd ℘ 396118, Fax 396073
🚗 – ❖ 🔟 ☎ ℗ – 🕍 350. 🆎 🞉
closed 24 and 25 December – Meals (bar lunch Monday to Saturday)/ dinner 13.95 st. ₰ 7.50 – 57 rm ⛌ 48.00/105.00 st. – SB.

⋔ Foxhollow
Knockanes, SE : 2 ¼ m. by N 21 on Croom rd ℘ 396776, Fax 396779
without rest., 🚗 – ⍻ 🔟 ℗. 🆎 𝑽𝑰𝑺𝑨. 🞉
3 rm ⛌ 22.00/34.00 t.

⋔ Adare Lodge
Kildimo Rd ℘ 396629
without rest. – ⍻ 🔟 ℗. 🆎 🅰🅴 𝑽𝑰𝑺𝑨 𝐉𝐂𝐁. 🞉
6 rm ⛌ 30.00/35.00 st.

⋔ Carrabawn House
Killarney Rd, SW : ½ m. on N 21 ℘ 396067, Fax 396925
without rest., 🚗 – 🔟 ☎ ℗. 🆎 𝑽𝑰𝑺𝑨
7 rm ⛌ 37.00/50.00 st.

⋔ Abbey Villa
Kildimo Rd ℘ 396113, Fax 396969
without rest. – 🔟 ℗. 🆎 𝑽𝑰𝑺𝑨. 🞉
closed 25 December – 6 rm ⛌ 17.50/40.00 st.

⋔ Village House
Main St. ℘ 396554, Fax 396903
without rest. – ℗. 🆎 𝑽𝑰𝑺𝑨. 🞉
April-October – 5 rm ⛌ 20.00/35.00 st.

⋔ Sandfield House
Castleroberts, SE : 3 ¼ m. by N 21 on Croom rd ℘ 396119, Fax 396119
without rest., 🚗 – ℗. 🆎 𝑽𝑰𝑺𝑨. 🞉
28 February-30 November – 4 rm ⛌ 24.00/42.00.

XX   Maigue (at Dunraven Arms H.)
     Main St.   ✆ 396633, Fax 396541
     🛋 – **P**. **MO** **AE** **O** **VISA**
     Meals (dinner only and Sunday lunch)/dinner 22.95 **t.** and a la carte ░ 5.35.

AHAKISTA (Áth an Chiste) Cork 405 D 13 – ⊠ Bantry – ☻ 027.

Dublin 217 – Cork 63 – Killarney 59.

XX   Shiro (Kei Pilz)
❀   ✆ 67030, Fax 67206
     ≤ Dunmanus Bay, 🛋 – **P**. **MO** **AE** **O** **VISA**
     Meals - Japanese - (booking essential) (dinner only) 42.00 **st.** ░ 10.00
     Spec. Sashimi, Tempura, Sushi.

ARAN ISLANDS (Oileáin Árann) Galway 405 CD 8 Ireland G.

See : Islands★ – Inishmore (Dun Aenghus★★★).

Access by boat or aeroplane from Galway city or by boat from Kilkieran, Rossaneel or Fisherstreet (Clare) and by aeroplane from Inverin.

🛈 ✆ 099 (Inishmore) 61263 (30 May-15 September).

Inishmore – ⊠ Aran Islands – ☻ 099.

⌂   Ard Einne
    Killeany ✆ 61126, Fax 61388
    ⌂, ≤ Killeany Bay – ☎. **MO** **VISA**. ❀
    March-9 November – **Meals** (by arrangement) 12.00 **st.** ░ 6.00 – **10 rm**
    ⇌ 28.00/33.00 **st.** – SB.

ATHLONE (Baile Átha Luain) Westmeath 405 I 7 Ireland G. – pop. 8 170 – ☻ 0902.

Exc. : Clonmacnois★★★ (Grave Slabs★, Cross of the Scriptures★) S : 13 m. by N 6 and N 62 – N : Lough Ree (Ballykeeran Viewpoint★★, Glassan★) – Clonfinlough Stone★, S : 11 ½m. by N 6 and N 62.

🛈₈ Hodson Bay ✆ 92073/92235.

🛈 Tourist Office, The Castle ✆ 94630/92856 (late April- mid October).

Dublin 75 – Galway 57 – Limerick 75 – Roscommon 20 – Tullamore 24.

🏰🏰🏰 Hodson Bay
       NW : 4 ¾ m. by N 61 ✆ 92444, Fax 92688
       ≤, 𝄈, ⩆, 🛋, 🟦, ❨, ❳ – ⧈ **TV** ☎ & **P** – 🔥 500. **MO** **AE** **O** **VISA**. ❀
       Meals 11.00/20.50 **st.** and dinner a la carte ░ 6.00 – **97 rm** ⇌ 92.00/150.00,
       2 suites – SB.

⌂   Shelmalier House
    Retreat Rd, Cartrontroy, E : 2 ½ m. by Dublin rd ✆ 72245, Fax 73190
    🛋 – **TV** ☎ **P**. **MO** **AE** **VISA**. ❀
    closed 24 and 25 December – **Meals** (by arrangement) 13.00 **st.** – **7 rm**
    ⇌ 21.00/32.00 **st.** – SB.

ATHY (Baile Átha Á) Kildare 405 L 9 – pop. 5 204 – ☻ 0507.

Dublin 40 – Kilkenny 29 – Wexford 59.

XX   Tonlegee House
     SW : 2 ¼ m. by N 78 ✆ 31473, Fax 31473
     ⌂ with rm – **TV** ☎ **P**. **MO** **AE** **VISA**
     closed 1 week spring, 2 weeks November and 23 to 27 December – **Meals**
     (closed Sunday to non-residents) (dinner only) a la carte 21.50/22.50 **st.** ░ 5.50
     – **9 rm** ⇌ 45.00/65.00 **st.** – SB.

AUGHRIM (Eachroim) Wicklow 🗍🗍🗍 N 9 – pop. 713 – 🌣 0402.

🗓 🖉 73939 (2 April-9 October).

Dublin 46 – Waterford 77 – Wexford 60.

🏠 Lawless's
🖉 36146, Fax 36384
🖙 – 📺 ☎ 🅿. 🕼 🖭 ⓪ 𝑉𝐼𝑆𝐴. ✼
closed 23-26 December – **Meals** (bar lunch Monday to Saturday)/dinner
18.50 **st.** and a la carte ⌖ 5.45 – **10 rm** ⇌ 58.50/78.25 **st.** – SB.

AVOCA (Abhóca) Wicklow 🗍🗍🗍 N 9 – pop. 494 – 🌣 0402.

Dublin 47 – Waterford 72 – Wexford 55.

🏠 Woodenbridge
Vale of Avoca, SW : 2 ¼ m. on R 752 🖉 35146, Fax 35573
🚗 – 📺 ☎ 🅿. 🕼 🖭 𝑉𝐼𝑆𝐴. ✼
Meals 10.95/15.95 **st.** and dinner a la carte ⌖ 5.50 – **23 rm** ⇌ 45.00/70.00 **st.**
– SB.

⋔ Keppel's Farmhouse
Ballanagh, S : 2 m. by unmarked road 🖉 35168
🖏, ≼, « Working farm », 🚗, park – ⋙. 🕼 𝑉𝐼𝑆𝐴. ✼
Easter-mid October – **Meals** (by arrangement) 14.00 **st.** – **5 rm** ⇌ 27.00/
36.00 **st.** – SB.

BAGENALSTOWN (Muine Bheag) Carlow 🗍🗍🗍 L 9 – 🌣 0503.

Dublin 63 – Carlow 10 – Kilkenny 13 – Wexford 37.

🏠 Kilgraney Country House
S : 3 ¾ m. by R 705 🖉 75283, Fax 75283
🖏, ≼, « Late Georgian house with collection of Philippine and other Eastern
furnishings and artefacts », 🚗 – ⋙ rm 🅿. 🕼 𝑉𝐼𝑆𝐴. ✼
March-November – **Meals** *(closed Sunday to Thursday, except June-August)*
(booking essential) (residents only) (communal dining) (dinner only) 22.00 **t.**
⌖ 5.00 – **5 rm** ⇌ 25.00/70.00 **t.** – SB.

BALLINA (Béal an Átha) Mayo 🗍🗍🗍 E 5 Ireland G. – pop. 6 563 – 🌣 096.

Env : Rosserk Abbey★, N : 4 m. by R 314.

Exc. : Moyne Abbey★, N : 7 m. by R 314 – Downpatrick Head★, N : 20 m. by R 314.

🏌 Mosgrove, Shanaghy 🖉 21050.

🗓 🖉 70848 (3 May-30 September).

Dublin 150 – Galway 73 – Roscommon 64 – Sligo 37.

🏠 Mount Falcon Castle
Foxford Rd, S : 4 m. on N 57 🖉 70811, Fax 71517
🖏, ≼, « Country house atmosphere », 🦢, park, ✕ – ☎ 🅿. 🕼 🖭 ⓪ 𝑉𝐼𝑆𝐴. ✼
closed February, March and 1 week Christmas – **Meals** (by arrangement)
(communal dining) (dinner only) 20.00 **st.** – **10 rm** ⇌ 33.00/49.00 **st.**

⋔ Brigown
Quay Rd, NE : 1 ¾ m. by N 59 🖉 22609, Fax 71247
without rest., 🚗 – 📺 🅿
4 rm ⇌ 20.00/32.00.

BALLINA (Béal an Átha) Tipperary 🗍🗍🗍 G 9 – 🌣 061.

🏠 Waterman's Lodge
🖉 376333, Fax 376333
🚗 – ⋙ rm ☎ 🅿. 🕼 𝑉𝐼𝑆𝐴. ✼
closed 24 to 26 December – **Meals** *(closed Monday)* (booking essential to
non-residents) (dinner only) 26.50 **t.** ⌖ 7.95 – **10 rm** ⇌ 40.00/90.00 **t.**

BALLINADEE (Baile na Daibhche) Cork **405** G 12 – ⊠ Bandon – ☎ 021.

Dublin 174 – Cork 20.

🏠 Glebe Country House
       𝒫 778294, Fax 778456
       ⤷, « Georgian rectory », 🐴 – ☎ 🅿. 🕮🕮 VISA
       Meals *(closed Sunday)* (by arrangement) (communal dining) (unlicensed) 5.00/
       16.50 **st.** – **3 rm** ⤶ 35.00/50.00 **st.** – SB.

BALLINASLOE (Béal Átha na Sluaighe) Galway **405** H 8 **Ireland G.** – pop. 5 793 –
☎ 0905.

Exc. : Turoe Stone, Bullaun★, SW : 18 m. by R 348 and R 350.

🏌 Ballinasloe 𝒫 42126 – 🏌 Mountbellew 𝒫 79259.

🅱 Main St. 𝒫 42131 (1 July-31 August).

Dublin 91 – Galway 41 – Limerick 66 – Roscommon 36 – Tullamore 34.

🏨 Haydens
       Dunlo St. 𝒫 42347, Fax 42895
       🐴 – 🛗 ▤ rest 📺 ☎ 🅿 – 🔬 250. 🕮🕮 🄰🄴 ① VISA. ✾
       closed 24 to 27 December – **Meals** 10.00/12.00 **t.** and dinner a la carte ᵢ 5.00 –
       ⤶ 5.75 – **48 rm** (dinner included) 33.00/58.00 **t.** – SB.

       "Short Breaks" (SB)
       Many hotels now offer a special rate for a stay of 2 or more nights
       which includes dinner, bed and breakfast.

BALLINCLASHET Cork **405** G 12 – see Kinsale.

BALLINDERRY (Baile an Doire) Tipperary **405** H 8 **Ireland G.** – ⊠ Nenagh –
☎ 067.

Exc. : Portumna★ (castle★) N : 9 ½m. by R 493 and N 65.

Dublin 111 – Galway 53 – Limerick 41.

🏠 Gurthalougha House
       W : 1 ¾ m. 𝒫 22080, Fax 22154
       ⤷, ≼, « Country house on banks of Lough Derg », ❧, 🐴, park, ✾ – ☎ 🅿.
       🕮🕮 🄰🄴 ① VISA
       March-October and weekends November and January – **Meals** (dinner
       only) 16.00 ᵢ 5.00 – **8 rm** ⤶ 38.00/76.00 **t.** – SB.

BALLINGARRY (Baile an GharraÁ) Limerick **405** F 10 – ☎ 069.

Dublin 141 – Killarney 56 – Limerick 18.

🏨 Mustard Seed at Echo Lodge
       𝒫 68508, Fax 68511
       ⤷, « Stylishly decorated Victorian house », 🐴 – 📺 & 🅿 – 🔬 25. 🕮🕮 🄰🄴
       VISA
       closed 24 to 27 December and late January-7 March – **Meals** (communal dining
       Sunday dinner residents only) (dinner only) 25.00/29.00 **t.** ᵢ 7.00 – **12 rm**
       ⤶ 75.00/150.00 **t.** – SB.

BALLYBOFEY (Bealach Féich) Donegal **405** I 3 – pop. 2 972 – ☎ 074.

🏌 Ballybofey & Stranorlar 𝒫 31093.

Dublin 148 – Londonderry 30 – Sligo 58.

🏨 Kee's
       Main St., Stranorlar, NE : ½ m. on N 15 𝒫 31018, Fax 31917
       🛁, 🛐, 🔲 – 📺 ☎ 🅿. 🕮🕮 🄰🄴 ① VISA
       Meals (bar lunch Monday to Saturday)/dinner 18.00 **st.** and a la carte ᵢ 6.00 –
       36 rm ⤶ 36.00/82.00 **st.** – SB.

BALLYBUNNION (Baile an Bhuinneánaigh) Kerry 405 D 10 Ireland G. – pop. 1 346 – ✪ 068.

Exc. : Carrigafoyle Castle★, NE : 13 m. by R 551 – Glin Castle★ *AC*, E : 19 m. by R 551 and N 69.

🛏, 🛏 Ballybunnion, Sandhill Rd ℘ 27146.

Dublin 176 – Limerick 56 – Tralee 26.

🏠 **Marine Links**
Sandhill Rd ℘ 27139, Fax 27666
≼ – 📺 ☎ 🅿. 🔟 AE ① VISA
10 March-October – **Meals** (bar lunch Monday to Saturday)/dinner 19.00 **t.**
and a la carte ⌀ 6.50 – **12 rm** ☑ 50.00/72.00 **t.** – SB.

🏠 **Teach de Broc**
Link Rd, S : 1 ½ m. by Golf Club rd on Ballyduff rd ℘ 27581, Fax 27919
without rest., ≼ – ⌇ ☎ & 🅿. 🔟 VISA. ⌾
6 rm ☑ 29.00/52.00 **t.**

BALLYCONNEELY (Baile Conaola) Galway 405 B 7 – ✉ Clifden – ✪ 095.

Dublin 189 – Galway 54.

🏠 **Erriseask House**
℘ 23553, Fax 23639
⌇, ≼ Mannin Bay and mountains, park – ☎ 🅿. 🔟 AE ① VISA. ⌾
Easter-October – **Meals** – (see below) – **13 rm** ☑ 58.50/94.00 **t.** – SB.

✕✕ **Erriseask House** (at Erriseask House H.)
℘ 23553, Fax 23639
🅿. 🔟 AE ①
Easter-October – **Meals** *(closed lunch Monday to Thursday except Wednesday July-August and Monday dinner to non-residents)* (booking essential) 14.90/24.00 **t.** and a la carte ⌀ 7.00.

BALLYCONNELL (Béal Atha Conaill) Cavan 405 J 5 – pop. 465 – ✪ 049.

Dublin 89 – Drogheda 76 – Enniskillen 23.

🏨 **Slieve Russell**
SE : 1 ¾ m. on R 200 ℘ 26444, Fax 26474
≼, ℔, ≋, 🔲, 🛏, ⌗, park, ✕, squash – ⌇ 📧 rest 📺 ☎ & 🅿 – 🛅 800. 🔟 AE ① VISA. ⌾
Meals (carvery lunch) 12.50/26.00 **st.** and dinner a la carte ⌀ 5.00 – **145 rm** ☑ 70.00/220.00 **st.** – SB.

BALLYCOTTON (Baile Choitán) Cork 405 H 12 – ✪ 021.

Dublin 165 – Cork 27 – Waterford 66.

🏨 **Bayview**
℘ 646746, Fax 646075
≼ Ballycotton Bay, harbour and island, ⌗ – ⌇ 📺 ☎ 🅿 – 🛅 40. 🔟 AE ① VISA. ⌾
28 March-1 November – **Meals** (bar lunch Monday to Saturday)/dinner 25.00 **st.** and a la carte ⌀ 8.80 – **33 rm** ☑ 67.00/110.00 **st.**, 2 suites – SB.

✕✕ **Spanish Point**
℘ 646177, Fax 646179
with rm, ≼ Ballycotton Bay – 📺 ☎ 🅿. 🔟 ① VISA
Meals *(closed 6 January-14 February and Monday to Wednesday October-May)* 10.50/19.00 **st.** and a la carte ⌀ 6.00 – **5 rm** ☑ 25.00/40.00 **st.**

Dans ce guide

un même symbole, un même mot,
imprimé en noir ou en rouge, en maigre ou en gras,
n'ont pas tout à fait la même signification.

Lisez attentivement les pages explicatives.

BALLYHACK (Baile Hac) Wexford 405 L 11 – pop. 221 – ⊠ New Ross – 🕿 051.

Dublin 105 – Waterford 8.5.

X   **Neptune**
    Ballyhack Harbour 𝒫 389284, Fax 389284
    MO AE O *VISA*
    April-October – **Meals** - Seafood - *(closed Sunday and Monday April-June,*
    September and October) (dinner only) 15.00 **t.** and a la carte 🍸 6.50.

BALLYHEIGE (Baile Uí Thaidhg) Kerry 405 C 10 – pop. 656 – 🕿 066.

Dublin 186 – Limerick 73 – Tralee 11.

🏨   **White Sands**
    𝒫 33102, Fax 33357
    TV ☎ P. MO *VISA* **JCB**
    April-mid October – **Meals** (bar lunch Monday to Saturday)/dinner
    16.00 **st.** and a la carte 🍸 6.50 – **75 rm** ⊆ 41.00/75.00 **st.** – SB.

BALLYLICKEY (Béal Átha Leice) Cork 405 D 12 Ireland G. – ⊠ Bantry – 🕿 027.

Env : Bantry Bay★ – Bantry House★ *AC*, S : 3 m. by R 584.

Exc. : Glengarriff★ (Garinish Island★★, access by boat) NW : 8 m. by N 71 – Healy
Pass★★ (≤★★) W : 23 m. by N 71, R 572 and R 574 – Slieve Miskish Mountains
(≤★★) W : 29 m. by N 71 and R 572 – Lauragh (Derreen Gardens★ *AC*) NW : 27 ½m.
by N 71, R 572 and R 574 – Allihies (copper mines★) W : 41 ½m. by N 71, R 572 and
R 575 – Garnish Island (≤★) W : 44 m. by N 71 and R 572.

🛉 Bantry Park, Donemark 𝒫 50579.

Dublin 216 – Cork 55 – Killarney 45.

🏨   **Ballylickey Manor House**
    𝒫 50071, Fax 50124
    🏖, ≤, « Extensive gardens », ⌨, 🏊, park – **TV ☎ P. MO AE** *VISA* 🛇
    April-early November – **Meals** *(closed Wednesday lunch)* 25.00 **t.** (dinner)
    and lunch a la carte 19.80/25.00 **t.** 🍸 8.00 – **5 rm** ⊆ 100.00 **t.**, **6 suites** 130.00/
    180.00 **t.** – SB.

🏨   **Sea View House**
    𝒫 50462, Fax 51555
    🏖, ≤, 🖙 – **TV ☎ & P. MO AE O** *VISA*
    mid March-mid November – **Meals** (bar lunch Monday to Saturday)/
    dinner 23.50 **t.** and a la carte – **17 rm** ⊆ 60.00/120.00 **st.** – SB.

🏠   **Reendesert**
    𝒫 50153, Fax 50597
    TV ☎ P. – 🔥 100. **MO AE O** *VISA*. 🛇
    14 March-2 November – **Meals** (bar lunch Monday to Saturday)/dinner
    16.00 **t.** and a la carte 🍸 4.50 – **18 rm** ⊆ 32.50/61.00 **t.** – SB.

XX   **Larchwood House**
    Pearsons Bridge, NE : 1 ¾ m. by R 584 𝒫 66181
    with rm, ≤, 🖙 – **P. MO AE O** *VISA*. 🛇
    closed 24 to 27 December – **Meals** *(closed Sunday)* (dinner only) 23.00 **t.** 🍸 7.00
    – **4 rm** ⊆ 22.00/44.00 **t.**

BALLYMACARBRY (Baile Mhac Cairbre) Waterford 405 I 11 Ireland G. – pop. 381
– ⊠ Clonmel – 🕿 052.

Exc. : W : Nier Valley Scenic Route★★.

Dublin 118 – Cork 49 – Waterford 39.

🏠   **Hanora's Cottage**
    Nire Valley, E : 4 m. by Nire Drive rd and Nire Valley Lakes rd 𝒫 36134,
    Fax 36540
    🏖, 🖙 – 🖙 **TV ☎ P. MO** *VISA*. 🛇
    closed 14 to 27 December – **Meals** (by arrangement) 20.00 **st.** – **8 rm**
    ⊆ 30.00/60.00 **st.**

BALLYMOTE (Baile an Mhóta) Sligo **405** G 5 – ⊠ Sligo – ✆ 071.

Dublin 124 – Longford 48 – Sligo 15.

⌂ **Mill House**
Keenaghan ✆ 83449
without rest., ⚘, ✗ – **P**. ✗
closed 21 December-7 January – **4 rm** ⌷ 14.00/32.00.

BALLYNAHINCH (Baile na hInse) Galway **405** C 7 – ⊠ Recess – ✆ 095.

Dublin 140 – Galway 41 – Westport 49.

🏰 **Ballynahinch Castle**
Ballinafad ✆ 31006, Fax 31085
⚲, ≼ Owenmore River and woods, ⚲, ⚘, park, ✗ – **TV** ☎ **P**. **MⒸ** **AE** **①**
VISA. ✗
closed February and 20 to 26 December – **Meals** (bar lunch)/dinner 25.30 **t.**
and a la carte – **28 rm** ⌷ 77.00/140.00 **t.**

BALLYSHANNON (Béal Atha Seanaion) Donegal **405** M 4 **Ireland G.** – pop. 2 426
– ✆ 072.

Env : Rossnowlagh Strand★★, N : 6 m. by R 231.

Dublin 157 – Donegal 13 – Sligo 27.

🏨 **Dorrian's Imperial**
Main St. ✆ 51147, Fax 51001
ᵯ⅚ – **TV** ☎ **P**. – ⚖ 30. **MⒸ** **VISA**. ✗
closed 23 to 31 December – **Meals** 10.00/13.00 **t.** and dinner a la carte ⌑ 5.50 –
26 rm ⌷ 46.00/79.00 **t.** – SB.

BALLYVAUGHAN (Baile Uí Bheacháin) Clare **405** E 8 **Ireland G.** – pop. 181 –
✆ 065.

Env : The Burren★★ (Cliffs of Moher★★★, Scenic Routes★★, Aillwee Cave★ *AC*
(Waterfall★), Corcomroe Abbey★, Kilfenora Crosses★).

Dublin 149 – Ennis 34 – Galway 29.

🏰 **Gregans Castle**
SW : 3 ¾ m. on N 67 ✆ 77005, Fax 77111
⚲, ≼ countryside and Galway Bay, ⚘, park – ☎ **P**. **MⒸ** **AE** **VISA** **JCB**. ✗
28 March-October – **Meals** 34.00 **st.** (dinner) and a la carte 12.00/36.00 **st.**
⌑ 15.00 – **18 rm** ⌷ 90.00/180.00 **st.**, 4 suites.

🏨 **Hyland's**
✆ 77037, Fax 77131
TV ☎ **P**. **MⒸ** **AE** **①** **VISA**. ✗
March-November – **Meals** (bar lunch)/dinner 18.00 **st.** and a la carte ⌑ 7.50 –
30 rm ⌷ 58.50/78.25 **st.** – SB.

🏚 **Rusheen Lodge**
SW : ¾ m. on N 67 ✆ 77092, Fax 77152
without rest., ⚘ – ⚡ **TV** ☎ **P**. **MⒸ** **AE** **VISA**. ✗
February-November – **6 rm** ⌷ 35.00/50.00 **t.**

BALTIMORE (Dún na Séad) Cork **405** D 13 – ✆ 028.

Dublin 214 – Cork 59 – Killarney 77.

🏰 **Baltimore Harbour**
✆ 20361, Fax 20466
⚘ – **TV** ☎ ⚥ **P**. – ⚖ 130. **MⒸ** **AE** **①** **VISA**. ✗
Easter-November and Christmas-New Year – **Meals** (bar lunch Monday to
Saturday)/dinner 15.50 **t.** ⌑ 7.50 – **30 rm** ⌷ 55.00/74.00 **st.** – SB.

BANAGHER (Beannchar) Offaly **405** I 8 **Ireland** G. – pop. 1 428 – ✆ 0509.

Env : Clonfert Cathedral★ (West doorway★★).

Dublin 83 – Galway 54 – Limerick 56 – Tullamore 24.

🏠 **Brosna Lodge**
Main St. 🖉 51350, Fax 51521
🚗 – 📺 📷 **P**. **MO** **VISA**
closed 25 December-30 January – **Meals** *(closed Sunday dinner)* (bar lunch
Monday to Saturday)/dinner 16.95 **st.** and a la carte ⌕ 6.00 – **14 rm** ⊇ 30.00/
56.00 **st.** – SB.

BANDON (Droichead na Bandan) Cork **405** F 12 – ✆ 023.

Dublin 174 – Cork 19.

🏨 **Munster Arms**
Oliver Plunkett St. 🖉 41562, Fax 41562
🍴✖ rm 📺 ☎ – 🔬 25. **MO** **AE** **①** **VISA**. 🎛
closed 25 and 26 December – **Meals** 9.95/18.50 **st.** and dinner a la carte ⌕ 6.50
– **34 rm** ⊇ 35.00/56.00 **st.** – SB.

⌂ **St. Anne's**
Clonakilty Rd, SW : ¾ m. on N 71 🖉 44239
without rest., 🚗 – 🍴✖ **P**. **MO** **VISA**. 🎛
5 rm ⊇ 21.00/32.00 **st.**

BANSHA (An Bháinseach) Co. Tipperary **405** H 10 – ✆ 062.

Dublin 103 – Cork 55 – Limerick 30 – Waterford 48.

⌂ **Bansha House**
🖉 54194, Fax 54215
🚗, park – 🍴✖ **P**. **MO** **VISA**. 🎛
closed 1 week Christmas – **Meals** 13.50 **st.** ⌕ 6.00 – **8 rm** ⊇ 25.00/44.00 **st.** –
SB.

BANTEER (Bántár) Cork **405** F 11 – ✆ 029.

Dublin 158 – Cork 30 – Killarney 29 – Limerick 48.

🏠 **Clonmeen Lodge**
E : 2 m. on Mallow rd 🖉 56238, Fax 56294
🎣, 🦌, 🚗, park – **P**. **MO** **AE** **①** **VISA**. 🎛
closed 23 to 28 December – **Meals** (booking essential) a la carte 15.00/18.00
⌕ 5.50 – **8 rm** ⊇ 35.00/60.00 **st.**

BAREFIELD (Gort Lomán) Clare **405** F 9 – see Ennis.

BIRR (Biorra) Offaly **405** I 8 **Ireland** G. – pop. 3 280 – ✆ 0509.

See : Town★ – Birr Castle Demesne★★ *AC* (Telescope★).

Exc. : Roscrea★ (Damer House★ *AC*) S : 12 m. by N 62 – Slieve Bloom Mountains★,
E : 13 m. by R 440.

🏌 The Glenns 🖉 20082.

🎫 🖉 20110 (16 May-11 September).

Athlone 28 – Dublin 87 – Kilkenny 49 – Limerick 49.

🏨 **Dooly's**
Emmet Sq. 🖉 20032, Fax 21332
📺 ☎ – 🔬 250
18 rm.

🏨 **County Arms**
Railway Rd 🖉 20791, Fax 21234
🚗, squash – 📺 ☎ **P** – 🔬 300. **MO** **AE** **①** **VISA** **JCB**. 🎛
Meals 12.00/19.00 **t.** and a la carte ⌕ 8.00 – **18 rm** ⊇ 48.00/90.00 **t.** – SB.

BLARNEY (An Bhlarna) Cork 405 G 12 Ireland G. – pop. 2 043 – ⊠ Cork – ☎ 021.

See : Blarney Castle★★ *AC* – Blarney House★ *AC*.

Dublin 167 – Cork 6.

🏨 **Blarney Park**
  ℰ 385281, Fax 381506
  ʃ₆, ≋, ▨, ≋, ℀ – ⊤⊽ ☎ �6 ℗ – ▟ 300. ⦿ ꬰ ⦿ *VISA*. ℀
  Meals (lunch by arrangement Monday to Saturday) 11.50/17.50 **t.** and
  dinner a la carte – **75 rm** ⊑ 65.00/110.00 **t.** – SB.

⋔ **Killarney House**
  Station Rd, NE : 1 m. ℰ 381841
  without rest., ≋ – Ꮓ⊁ ⊤⊽ ℗. ℀
  closed 23 to 28 December – **4 rm** ⊑ 22.00/34.00.

  at Tower W : 2 m. on R 617 – ⊠ Cork – ☎ 021 :

⋔ **Ashlee Lodge**
  ℰ 385346
  without rest., ≋ – Ꮓ⊁ ℗. ℀
  April-October – **5 rm** ⊑ 25.00/34.00 **st.**

BLESSINGTON (Baile Coimán) Wicklow 405 M 8 – ☎ 045.

Dublin 19 – Kilkenny 56 – Wexford 70.

🏨 **Tulfarris House**
  S : 6 m. by N 81 ℰ 864574, Fax 864423
  ⩟, ≤, ʃ₆, ≋, ▨, ⌧₉, ⌑, ≋, park, ℀ – ⊤⊽ ☎ ℗ – ▟ 150. ⦿ ꬰ ⦿ *VISA*. ℀
  closed 22 to 28 December – **Meals** (bar lunch Monday to Saturday)/
  dinner 23.00 and a la carte ▮ 4.75 – **21 rm** ⊑ 79.00/112.00 **st.** – SB.

BRAY (Bré) Wicklow 405 N 8 Ireland G. – pop. 25 096 – ☎ 01.

Env : Powerscourt★★ (Waterfall★★★ *AC*) W : 4 m. - Killruddery House and Gardens★ *AC*, S : 2 m. by R 761.

🏌 Woodbrook, Dublin Rd ℰ 282 4799 – 🏌 Old Conna, Ferndale Rd ℰ 282 6055.

Dublin 13 – Wicklow 20.

✗✗ **Tree of Idleness**
  Seafront ℰ 286 3498
  ⦿ ꬰ ⦿ *VISA*
  closed Monday, 2 weeks August-September and Christmas – **Meals** - Greek-
  Cypriot - (dinner only) 19.50 **t.** and a la carte ▮ 8.00.

BUNCRANA (Bun Cranncha) Donegal 405 J 2 Ireland G. – ☎ 077.

Exc. : – Malin Head★★★ (≤★★★), NE : 31½m. by R 238 and R 242 – Inishowen
Peninsula★★ – Carndonagh High Cross★, NE : 18½m. by R 238 – Gap of Mamore★,
NW : 8 m. – Lag Sand Dunes★, NE : 24½m. by R 238 and R 242.

Dublin 160 – Londonderry 15 – Sligo 99.

🏨 **Lake of Shadows**
  Grianan Park ℰ 61005, Fax 62131
  ⊤⊽ ☎ ℗. ⦿ ꬰ *VISA*. ℀
  closed 24 and 25 December – **Meals** 13.60 **st.** and a la carte ▮ 4.50 – **23 rm**
  ⊑ 25.00/48.00 **st.** – SB.

BUNDORAN (Bun Dobhráin) Donegal 405 H 4 – ☎ 072.

🖪 Main St. ℰ 41350 (June-September).

Dublin 161 – Donegal 17 – Sligo 23.

🏨 **Great Northern**
  N : ¼ m. ℰ 41204, Fax 41114
  ⩟, ≤, ʃ₆, ≋, ▨, ⌧₈, ≋, ℀ – ⥮ ⊤⊽ ☎ �6 ℗. ⦿ ꬰ *VISA*. ℀
  Meals 9.50/23.00 **t.** and a la carte ▮ 10.00 – **94 rm** ⊑ 48.00/62.00 **t.** – SB.

🏨 Holyrood
    📞 41232, Fax 41100
    🛏, ⬛, 🔟, 📶, ✂ – 📶 📺 📺 ☎ 🚿 🅿. 🆎 🆎 ⓪ *VISA*. 🍽
    Meals (bar lunch Monday to Saturday)/dinner 15.00 **t.** ♦ 10.00 – **85 rm**
    ⚏ 48.00/70.00 **st.** – SB.

🏨 Allingham Arms
    📞 41075, Fax 41171
    📺 ☎ 🚿 🅿. 🆎 🆎 ⓪ *VISA*. 🍽
    closed 25 and 26 December – **Meals** 9.50/17.00 **st.** and dinner a la carte –
    88 rm ⚏ 45.00/70.00 **st.** – SB.

🏠 Bay View
    Main St. *📞* 41296, Fax 41147
    without rest., ≼, 🛏 – 📺 ☎. 🆎 *VISA*. 🍽
    closed 25 and 26 December – **19 rm** ⚏ 17.00/34.00 **st.**

🍽🍽 Le Chateaubrianne
    Sligo Rd, W : 1 m. on N 5 *📞* 42160, Fax 42160
    🅿. 🆎 🆎 *VISA*
    closed Monday in winter, 3 weeks November and 24 to 26 December – **Meals**
    (dinner only and Sunday lunch)/dinner 20.00 **t.** ♦ 7.50.

BUNRATTY (Bun Raite) Clare 👁👁👁 F 9 Ireland G. – 🕾 061.

See : Castle and Folk Park★★ *AC* – Town★★.

Dublin 129 – Ennis 15 – Limerick 8.

🏨 Fitzpatrick Bunratty Shamrock
    📞 361177, Fax 471252
    🛏, ⬛, 🏊 – 📶 rest 📺 ☎ 🅿 – 🔺 200. 🆎 🆎 ⓪ *VISA*. 🍽
    closed 24 and 25 December – **Meals** *(closed Saturday lunch)* 10.50/19.50 **t.**
    and dinner a la carte ♦ 6.80 – ⚏ 8.50 – **115 rm** 83.00/121.00 **t.** – SB.

🏠 Bunratty Lodge
    N : 1 ½ m. *📞* 369402, Fax 369363
    without rest., 🏊 – 🍴 📺 🅿. 🍽
    mid March-October – **6 rm** ⚏ 30.00/35.00 **st.**

🏠 Shannon View
    NW : 1 m. on N 18 (south-eastbound carriageway) completing U-turn at
    junction with R 471 *📞* 364056, Fax 364056
    without rest., 🏊 – 🅿. 🍽
    March-November – **4 rm** ⚏ 22.00/34.00 **st.**

🍽🍽 MacCloskey's
    Bunratty House Mews *📞* 364082, Fax 364350
    « Cellars of Georgian house » – 🅿. 🆎 🆎 ⓪ *VISA*
    closed Sunday, Monday and February – **Meals** (dinner only) 26.00 **t.**

BUTLERSTOWN (Baile an Bhuitléaraigh) Cork 👁👁👁 F 13 Ireland G. – ✉ Bandon – 🕾 023.

Env : Courtmacsherry★, N : 3 m..

Dublin 193 – Cork 32.

🍴 Dunworley Cottage
    Dunworley, S : 2 m. *📞* 40314, Fax 40314
    🅿. 🆎 🆎 ⓪ *VISA*
    closed Monday, Tuesday and November-mid March except Christmas – **Meals**
    (lunch by arrangement)/dinner 21.75 **st.**

CAHERDANIEL (Cathair Dónall) Kerry 👁👁👁 B 12 – ✉ Killarney – 🕾 066.

Dublin 238 – Killarney 48.

🏠 Derrynane Bay House
    W : ½ m. on N 70 *📞* 75404, Fax 75436
    ≼ – 🍴 rm 📺 ☎ 🅿. 🆎 *VISA*. 🍽
    closed February – **Meals** 13.50 **s.** ♦ 6.00 **6 rm** ⚏ 24.00/38.00 **s.** – SB.

CAMP (An Com) Kerry **405** C 11 – ⊠ Tralee – ☎ 066.

⋔   **Barnagh Bridge**
    Cappalough, W : 2 m. on R 560 ℘ 30145, Fax 30299
    without rest., ≤, ☞ – ⁕⊁ 🖵 ☎ 🅿. 🆖 𝘝𝘐𝘚𝘈. ⅌
    March-October – **5 rm** ⊇ 34.00/44.00 **st.**

CAPPOQUIN (Ceapach Choinn) Waterford **405** I 11 Ireland G. – pop. 829 – ☎ 058.

Env : Lismore★ (Lismore Castle Gardens★ *AC*, St. Carthage's Cathedral★), W : 4 m.
by N 72 – Mount Melleray Abbey★, N : 4 m. by R 669.

Exc. : The Gap★ (≤★) NW : 9 m. by R 669.

Dublin 136 – Cork 31 – Waterford 40.

✗✗   **Richmond House**
    SE : ½ m. on N 72 ℘ 54278, Fax 54988
    with rm, « Georgian house », ☞ – 🖵 ☎ 🅿. 🆖 ⓞ 𝘝𝘐𝘚𝘈. ⅌
    closed 23 December-12 February – **Meals** *(closed Sunday and Monday to
    non-residents)* (dinner only) 25.00 **st.** ▯ 7.00 – **10 rm** ⊇ 25.00/70.00 **st.** – SB.

CARAGH LAKE (Loch Cárthaí) Kerry **405** C 11 Ireland G. – ☎ 066.

See : Lough Caragh★.

Exc. : Iveragh Peninsula★★★ (Ring of Kerry★★).

🏌 Dooks, Glenbeigh ℘ 68205/68200.

Dublin 212 – Killarney 22 – Tralee 25.

🏰   **Ard-Na-Sidhe**
    ℘ 69105, Fax 69282
    ⏶, ≤, « Country house furnished with antiques, lakeside setting », 🐾, ☞,
    park – ⁕⊁ rest ☎ 🅿. 🆖 🅰🅴 ⓞ 𝘝𝘐𝘚𝘈. ⅌
    May-September – **Meals** (dinner only) 25.00 **st.** – **19 rm** ⊇ 70.00/135.00 **st.**

🏰   **Caragh Lodge**
    ℘ 69115, Fax 69316
    ⏶, ≤, « Country house atmosphere, lakeside setting », ⥲s, 🐾, ☞, ✗✗ – ☎
    🅿. 🆖 🅰🅴 𝘝𝘐𝘚𝘈. ⅌
    25 April-27 October – **Meals** (dinner only) 25.00 **t.** ▯ 6.00 – **10 rm** ⊇ 60.00/
    100.00 **t.**

CARLINGFORD (Cairlinn) Louth **405** N 5 Ireland G. – pop. 850 – ☎ 042.

See : Town★.

Exc. : Windy Gap★, NW : 8 m. by R 173.

Dublin 66 – Dundalk 13.

🏠   **McKevitt's Village**
    Market Sq. ℘ 73116, Fax 73144
    ☞ – 🖵 ☎. 🆖 🅰🅴 ⓞ 𝘝𝘐𝘚𝘈. ⅌
    closed 25 December – **Meals** 9.95/17.50 **st.** and dinner a la carte ▯ 5.50 –
    13 rm ⊇ 35.00/65.00 **t.** – SB.

⋔   **Carlingford House**
    ℘ 73118
    without rest., ☞ – 🖵 🅿. ⅌
    March-November – **5 rm** ⊇ 20.00/35.00.

CARLOW (Ceatharlach) Carlow **405** L 9 – ☎ 0503.

Dublin 50 – Kilkenny 23 – Wexford 47.

🏠   **Barrowville Town House**
    Kilkenny Rd ℘ 43324, Fax 41953
    without rest., ☞ – ⁕⊁ 🖵 ☎ 🅿. 🆖 𝘝𝘐𝘚𝘈. ⅌
    7 rm ⊇ 25.00/42.50 **st.**

⋔ Goleen
  Milford, SW : 5 ¼ m. on N 9 ℰ 46132, Fax 46132
  without rest., ⌿ – ⊹⊠ 📺 ☎ 🅿. 📢🅾 🄰🄴 𝗩𝗜𝗦𝗔. ⅏
  April-November – **6 rm** ⌷ 18.00/34.00 **st.**

CARRICKMACROSS (Carraig Mhachaire Rois) Monaghan 405 L 6 Ireland G. –
pop. 1 678 – ✪ 042.

Env : Dún a' Rá Forest Park★, SW : 5 m. by R 179 – St. Mochta's House★, E : 7 m. by
R 178.

🛇₁₈ Nuremore ℰ 61438.

Dublin 57 – Dundalk 14.

🏨 Nuremore (Virgin)
  S : 1 m. on N 2 ℰ 61438, Fax 61853
  🐟, ≼, ℔, ⇖, ⛳, 🛇₁₈, 🢒, ⌿, park, ✂, squash – ⧉ ▤ rest 📺 ☎ ♿ 🅿 –
  🕍 600. 📢🅾 🄰🄴 🅾 𝗩𝗜𝗦𝗔. ⅏
  Meals 13.50/24.00 **st.** and a la carte ≬ 7.00 – **69 rm** ⌷ 85.00/125.00 **st.** – SB.

CARRICK -ON- SHANNON (Cora Droma Rúisc) Leitrim 405 H 6 Ireland G. –
pop. 1 858 – ✪ 078.

See : Town★.

Exc. : Lough Rynn Demesne★.

Dublin 97 – Ballina 50 – Galway 74 – Roscommon 26 – Sligo 34.

⋔ Hollywell
  Liberty Hill ℰ 21124, Fax 21124
  🐟 without rest., ≼, « Part 18C country house », ⌿ – 🅿. 📢🅾 𝗩𝗜𝗦𝗔. ⅏
  closed 23 to 30 December – **4 rm** ⌷ 35.00/60.00 **st.**

CARRICK-ON-SUIR (Carraig na Siúire) Tipperary 405 J 10 – pop. 5 143 – ✪ 051.

🛇₉ Garravone ℰ 40047.

Dublin 95 – Cork 68 – Limerick 62 – Waterford 16.

🏨 Carraig
  Main St. ℰ 641455, Fax 641604
  ▤ rest 📺 ☎ 🅿 – 🕍 250. 📢🅾 🄰🄴 🅾 𝗩𝗜𝗦𝗔. ⅏
  closed Good Friday and 25 December – **Meals** 10.00/16.95 **st.** and a la carte –
  14 rm ⌷ 35.00/60.00 **st.** – SB.

CARRIGALINE (Carraig Uí Leighin) Cork 405 G 12 – ✪ 021.

Dublin 163 – Cork 9.

🏠 Glenwood House
  Ballinrea Rd, N : ¾ m. by R 611 (Cork rd) ℰ 373878, Fax 373878
  without rest., ⌿ – 📺 ☎ ♿ 🅿. 📢🅾 𝗩𝗜𝗦𝗔. ⅏
  closed 24 December-1 January – **8 rm** ⌷ 30.00/50.00.

⋔ Raffeen Lodge
  Ringaskiddy Rd, Monkstown, NE : 2 ½ m. by R 611 and N 28 off R 610
  ℰ 371632, Fax 371632
  without rest. – 📺 🅿. 📢🅾 𝗩𝗜𝗦𝗔. ⅏
  March-October – **6 rm** ⌷ 20.00/33.00 **st.**

CASHEL (Caiseal) Tipperary 405 I 10 Ireland G. – pop. 2 473 – ✪ 062.

See : Town★★★ – Rock of Cashel★★★ *AC* – Cormac's Chapel★★ – Round Tower★ –
Museum★ – Cashel Palace Gardens★ – Cathedrals★ – GPA Bolton Library★ *AC* –
Hore Abbey★ – Dominican Friary★.

Env : Holy Cross Abbey★★, N : 9 m. by R 660 – Athassel Abbey★, W : 5 m. by N 74.

🛈 Bolton Library ℰ 61333 (1 April-1 October).

Dublin 101 – Cork 60 – Kilkenny 34 – Limerick 36 – Waterford 44.

🏨 **Cashel Palace**
     🖉 62707, Fax 61521
     🅦, « Former Archbishop's palace, gardens », park – 🛗 ✵ rm 📺 ☎ 🅿 –
     🅰 50. 🆗 🆎 ⓪ 𝑽𝑰𝑺𝑨. ✵
     Three Sisters : Meals (dinner only) a la carte 25.50/35.00
     Bishops Buttery : Meals a la carte 10.45/22.95 – **13 rm** ⯑ 130.00/175.00 **st.** –
     SB.

🏠 **Ros Guill House**
     NE : ¾ m. on R 691 🖉 61507
     without rest., 🍴 – 🅿. 🆗 𝑽𝑰𝑺𝑨. ✵
     May-20 October – **5 rm** ⯑ 26.00/36.00 **st.**

XXX **Chez Hans**
     Rockside 🖉 61177
     « Converted synod hall » – 🅿. 🆗 𝑽𝑰𝑺𝑨
     closed Sunday, Monday, 1 week Christmas and 3 weeks January – **Meals**
     (dinner only) a la carte 24.20/32.50 **t.** ⓙ 7.50.

X **Spearman**
     97 Main St. 🖉 61143
     🆗 🆎 𝑽𝑰𝑺𝑨
     closed Sunday dinner, Monday October-May, last 2 weeks November and 24 to
     27 December – **Meals** (restricted lunch) a la carte 8.75/20.50 **t.** ⓙ 4.95.

CASHEL BAY (Cuan an Chaisil) Galway 🚰 C 7 **Ireland G.** – ⓣ 095.

See : Town★.

Dublin 173 – Galway 41.

🏨 **Cashel House**
     🖉 31001, Fax 31077
     🅦, ≤, « Country house atmosphere, gardens », 🦢, park, ✵ – 📺 ☎ 🅿. 🆗
     🆎 𝑽𝑰𝑺𝑨
     closed 10 January-10 February – **Meals** (booking essential to non-residents)
     (bar lunch)/dinner 30.00 **t.** and a la carte 29.85/35.85 **t.** ⓙ 7.95 – **32 rm**
     ⯑ 49.00/182.00 **t.** – SB.

🏨 **Zetland Country House**
     🖉 31111, Fax 31117
     🅦, ≤ Cashel Bay, « Country house, gardens », 🦢, ✵ – 📺 ☎ 🅿. 🆗 🆎 ⓪
     𝑽𝑰𝑺𝑨
     16 April-October – **Meals** 29.00 **t.** (dinner) and a la carte 18.50/34.50 **t.** ⓙ 7.60 –
     19 rm ⯑ 83.50/165.00 **t.** – SB.

🏠 **Glynsk House**
     SW : 5 ¾ m. on R 340 🖉 32279, Fax 32342
     🅦, ≤ – 📺 ☎ 🅿. 🆗 𝑽𝑰𝑺𝑨
     Meals 9.00/17.00 **t.** and a la carte ⓙ 6.00 – **12 rm** ⯑ 37.00/60.00 **st.** – SB.

CASTLEBALDWIN (Béal Átha na gCarraigíní) Sligo 🚰 G 5 **Ireland G.** – ✉ Boyle
(Roscommon) – ⓣ 071.

Env : Carrowkeel Megalithic Cemetery (≤★★), S : 3 m..

Exc. : Arigna Scenic Drive★★, N : 2 m. by N 4 – Lough Key Forest Park★★ *AC*, SE :
10 m. by N 4 – View★★, N : 9 m. by N 4 on R 280 – Mountain Drive★, N : 6 m. on
N 4 – Boyle Abbey★ *AC*, SE : 8 m. by N 4.

Dublin 118 – Longford 42 – Sligo 15.

🏨 **Cromleach Lodge**
     Ballindoon, SE : 3 ½ m. 🖉 65155, Fax 65455
     🅦, ≤ Lough Arrow and Carrowkeel Cairns, 🦢, 🍴, park – ✵ 📺 ☎ 🅿. 🆗 🆎
     ⓪ 𝑽𝑰𝑺𝑨. ✵
     February-2 November – **Meals** (dinner only) 25.00/30.00 **t.** ⓙ 6.50 – **10 rm**
     ⯑ 99.00/178.00 **t.** – SB.

| **Prices** | *For full details of the prices quoted in the guide,*
consult the introduction. |

CASTLEBLAYNEY (Baile na Lorgan) Monaghan 405 L 5 – pop. 2 029 – ✆ 042.

🇫🇮 Muckno Park ✐ 40197.

Dublin 68 – Belfast 58 – Drogheda 39 – Dundalk 17 – Londonderry 80.

🏨 Glencarn
Monaghan Rd ✐ 46666, Fax 46521
⌫, 🔲 – ▤ rest 📺 ☎ ℗
27 rm.

CASTLECONNELL (Caisleán Uí Chonaill) Limerick 405 G 9 Ireland G. – pop. 1 391
– ✉ Limerick – ✆ 061.

See : Town★.

Dublin 111 – Limerick 9.

🏨 Castle Oaks House
✐ 377666, Fax 377717
⌫, ≼, 🔲, ⌁, 🛏, ⌁, ☂, park, ✗ – 📺 ☎ ℗ – 🔏 200. ⬤⬤ 🅰🅴 ⬤ 𝘝𝘐𝘚𝘈. ✗
closed 24 to 29 December – **Meals** (bar lunch Monday to Saturday)/
dinner 18.50 **t.** and a la carte ⓘ 5.25 – **11 rm** ⌷ 59.40/132.00 **st.** – SB.

CASTLEDERMOT (Díseart Diarmada) Kildare 405 L 9 Ireland G. – pop. 741 –
✆ 0503.

Exc. : Carlow Cathedral (Marble Monument★) NE : 7 m. by N 9.

Dublin 44 – Kilkenny 30 – Wexford 54.

🏰 Kilkea Castle
Kilkea, NW : 3 ¾ m. on R 418 ✐ 45156, Fax 45187
⌫, ≼, « Part 12C », 🛉, ⌁, 🔲, 🛏, ⌁, ☂, park, ✗ – 🔌 📺 ☎ ℗ – 🔏 200.
⬤⬤ 🅰🅴 ⬤ 𝘝𝘐𝘚𝘈. ✗
closed 23 to 28 December – **Meals** 16.00/28.50 **t.** and a la carte ⓘ 8.00 – **29 rm**
⌷ 115.00/170.00 **t.**, 7 suites – SB.

CASTLEISLAND (Oileán Ciarraí) Kerry 405 D 11 – ✆ 066.

Dublin 170 – Cork 59 – Killarney 16 – Limerick 52 – Tralee 12.

🏨 River Island
Lower Main St. ✐ 42555, Fax 42544
🔌 📺 ☎ ℗. ⬤⬤ 🅰🅴 ⬤ 𝘝𝘐𝘚𝘈. ✗
Meals (dinner only) 14.50 **st.** and a la carte ⓘ 6.25 – **51 rm** ⌷ 30.00/60.00 **st.** –
SB.

CAVAN (An Cabhán) Cavan 405 J 6 Ireland G. – pop. 3 332 – ✆ 049.

Env : Killykeen Forest Park★, W : 6 m. by R 198.

🄳 Farnham St. ✐ 31942 (June-September).

Dublin 71 – Drogheda 58 – Enniskillen 40.

🏨 Kilmore
Dublin Rd, E : 2 m. on N 3 ✐ 32288, Fax 32458
📺 ☎ 🛆 ℗ – 🔏 550. ⬤⬤ 🅰🅴 ⬤ 𝘝𝘐𝘚𝘈
Meals 9.95/18.50 **st.** and dinner a la carte ⓘ 4.50 – **39 rm** ⌷ 42.00/72.00 **st.** –
SB.

CHEEKPOINT (Pointe na Ságe) Waterford 405 K/L 11 – see Waterford.

CLIFDEN (An Clochán) Galway 405 B 7 Ireland G. – pop. 808 – ✆ 095.

Exc. : Connemara★★★, NE : by N 59 – Sky Road★★★, NE : by N 59 – Connemara
National Park★, NE : 1 m by N 59.

🄳 Market St. ✐ 21163 (3 May-30 September).

Dublin 181 – Ballina 77 – Galway 49.

CLIFDEN

🏛 **Rock Glen Manor House**
S : 1 ¼ m. by R 341 ℘ 21035, Fax 21737
👪, ☞, ✖ – 📺 ☎ 🅿. 🆎 ⓪ 🆚 JCB. ✖
16 March-October – **Meals** (bar lunch)/dinner a la carte approx. 25.00 **t.** 🍷 6.00
– **29 rm** ⊇ 66.50/110.00 **st.** – SB.

🏛 **Ardagh**
Ballyconneely rd, S : 1 ¾ m. on R 341 ℘ 21384, Fax 21314
👪, ≼ Ardbear Bay, ☜ – 📺 ☎ 🅿. 🆎 ⓪ 🆚. ✖
April-October – **Meals** (dinner only) 26.00 and a la carte 🍷 7.25 – **21 rm**
⊇ 65.00/95.00 **st.** – SB.

↟ **Mal Dua**
Galway Rd, E : ½ m. on N 59 ℘ 21171, Fax 21739
without rest. – ✖ 📺 ☎ 🅿. 🆎 🆚. ✖
closed December – **9 rm** ⊇ 30.00/50.00 **st.**

↟ **Sunnybank House**
Sunny Bank, Church Hill ℘ 21437, Fax 21976
without rest., ☜s, ☾, ☞, ✖ – 📺 ☎ 🅿. 🆚. ✖
March-October – **10 rm** ⊇ 40.00/55.00 **st.**

↟ **Failte**
S : 1 ¼ m. by R 341 ℘ 21159
👪 without rest., ≼ – 🅿. 🆎 🆚. ✖
April-September – **5 rm** ⊇ 14.00/32.00 **st.**

✗ **Quay House**
Beach Rd ℘ 21369, Fax 21369
≼ – 🆚
closed Sunday and November-15 March – **Meals** 10.00/19.50 **t.** and a la carte
🍷 6.50.

CLONAKILTY (Cloich na Coillte) Cork 🗺 F 13 Ireland G. – pop. 2 576 – 🕾 023.

See : West Cork Regional Museum★ *AC.*

Env : Timoleague★ (Franciscan Friary★) E : 5 m. by R 600.

Dublin 193 – Cork 32.

↟ **Árd na Gréine Farm House**
Ballinascarthy, NW : 5 ¾ m. by N 71 ℘ 39104, Fax 39397
👪, ☞ – 📺 🅿. 🆚
Meals 15.00 **st.** – **6 rm** ⊇ 18.00/36.00 – SB.

CLONMEL (Cluain Meala) Tipperary 🗺 I 10 – pop. 14 531 – 🕾 052.

🏌 Lyreanearla, Mountain Rd ℘ 21138.

🛈 Community Office, Town Centre ℘ 22960.

Dublin 108 – Cork 59 – Kilkenny 31 – Limerick 48 – Waterford 29.

🏛 **Minella**
Coleville Rd ℘ 22388, Fax 24381
👪, ☾, ☞, park – 📺 ☎ 🅿 – 🏃 600. 🆎 🆚 ⓪ 🆚
closed 24 to 28 December – **Meals** 13.00/22.00 **t.** and a la carte 🍷 7.00 – **67 rm**
⊇ 70.00/100.00 **st.**, 3 suites – SB.

🏛 **Clonmel Arms**
Sarsfield St. ℘ 21233, Fax 21526
🔌 📺 ☎ – 🏃 450. 🆎 🆚 ⓪ 🆚. ✖
Meals *(closed Saturday lunch)* 10.00/14.00 **t.** and a la carte 🍷 5.00 – ⊇ 6.50 –
30 rm 70.00/80.00 **t.** – SB.

COBH (An Cóbh) Cork 🗺 H 12 – pop. 6 227 – 🕾 021.

Dublin 173 – Cork 13 – Waterford 71.

↟ **Tearmann**
Ballynoe, N : 2 ½ m. by R 624 ℘ 813182, Fax 814011
👪, ☞ – 🅿. ✖
March-October – **Meals** (by arrangement) 12.00 **s.** – **3 rm** ⊇ 19.50/32.00 **s.**

88

CONG (Conga) Mayo 405 E 7 Ireland G. – pop. 183 – © 092.

See : Town★.

Env : Lough Corrib★★.

Exc. : Ross Abbey★★ (Tower ≤★) – Joyce Country★★ (Lough Nafooey★★) W : by R 345.

Dublin 160 – Ballina 49 – Galway 28.

🏰 **Ashford Castle**
    🖉 46003, Fax 46260
    🏊, ≤, « Part 13C and 18C castle, in extensive formal gardens on shores of Lough Corrib », 🏋, ≦s, 🦅, 🎣, park, 🎾 – 🛗 📺 ☎ 🅿 – 🛐 110. 🐵 🅰🅴 🅾 𝑽𝑰𝑺𝑨 🥃 🦀
    George V Room : Meals 22.00/36.00 **t.** and a la carte – (see also **Connaught Room** below) – ⌑ 12.50 – **77 rm** 210.00/304.00 **st.**, 6 suites – SB.

🍴🍴🍴🍴 **Connaught Room** (at Ashford Castle H.)
    🖉 46003, Fax 46260
    ≤ gardens, Lough Corrib and islands – 🅿. 🐵 🅰🅴 🅾 𝑽𝑰𝑺𝑨 🥃
    April-October – **Meals** (booking essential) (dinner only) a la carte 38.20/59.95 **t.**
    🍷 9.00.

    For business or tourist interest :
    MICHELIN Red Guide : EUROPE.

CORK (Corcaigh) Cork 405 G 12 Ireland G. – pop. 174 400 – © 021.

See : City★★ – Shandon Bells★★ EY, St. Fin Barre's Cathedral★★ AC Z, Cork Public Museum★★ X **M** – Grand Parade★ Z , South Mall★ Z , St. Patrick Street★ Z , Crawford Art Gallery★ Y – Christ the King Church★ X **D** , Elizabethan Fort★ Z , Cork Lough★ X.

Env : Dunkathel House★ AC, E : 5¾m. by N 8 and N 25 X.

Exc. : Fota Island★★ (Fota House★★) E : 8 m. by N 8 and N 25 X – Cobh★ (St. Colman's Cathedral★, Lusitania Memorial★) SE : 15 m. by N 8, N 25 and R 624 X.

🏌 Douglas 🖉 891086, X – 🏌 Mahon, Cloverhill, Blackrock 🖉 362480 X – 🏌 Monkstown, Parkgarriffe 🖉 841376, X – 🏌 Harbour Point, Clash, Little Island 🖉 353094, X.

✈ Cork Airport : 🖉 313131, S : 4 m. by L 42 X – **Terminal :** Bus Station, Parnell Pl.

🚢 to France (Le Havre) (Irish Ferries) (summer only) (21 h 30 mn), (Roscoff) (Brittany Ferries and Irish Ferries), (St. Malo) (Brittany Ferries) weekly (17 h 30 mn) – to Pembroke (Swansea Cork Ferries) 3 weekly (10 h) – to Swansea (Swansea Cork Ferries) (10 h).

🏢 Cork City, Grand Parade 🖉 273251.

Dublin 154.

Plans on following pages

🏨 **Fitzpatrick's Silver Springs**   X **c**
    Tivoli, E : 2 ½ m. on N 8 🖉 507533, Fax 507641
    🏋, ≦s, 🏊, 🦅, 🌳, park, 🎾, squash – 🛗 🖐 rm 🍽 rest 📺 ☎ 🅿 – 🛐 800. 🐵 🅰🅴 🅾 𝑽𝑰𝑺𝑨 🥃
    closed 25 December – **Meals** 11.00/18.75 **t.** and a la carte 🍷 6.00 – ⌑ 7.50 – **106 rm** 79.00/96.00 **st.**, 3 suites – SB.

🏨 **Jurys**   Z **v**
    Western Rd, by Washington St. 🖉 276622, Fax 274477
    🏋, ≦s, 🏊, 🌳, squash – 🛗 🖐 rm 🍽 rest 📺 ☎ 🦽 🅿 – 🛐 500. 🐵 🅰🅴 🅾 𝑽𝑰𝑺𝑨 🥃
    closed 25 to 27 December – **Glandore : Meals** 16.00 **t.** (dinner) and a la carte 12.45/24.05
    Fastnet : Meals *(closed Sunday and Monday)* (dinner only) 16.95/22.00 **t.** and a la carte – ⌑ 9.75 – **184 rm** 100.00/119.00 **t.**, 1 suite – SB.

🏨 **Rochestown Park**
    Rochestown Rd, Douglas, SE : 3 m. by R 609 🖉 892233, Fax 892178
    🏋, ≦s, 🏊, 🌳 – 🖐 🖐 rm 📺 ☎ 🅿 – 🛐 150. 🐵 🅰🅴 🅾 𝑽𝑰𝑺𝑨 🥃
    Windsor : Meals 12.00/16.50 **t.** and a la carte – **63 rm** ⌑ 57.00/85.00 **t.** – SB.

CORK
BUILT UP AREA

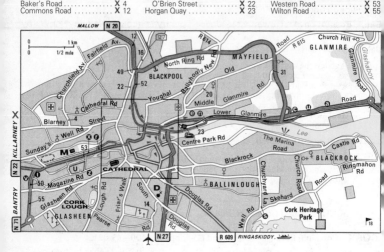

🏨 **Hayfield Manor**   X **z**
Perrott Av., College Rd ℰ 315600, Fax 316839
ℐ𝒔, 🔲, 🐾 – ⫴ ⇥ rm 🗏 📺 ☎ 🕭 🅿 – 🔏 130. 🐠 🕮 ① 𝓥𝓘𝓢𝓐. ⅍
closed 24 to 27 December – **Meals** 16.50/28.00 **st.** and dinner a la carte 🍷 6.50 – **51 rm** ⇌ 125.00/180.00 **st.**, 2 suites – SB.

🏨 **Morrisons Island**   Z **a**
Morrisons Quay ℰ 275858, Fax 275833
⫴ ⇥ rm 🗏 rest 📺 ☎ 🅿. 🐠 🕮 ① 𝓥𝓘𝓢𝓐. ⅍
closed 25 and 26 December – **Riverbank : Meals** 13.00 **t.** (lunch) and dinner a la carte 17.50/26.00 – ⇌ 8.00 – **12 rm** 80.00/110.00 **t.**, **28 suites** 160.00 **t.** – SB.

🏨 **Arbutus Lodge**   X **e**
Middle Glanmire Rd, Montenotte ℰ 501237, Fax 502893
🐾, 🍴 – 📺 ☎ 🅿 – 🔏 100. 🐠 🕮 ① 𝓥𝓘𝓢𝓐. ⅍
closed 24 to 28 December – **Meals** – (see Arbutus Lodge below) – **16 rm** ⇌ 45.00/115.00 **st.**, 4 suites.

🏨 **Country Club**   X **n**
Middle Glanmire Rd, Montenotte ℰ 502922, Fax 502082
🐾 – 📺 ☎ 🅿 – 🔏 300. 🐠 🕮 ① 𝓥𝓘𝓢𝓐
closed 24 to 26 December – **Meals** (bar lunch)/dinner 20.00 **st.** and dinner a la carte – **60 rm** ⇌ 39.50/52.00 **st.** – SB.

🏨 **Imperial**   Z **n**
South Mall ℰ 274040, Fax 275375
⫴ 📺 ☎ 🅿 – 🔏 500. 🐠 🕮 ① 𝓥𝓘𝓢𝓐 𝗝𝗖𝗕. ⅍
closed 24 to 31 December – **Meals** a la carte 11.70/24.05 **t.** 🍷 5.50 – ⇌ 6.50 – **99 rm** 65.00/85.00 **t.** – SB.

🏨 **Jurys Cork Inn**   Y **c**
Anderson's Quay ℰ 276444, Fax 276144
⫴ ⇥ rm 📺 ☎ 🕭 🅿 – 🔏 40. 🐠 🕮 ① 𝓥𝓘𝓢𝓐. ⅍
closed 24 to 27 December – **Meals** (bar lunch)/dinner 14.50 **t.** and a la carte – ⇌ 6.00 – **133 rm** 53.00 **t.**

🏨 **Victoria Lodge**   X **v**
Victoria Cross ℰ 542233, Fax 542572
without rest., 🐾 – ⫴ ⇥ 📺 ☎ 🅿. 🐠 🕮 𝓥𝓘𝓢𝓐
closed 24 to 27 December – **30 rm** ⇌ 30.00/48.00 **st.**

CORK

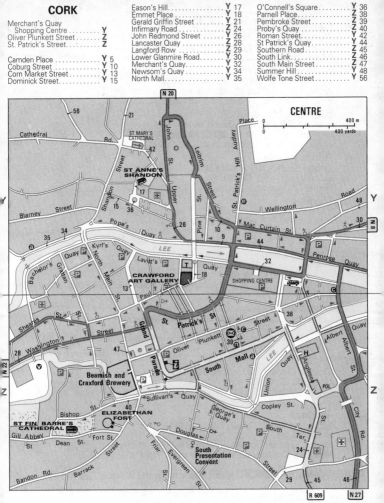

CENTRE

🏠 **Holiday Inn Express**
Dunkette Roundabout, E : 4 ¾ m. by N 8 and N 25 on R 639 ℘ 354354,
Fax 354202
📶 ✖ rm 📺 ☎ & 🅿 – 🔏 90. 🐵 AE ① VISA JCB
Meals (carving lunch) 4.50/12.95 **st.** and a la carte ⅃ 5.50 – **100 rm** ⊊ 39.95/
49.95 **st.**

🏠 **Lotamore House**   X **a**
Tivoli, E : 3 ¼ m. on N 8 ℘ 822344, Fax 822219
without rest., 🌲 – 📺 ☎ 🅿. 🐵 AE VISA
closed 24 December-5 January – **20 rm** ⊊ 27.00/52.00 **st.**

🏠 Travelodge (Granada)
Blackash, S : 2 ¼ m. by R 600 ℘ 310722
Reservations (Freephone) 0800 850950 (UK), 1800 709709 (Republic of
Ireland) – 📺 & 🅿
40 rm.

CORK

↑ **Garnish House**   X r
Western Rd ℰ 275111, Fax 273872
without rest. – ⭐ TV ☎ P. MO AE ① VISA. ⚅
14 rm � 30.00/55.00 **st.**

↑ **Seven North Mall**   Y a
7 North Mall ℰ 397191, Fax 300811
without rest. – TV ☎ P. MO VISA. ⚅
closed 9 December-15 January – **5 rm** ⊇ 40.00/60.00.

↑ **Killarney House**   X x
Western Rd ℰ 270290, Fax 271010
without rest. – TV ☎ P. MO AE ① VISA. ⚅
closed Christmas – **18 rm** ⊇ 44.00/55.00 **st.**

↑ **Acorn House**   Y e
14 St. Patrick's Hill ℰ 502474
without rest. – TV. MO VISA. ⚅
closed 22 December-10 January – **9 rm** ⊇ 28.00/50.00 **st.**

XXX **Flemings**   X u
Silver Grange House, Tivoli, E : 2 ¾ m. on N 8 ℰ 821621, Fax 821800
with rm, 🍴 – TV ☎ P. MO AE ① VISA. ⚅
closed 24 to 27 December – **Meals** 13.50/21.00 **st.** and a la carte 20.00/
25.50 **st.** ₰ 6.25 – **4 rm** ⊇ 45.00/65.00 **st.** – SB.

XXX **Arbutus Lodge** (at Arbutus Lodge H.)   X e
Middle Glanmire Rd, Montenotte ℰ 501237, Fax 502893
🍴 – ▤ P. MO AE ① VISA
closed Sunday and 24 to 28 December – **Meals** 16.50/24.50 **st.** and a la carte
₰ 7.25.

XX **Lovett's** (Restaurant)   X s
Churchyard Lane, off Well Rd, Douglas ℰ 294909
P. MO AE ① VISA
closed Saturday lunch, Sunday and 1 week Christmas – **Meals** 14.50/24.00 **t.**
and dinner a la carte ₰ 6.50.

XX **Wylam**   X i
Victoria Cross ℰ 341063, Fax 272146
▤ P. MO AE ① VISA JCB
closed 24 and 25 December – **Meals** - Chinese - (dinner only) 16.00 **t.**
and a la carte ₰ 6.00.

X **Jacques**   Z c
9 Phoenix St. ℰ 277387, Fax 270634
▤. MO AE VISA
closed Saturday lunch, Sunday, 24 to 29 December and Bank Holidays –
Meals 21.50 **t.** (dinner) and a la carte 15.90/24.30 **t.** ₰ 6.90.

COURTOWN HARBOUR (Cuan Bhaile na Cúirte) Wexford 405 N 10 – pop. 343 –
✉ Gorey – ☎ 055.

Dublin 62 – Waterford 59 – Wexford 42.

🏠 **Courtown**
ℰ 25108, Fax 25304
₰, ☎, 🏊, 🍴 – TV ☎ P. MO AE ① VISA. ⚅
16 March-October – **Meals** 10.00/19.00 and a la carte ₰ 5.00 – **21 rm**
⊇ 40.00/80.00 **t.** – SB.

CRATLOE (An Chreatalach) Clare 405 F 9 – pop. 510 – ✉ Bunratty – ☎ 061.

Dublin 127 – Ennis 17 – Limerick 7.

↑ **Bunratty View**
ℰ 357352, Fax 357491
≤, 🍴 – ⭐ TV ☎ P
6 rm.

*Great Britain and Ireland are covered entirely
at a scale of 16 miles to 1 inch by our map «Main Roads»* 986

CROOKEDWOOD (Tigh Munna) Westmeath 405 K 7 – ⊠ Mullingar – ☎ 044.

Dublin 55 – Drogheda 30 – Mullingar 6.

🏨 Crookedwood House
E : 1 ½ m. on Delvin rd ℰ 72165, Fax 72166
⏃, ≼, « 18C rectory », ☞ – 📺 ☎ 🅿. ⓜⓞ 🆎 ⓞ 𝑉𝐼𝑆𝐴. ❀
closed 2 weeks November – **Meals** – (see below) – **8 rm** ⊇ 45.00/90.00 **st.** –
SB.

✕✕ Crookedwood House (at Crookedwood House H.)
E : 1 ½ m. on Delvin rd ℰ 72165, Fax 72166
« 18C rectory », ☞ – 🅿. ⓜⓞ 🆎 ⓞ 𝑉𝐼𝑆𝐴
closed Sunday dinner, Monday and 2 weeks November – **Meals** (dinner only
and Sunday lunch)/dinner 22.00 **st.** and a la carte 🛇 5.95.

CROSSMOLINA (Crois Mhaoilíona) Mayo 405 E 5 **Ireland** G. – pop. 1 202 –
☎ 096.

Env : Errew Abbey★, SE : 6 m. by R 315.

Exc. : Broad Haven★, NW : 27 m. by N 59 and R 313.

Dublin 157 – Ballina 6.5.

🏨 Enniscoe House
Castlehill, S : 2 m. on R 315 ℰ 31112, Fax 31773
⏃, ≼, « Georgian country house, antiques », 🐾, park – 🅿. ⓜⓞ 🆎 ⓞ 𝑉𝐼𝑆𝐴. ❀
April-14 October – **Meals** (dinner only) 25.00 **t.** 🛇 8.00 – **6 rm** ⊇ 58.00/
108.00 **st.** – SB.

In this guide

*a symbol or a character, printed in red or black, in **bold** or light type,
does not have the same meaning.*

Pay particular attention to the explanatory pages.

DELGANY (Deilgne) Wicklow 405 N 8 – pop. 6 682 (inc. Greystones) – ⊠ Bray –
☎ 01.

🛺 Delgany ℰ 287 4645/287 4536.

Dublin 19.

🏨 Glenview
Glen of the Downs, NW : 2 m. by L 164 on N 11 ℰ 287 3399, Fax 287 7511
⏃, ≼, 🛁, 🏊, 🔲, ☞, park – 📳 ⇌ rm 📺 ☎ 🅿. 🅿 – 🔼 250. ⓜⓞ 🆎 ⓞ 𝑉𝐼𝑆𝐴.
❀
closed 25 December – **Meals** 17.00/25.00 **t.** and a la carte 🛇 5.50 – ⊇ 8.00 –
40 rm 77.00/115.00 **t.** – SB.

DINGLE (An Daingean) Kerry 405 B 11 **Ireland** G. – pop. 1 272 – ☎ 066.

See : Town★ – Pier★, St. Mary's Church★.

Env : Gallarus Oratory★★★, NW : 5 m. by R 559 – NE : Connor Pass★★ – Kilmalke-
dar★, NW : 5 ½m. by R 559.

Exc. : Mount Eagle (Beehive Huts★★) W : 9 m. by R 559 – Slea Head★★, W : 10 ½m.
by R 559 – Stradbally Strand★★, NE : 10 ½m. via Connor Pass – Ballyferriter Heritage Centre★ *AC*, NW : 8 m. by R 559 – Mount Brandon★, N : 12 ½m. by R 559 via
Kilmalkedar – Blasket Islands★, W : 13 m. by R 559 and ferry from Dunquin.

🎫 Main St. ℰ 51188 (April-October).

Dublin 216 – Killarney 51 – Limerick 95.

🏨 Dingle Skellig
SE : ½ m. by T 68 ℰ 51144, Fax 51501
≼, 🔲, ☞, ✕ – 📳 📺 ☎ 🅿. ⓜⓞ 🆎 ⓞ 𝑉𝐼𝑆𝐴. ❀
28 March-15 November – **Meals** (bar lunch Monday to Saturday)/dinner
21.95 **t.** and a la carte 🛇 6.50 – **99 rm** ⊇ 80.00/115.00 **t.**, 1 suite – SB.

93

🏠 **Milltown House**
W : ¾ m. by Slea Head Drive 🖉 51372, Fax 51095
🦢 without rest., ≤, 🚗 – TV ☎ & ℗. M◉ VISA
closed 14 November-14 March – **10 rm** 🖙 40.00/60.00 **st.**

🏠 **Greenmount House**
Gortonora, by John St. 🖉 51414, Fax 51974
without rest., ≤ – ✕ TV ☎ ℗. M◉ VISA . 🛠
closed 20 to 26 December and 14 January-4 February – **12 rm** 🖙 30.00/
60.00 **t.**

🏠 **Doyle's Townhouse**
5 John St. 🖉 51174, Fax 51816
TV ☎. M◉ ◍ VISA . 🛠
mid March-mid November – **Meals** – (see **Doyle's Seafood Bar** below) – **8 rm**
🖙 42.00/66.00 **t.**

↑ **Cleevaun**
Lady's Cross, Milltown, W : 1 ¼ m. on R 559 following signs for Slea Head
Drive 🖉 51108, Fax 51108
without rest., ≤, 🚗 – TV ☎ ℗. M◉ VISA . 🛠
mid March-mid November – **9 rm** 🖙 40.00/50.00 **t.**

↑ **Captains House**
The Mall 🖉 51531, Fax 51079
without rest., 🚗 – TV ☎. M◉ AE ◍ VISA . 🛠
April-November – **7 rm** 🖙 25.00/44.00 **st.**

↑ **Bambury's**
Mail Rd, E : on T 68 🖉 51244, Fax 51786
without rest., ≤ – TV ☎ ℗. M◉ VISA . 🛠
12 rm 🖙 35.00/50.00 **st.**

↑ **Alpine House**
Mail Rd, E : on T 68 🖉 51250, Fax 51966
without rest., 🚗 – TV ☎ ℗. M◉ VISA . 🛠
12 rm 🖙 35.00/40.00 **t.**

XX **Beginish**
Green St. 🖉 51588, Fax 51591
🚗 – M◉ AE ◍ VISA
mid March-mid November – **Meals** - Seafood - *(closed Monday)* (light lunch)
dinner a la carte 17.50/24.95 **t.** 🍷 5.50.

X **Waterside**
🖉 51458
M◉ VISA
closed Tuesday and November-March – **Meals** 23.00 **t.** (dinner) and
a la carte 10.45/25.00 **t.** 🍷 5.00.

X **Doyle's Seafood Bar**
4 John St. 🖉 51174, Fax 51816
M◉ ◍ VISA . 🛠
mid March-mid November – **Meals** *(closed Sunday)* (dinner only) 14.50 **t.**
and a la carte 17.50/24.00 **t.** 🍷 7.60.

DONEGAL (Dún na nGall) Donegal 405 H 4 Ireland G. – pop. 2 193 – ✿ 073.

See : Donegal Castle★ *AC.*

Exc. : Cliffs of Bunglass★★★, W : 30 m. by N 56 and R 263 – Glencolumbkille Folk
Village★★ *AC*, W : 33 m. by N 56 and R 263 – Trabane Strand★★, W : 36 m. by N 56
and R 263 – Glenmalin Court Cairn★, W : 37 m. by N 56 and R 263 at Malin Beg.

✈ Donegal Airport 🖉 (075) 48232.

🚹 The Quay 🖉 21148 (April-October).

Dublin 164 – Londonderry 48 – Sligo 40.

🏠 **St. Ernan's House**
St. Ernan's Island, SW : 2 ¼ m. by N 15 ℰ 21065, Fax 22098
🍴, « Wooded island setting ≤ Donegal Bay », park – ⅍ rest 📺 ☎ 🅿. 🕸
VISA. ⅍
30 March-October – **Meals** (dinner only) 28.00 **st.** ⌀ 7.00 – **12 rm** ⌷ 130.00/
164.00 **st.** – SB.

🏠 **Harvey's Point Country**
Lough Eske, NE : 4 ½ m. by T 27 (Killibegs rd) ℰ 22208, Fax 22352
🍴, ≤, « Loughside setting », 🐟, 🌷, park, ⅍ – 📺 ☎ 🅿 – 🔏 50. 🕸 AE ①
VISA
April-October and restricted opening November-March – **Meals** – (see below) –
20 rm ⌷ 60.50/121.00 **st.** – SB.

⌂ **Island View House**
Ballyshannon rd, SW : ¾ m. ℰ 22411
without rest., ≤, 🌷 – 📺 🅿. ⅍
4 rm ⌷ 25.00/33.00 **t.**

🍴🍴 **Harvey's Point Country** (at Harvey's Point Country H.)
Lough Eske, NE : 4 ½ m. by T 27 (Killibegs rd) ℰ 22208, Fax 22352
≤, « Loughside setting », 🌷 – 🅿. 🕸 AE ① *VISA*
April-October and restricted opening November-March – **Meals** 12.50/22.50 **t.**
and a la carte ⌀ 5.75.

DOOGORT (Dumha Goirt) Mayo 405 B 5/6 – see Achill Island.

DOOLIN (Dúlainm) Clare 405 D 8 – ✆ 065.

Dublin 171 – Galway 43 – Limerick 50.

🏠 **Aran View House**
NE : ½ m. ℰ 74061, Fax 74540
🍴, ≤, « Working farm », 🌷, park ⅍ rm 📺 ☎ 🅿. 🕸 AE ① *VISA*. ⅍
17 March-October – **Meals** (bar lunch Monday to Saturday and Bank Holidays)/
dinner 18.00 **t.** and a la carte ⌀ 4.95 – **19 rm** ⌷ 40.00/80.00 **t.** – SB.

⌂ **Doonmacfelim House**
ℰ 74503, Fax 74129
without rest., 🍴 – ☎ 🅿. 🕸 *VISA*. ⅍
closed 24 to 28 December – **6 rm** ⌷ 20.00/38.00.

DROGHEDA (Droichead Átha) Louth 405 M 6 **Ireland G.** – pop. 23 848 – ✆ 041.

Env : Monasterboice★★, N : 6 ½ m. by N 1 – Boyne Valley★★, on N 51 – Termonfeckin (Tower House★) NE : 5 m. by R 166.

Exc. : Newgrange★★, W : 3 m. by N 51 on N 2 – Old Mellifont★.

Dublin 29 – Dundalk 22.

🏠 **Boyne Valley H. and Country Club**
SE : 1 ¼ m. on N 1 ℰ 37737, Fax 39188
🏋, 🏊, 🎱, 🌷, park, ⅍ – ⅍ rm 📺 ☎ 🅿 – 🔏 350. 🕸 AE ① *VISA*. ⅍
Meals 10.10/22.00 **st.** ⌀ 5.10 – **37 rm** ⌷ 46.00/120.00 **st.** – SB.

⌂ **Tullyesker House**
Tullyesker, Monasterboice, N : 3 ½ m. by N 1 ℰ 30430, Fax 32624
without rest., 🌷 – 📺 🅿. ⅍
March-October – **5 rm** ⌷ 33.00/38.00 **st.**

at Termonfeckin NE : 5 m. on R 166 – ✉ Drogheda – ✆ 041 :

🍴🍴 **Triple House**
on R 166 ℰ 22616, Fax 22616
🌷 – 🅿. 🕸 *VISA*
closed Monday – **Meals** (dinner only and Sunday lunch)/dinner 16.00 **st.**
and a la carte ⌀ 5.00.

Die Preise *Einzelheiten über die in diesem Führer angegebenen Preise
finden Sie in der Einleitung.*

DUBLIN (Baile Átha Cliath) Dublin 𝟜𝟘𝟝 N 7 **Ireland G.** – pop. 859 976 – ✪ 01.

See : City★★★ – Trinity College★★★ (Library★★★ *AC*) JY – Chester Beatty Library★★★ FV – Phoenix Park★★★ AS – Dublin Castle★★ HY – Christ Church Cathedral★★ HY – St. Patrick's Cathedral★★ HZ – Marsh's Library★★ HZ – National Museum★★ (Treasury★★), KZ – National Gallery★★ KZ – Merrion Square★★ KZ – Rotunda Hospital Chapel★★ JX – Kilmainham Hospital★★ AT – Kilmainham Gaol Museum★★ AT **M6** – National Botanic Gardens★★ BS – No 29★ KZ **D** – Liffey Bridge★ JY – Taylors' Hall★ HY – City Hall★ HY – St. Audoen's Gate★ HY **B** – St. Stephen's Green★ JZ – Grafton Street★ JYZ – Powerscourt Centre★ JY – Civic Museum★ JY **M1** – Bank of Ireland★ JY – O'Connell Street★ (Anna Livia Fountain★) JX – St. Michan's Church★ HY **E** – Hush Lane Municipal Gallery of Modern Art★ JX **M4** – Pro-Cathedral★ JX – Garden of Remembrance★ JX – Custom House★ KX – Bluecoat School★ BS **F** – Guinness Museum★ BT **M7** – Marino Casino★ CS – Zoological Gardens★ AS – Newman House★ *AC* JZ.

Exc. : Powerscourt★★ (Waterfall★★★ *AC*), S : 14 m. by N 11 and R 117 EV – Russborough House★★★, SW : 22 m. by N 81 BT – Rathfarnham Castle★, S : 3 m. by N 81 and R 115 BT.

⛳ Elm Park G. & S.C., Nutley House, Donnybrook ✆ 269 3438/269 3014, GV – ⛳ Milltown, Lower Churchtown Rd ✆ 977060/976090, EV – ⛳ Royal Dublin, North Bull Island, Dollymount ✆ 833 6346, CS – ⛳ Forrest Little, Cloghran ✆ 840 1183/840 1763, BS – ⛳ Lucan, Celbridge Rd, Lucan ✆ 628 0246, AS – ⛳ Edmondstown, Rathfarnham ✆ 493 2461, BT – ⛳ The Open Golf Centre, Newtown House, St. Margaret's ✆ 864 0324, BS.

✈ Dublin Airport : ✆ 8444900, N : 5 ½m. by N 1 BS – **Terminal** : Busaras (Central Bus Station) Store St.

🚢 to Holyhead (Irish Ferries) 2 daily (3 h 30 mn) – to the Isle of Man (Douglas) (Isle of Man Steam Packet Co. Ltd) (4 h 30 mn).

🛈 Suffolk St., D2 ✆ 605 7797/605 7777 – Baggot Street Bridge, D2 – Arrivals Hall, Dublin Airport – Tallaght, D24.

Belfast 103 – Cork 154 – Londonderry 146.

Plans on following pages

🏨 **Conrad International Dublin**   JZ **w**
Earlsfort Terr. D2 ✆ 676 5555, Fax 676 5424
📶 ⍟ rm ▤ 📺 ☎ ᵹ 🄿 – 🔬 300. 🐼 🄰🄴 🄾 💳 🎌. ⌘
Alexandra : Meals *(closed Saturday lunch and Sunday)* 17.00/ 29.50 **t.** and a la carte
Plurabelle Brasserie : Meals 14.00/16.50 **t.** and a la carte – ⌻ 12.50 – **182 rm** 165.00/190.00 **t.**, 9 suites.

🏨 **Berkeley Court**   FU **c**
Lansdowne Rd, Ballsbridge D4 ✆ 660 1711, Fax 661 7238
📶 ⍟ rm ▤ rest 📺 ☎ ᵹ ⇔ 🄿 – 🔬 440. 🐼 🄰🄴 🄾 💳. ⌘
Berkeley Room : Meals 16.75/26.50 **t.** and a la carte
Conservatory Grill : Meals 9.75/15.00 **t.** and a la carte – ⌻ 10.75 – **181 rm** 165.00/185.00 **t.**, 5 suites.

🏨 **Shelbourne** (Forte)   JZ **s**
27 St. Stephen's Green D2 ✆ 676 6471, Fax 661 6006
📶 ⍟ rm 📺 ☎ ⇔ – 🔬 400. 🐼 🄰🄴 🄾 💳
Meals 18.00/25.50 **t.** and a la carte ⌀ 7.50 – ⌻ 12.50 – **155 rm** 138.00/ 207.00 **t.**, 9 suites – SB.

🏨 **Westbury**   JY **b**
Grafton St. D2 ✆ 679 1122, Fax 679 7078
📶 ⍟ rm ▤ rest 📺 ☎ ⇔ – 🔬 150. 🐼 🄰🄴 🄾 💳 🎌. ⌘
Meals 17.50/27.50 **t.** and a la carte ⌀ 7.50 – ⌻ 11.00 – **195 rm** 175.00/ 195.00 **t.**, 8 suites.

97

🏨 **Burlington**   EU **e**
Upper Leeson St. D4 ℰ 660 5222,
Fax 660 3172
|🛗| ⇔ rm 🍽 rest 📺 ☎ ⅙ 🅿 – 🔼 1000.
🔘 🆎 ⓪ *VISA* ᴶᶜᴮ. ⅌
Meals 12.50/17.50 **t.** and a la carte ⅙ 6.00
– 🖃 9.65 – **447 rm** 115.00/135.00 **t.**,
4 suites.

🏨 **Jurys**   FU **p**
Pembroke   Rd,   Ballsbridge   D4
ℰ 660 5000, Fax 660 5540
🏊 – |🛗| ⇔ rm 🍽 rest 📺 ☎ ⅙ 🅿 –
🔼 850. 🔘 🆎 *VISA* ⅌
Kish : Meals - Seafood - (dinner only)
27.50 **t.** and a la carte
Embassy   Garden   :   Meals   17.00/
23.50 **t.** and a la carte – 🖃 9.50 – **274 rm**
129.00/149.00 **t.**, 2 suites – SB.

🏨 **The Towers** Lansdowne Rd D4
ℰ 667 0033, Fax 660 5324, ⇆s, 🏊 – |🛗|
⇔ rm 🍽 📺 ☎ ⅙ 🅿
Meals – (see Jurys H. above) – **96 rm**
176.00/196.00 **t.**, 4 suites – SB.

🏨 **Gresham**   JX **k**
O'Connell   St.   D1   ℰ   874 6881,
Fax 878 7175
|🛗| 🍽 rest 📺 ☎ ⅙ ⇌ – 🔼 250. 🔘 🆎
⓪ *VISA*. ⅌
Meals 15.00/22.00 **t.** and a la carte ⅙ 7.00
– 🖃 15.00 – **194 rm** 160.00 **t.**, 6 suites.

🏨 **The Clarence**   HY **a**
6-8 Wellington Quay D2 ℰ 670 9000,
Fax 670 7800
« Contemporary   interior   design » – |🛗|
⇔ rm 📺 ☎ ⅙ 🅿 – 🔼 40. 🔘 🆎 ⓪ *VISA*
The Tea Room : Meals *(closed lunch Saturday and Sunday)* 17.50 **st.** (lunch) and a
la carte 19.85/34.45 – 🖃 13.00 – **49 rm**
165.00 **st.**, 4 suites.

🏨 **Hibernian**   EU **x**
Eastmoreland   Pl.,   Ballsbridge   D4
ℰ 668 7666, Fax 660 2655
|🛗| ⇔ rm 📺 ☎ ⅙ 🅿. 🔘 🆎 ⓪ *VISA* ᴶᶜᴮ.
⅌
closed 25 and 26 December
Patrick Kavanagh Room : Meals *(closed
Saturday lunch)* (residents only Sunday
dinner) 13.95/23.50 **t.** and dinner a la
carte – **40 rm** 🖃 110.00/180.00 **st.** – SB.

🏨 **Doyle Montrose**   GV **y**
Stillorgan Rd D4, SE : 4 m. by N 11
ℰ 269 3311, Fax 269 1164
|🛗| 📺 ☎ ⅙ 🅿 – 🔼 80. 🔘 🆎 ⓪ *VISA*
ᴶᶜᴮ. ⅌
Meals 10.30/18.20 **t.** and a la carte ⅙ 5.00 – 🖃 7.40 – **179 rm** 83.00/173.00 **t.**

🏨 **Mespil**   EU **u**
Mespil Rd D4 ℰ 667 1222, Fax 667 1244
|🛗| ⇔ rm 🍽 rest 📺 ☎ ⅙ 🅿 – 🔼 40. 🔘 🆎 ⓪ *VISA*. ⅌
closed 24 to 26 December – **Meals** (buffet lunch)/dinner 15.95 **st.** and
a la carte ⅙ 5.75 – 🖃 7.00 – **153 rm** 72.00 **st.**

🏨 **Royal Dublin**   JX **m**
O'Connell St. D1 ℰ 873 3666, Fax 873 3120
|🛗| 📺 ☎ ⇌ – 🔼 220. 🔘 🆎 ⓪ *VISA*. ⅌
closed 24 and 25 December – **Meals** 12.50/18.50 **st.** and a la carte ⅙ 6.50 –
117 rm 🖃 95.00/120.00 **st.**, 3 suites.

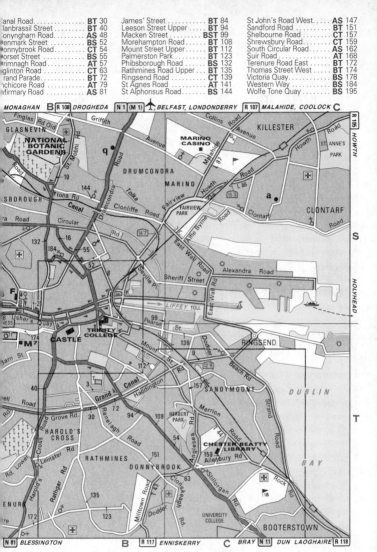

🏠 **Stephen's Hall**　　　　　　　　　　　　　　　　　　　　JZ **t**
Earlsfort Centre, 14-17 Lower Leeson St. D2 ✆ 661 0585, Fax 661 0606
📶 📺 ☎ 🚗 ⬛ 🅼🅒 🅰🅴 ① 𝘝𝘐𝘚𝘈 ✠
closed 25 to 27 December – **Morels : Meals** *(closed Saturday lunch, Sunday and Bank Holidays)* 12.50/25.00 **t.** and dinner a la carte – ☕ 8.00 – **3 rm** 105.00/145.00 **st.**, **34 suites** 145.00 **st.**

🏠 **Temple Bar**　　　　　　　　　　　　　　　　　　　　　　JY **e**
Fleet St. D2 ✆ 677 3333, Fax 677 3088
📶 📺 ☎ 🚹 – 🔬 30. 🅼🅒 🅰🅴 ① 𝘝𝘐𝘚𝘈 ✠
closed 24 to 27 December – **Meals** 9.25/15.00 **st.** and a la carte ▪ 6.50 – **108 rm** ☕ 95.00/120.00 **st.**

DUBLIN
SOUTH EAST
BUILT UP AREA

Ailesbury Road	**FV** 4
Baggot Street Upper	**EU** 7
Beech Hill Avenue	**FV** 10
Beechwood Road	**EV** 12
Belgrave Road	**DV** 13

Bloomfield Avenue	**DU** 18
Brighton Road	**DV** 22
Camden Street	**DU** 28
Castlewood Avenue	**DV** 31
Charlemont Street	**DU** 34
Charlotte Street	**DU** 36
Chelmsford Road	**EV** 37
Church Avenue	**FU** 39
Clyde Road	**EFU** 43
Eastmoreland Place	**EU** 61

Elgin Road	**EFU** 64
Harrington Street	**DU** 73
Herbert Place	**EU** 76
Irishtown Road	**FU** 82
Lansdowne Road	**FU** 90
Lea Road	**GU** 91
Leeson Street Lower	**EU** 93
Leinster Road West	**DV** 96
Londonbridge Road	**FU** 97
Maxwell Road	**DV** 10

Pour visiter une ville ou une région :
utilisez les Guides Verts Michelin.

100

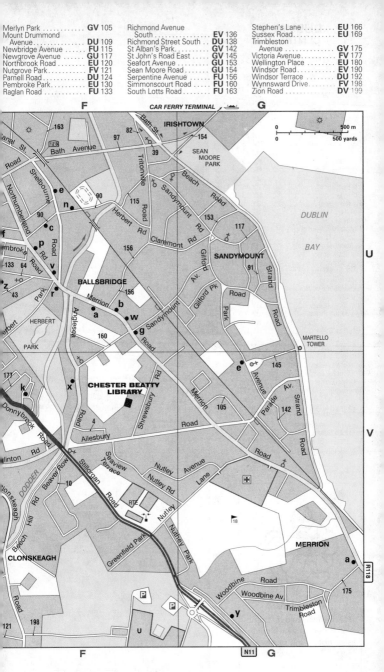

Benutzen Sie die Grünen Michelin-Reiseführer.
wenn Sie eine Stadt oder Region kennenlernen wollen.

4

DUBLIN CENTRE

Town plans:

roads most used by traffic
and those on which guide-
listed hotels and restaurants
stand are fully drawn;
the beginning only
of lesser roads is indicated.

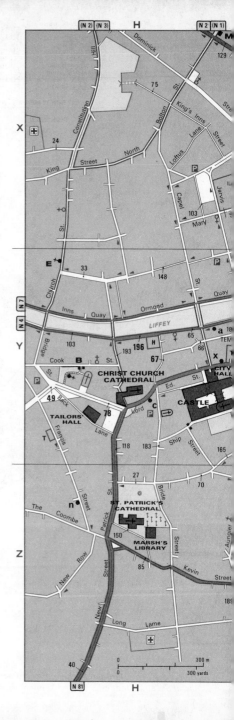

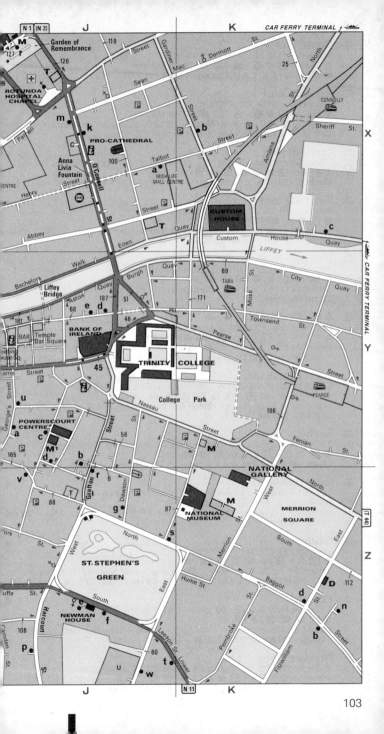

🏨 **Doyle Tara**   GV **a**
Merrion Rd D4, SE : 4 m. on T 44 ℰ 269 4666, Fax 269 1027
📶 ▤ rest 📺 ☎ 🅿 – 🔬 300. 🅜🅞 🅐🅔 🅞 *VISA* 🅙🅒🅑
Meals 8.40/13.50 **t.** and a la carte ▯ 4.90 – ☑ 7.35 – **113 rm** 85.00/105.00 **t.**

🏨 **Russell Court**   JZ **p**
21-25 Harcourt St. D2 ℰ 478 4066, Fax 478 1576
📶 ✎ 📺 ☎ 🅿 – 🔬 150. ☑ 🅞
closed 24 to 28 December – **Meals** 9.95/17.00 **st.** and dinner a la carte ▯ 6.00 –
☑ 6.50 – **42 rm** 65.00/140.00 **t.**, 6 suites – SB.

🏨 **Doyle Skylon**   BS **q**
Upper Drumcondra Rd, N : 2 ½ m. on N 1 ℰ 837 9121, Fax 837 2778
📶 ▤ rest 📺 ☎ 🅿. 🅜🅞 🅐🅔 🅞 *VISA* 🅙🅒🅑. ✑
Meals 11.00/14.00 **t.** and a la carte ▯ 4.90 – ☑ 7.35 – **92 rm** 85.00/105.00 **t.**

🏨 **Grafton Plaza**   JZ **v**
Johnsons Pl. D2 ℰ 475 0888, Fax 475 0908
📶 📺 ☎ &. 🅜🅞 🅐🅔 🅞 *VISA*. ✑
closed 24 to 26 December – **Meals** *(closed Sunday)* a la carte 10.50/23.00 **st.**
▯ 8.50 – ☑ 7.50 – **75 rm** 90.00/115.00 **st.**

🏨 **Bewley's**   JY **d**
19-20 Fleet St. D2 ℰ 670 8122, Fax 670 8103
📶 ✎ rm 📺 ☎. 🅜🅞 🅐🅔 🅞 *VISA*. ✑
closed 24 to 26 December – **Meals** a la carte 13.00/16.00 **st.** ▯ 7.00 – ☑ 6.00 –
70 rm 74.00/94.00 **st.**

🏨 **Jurys Custom House Inn**   KX **c**
Custom House Quay D1 ℰ 607 5000, Fax 829 0400
🎵 – 📶 ✎ rm 📺 ☎ &. – 🔬 100. 🅜🅞 🅐🅔 🅞 *VISA*. ✑
closed 24 to 26 December – **Meals** *(closed lunch Saturday and Sunday)* (buffet
lunch)/dinner 14.50 **t.** and a la carte ▯ 5.25 – ☑ 6.00 – **234 rm** 55.00 **t.**

🏨 **Jurys Christchurch Inn**   HY **c**
Christchurch Pl. D8 ℰ 454 0000, Fax 454 0012
📶 ✎ rm ▤ rest 📺 ☎ &. 🅿. 🅜🅞 🅐🅔 🅞 *VISA*. ✑
closed 24 to 26 December – **Meals** (bar lunch)/dinner 14.50 **st.** and a la carte –
☑ 6.00 – **182 rm** 55.00 **t.**

🏨 **Sachs**   EU **a**
12-29 Morehampton Rd, Donnybrook D4 ℰ 668 0995, Fax 668 6147
📶 📺 ☎ 🅿 – 🔬 120. 🅜🅞 🅐🅔 🅞 *VISA*. ✑
Meals 14.50/23.50 **st.** and a la carte ▯ 5.50 – **20 rm** ☑ 64.60/95.50 **st.** – SB.

🏨 **Ariel House**   FU **n**
52 Lansdowne Rd, Ballsbridge D4 ℰ 668 5512, Fax 668 5845
without rest., 🚂 – 📺 ☎ 🅿. 🅜🅞 *VISA*. ✑
closed 23 December-13 January except 31 December – ☑ 7.50 – **28 rm**
60.00/150.00 **t.**

🏨 **Central**   JY **u**
1-5 Exchequer St. D2 ℰ 679 7302, Fax 679 7303
📶 📺 ☎ – 🔬 80. 🅜🅞 🅐🅔 🅞 *VISA*. ✑
closed 24 to 26 December – **Meals** (bar lunch Monday to Friday)/dinner
a la carte 8.25/13.50 **t.** ▯ 5.25 – ☑ 7.50 – **69 rm** 75.00/110.00 **t.**, 1 suite – SB.

🏨 **Longfield's**   KZ **d**
10 Lower Fitzwilliam St. D2 ℰ 676 1367, Fax 676 1542
📶 📺 ☎. 🅜🅞 🅞 *VISA*. ✑
closed 25 December and 2 January – **Meals** – (see **Number 10** below) –
☑ 8.50 – **26 rm** 80.00/115.00 **st.** – SB.

🏨 **Number Eighty Eight**   FU **f**
88 Pembroke Rd, Ballsbridge D4 ℰ 660 0277, Fax 660 0291
without rest. – 📶 ✎ 📺 ☎ &. 🅿. 🅜🅞 🅐🅔 🅞 *VISA*. ✑
closed 1 week Christmas – **50 rm** ☑ 80.00/140.00 **st.**

🏨 **Stauntons on the Green**　　　　　　　　　　　　JZ **f**
83 St. Stephen's Green South D2 🕿 478 2300, Fax 478 2263
without rest., 🚗 – 📺 🕿 ⇦, 🐵 🖭 ⓪ *VISA*. ⅍
closed 24 to 27 December – **30 rm** ⴲ 59.00/94.00 **st.**

🏨 **Talbot**　　　　　　　　　　　　　　　　　　JX **a**
95-98 Talbot St. D1 🕿 874 9202, Fax 874 9672
without rest. – 🔌 📺 🕿 🅿 🐵 🖭 *VISA*. ⅍
closed 24 to 28 December – **48 rm** ⴲ 36.00/60.00 **st.**

🏨 **Aberdeen Lodge**　　　　　　　　　　　　　　GV **e**
53-55 Park Av. D4 🕿 283 8155, Fax 283 7877
🚗 – 📺 🕿 🅿. 🐵 🖭 ⓪ *VISA*. ⅍
Meals (dinner only) 19.00 **t.** and a la carte � 8.50 – **16 rm** ⴲ 49.50/95.00 **t.** –
SB.

🏨 **Raglan Lodge**　　　　　　　　　　　　　　　FU **z**
10 Raglan Rd, off Pembroke Rd, Ballsbridge D4 🕿 660 6697, Fax 660 6781
without rest., 🚗 – ⅙ 📺 🕿 🅿. 🐵 🖭 ⓪ *VISA*. ⅍
closed 22 December-7 January – **7 rm** ⴲ 50.00/90.00 **st.**

🏨 **Glenogra House**　　　　　　　　　　　　　　FU **w**
64 Merrion Rd D4 🕿 668 3661, Fax 668 3698
without rest. – 📺 🕿 🐵 🖭 ⓪ *VISA*. ⅍
closed 2 weeks February and 1 week Christmas – **10 rm** ⴲ 50.00/80.00 **st.**

🏨 **Merrion Hall**　　　　　　　　　　　　　　　FU **b**
54-56 Merrion Rd, Ballsbridge D4 🕿 668 1426, Fax 668 4280
without rest., 🚗 – 📺 🕿 🅿. 🐵 *VISA*. ⅍
closed 19 December-4 January – **15 rm** ⴲ 60.00/80.00 **st.**

🏨 **Cedar Lodge**　　　　　　　　　　　　　　　FU **g**
98 Merrion Rd, Ballsbridge D4 🕿 668 4410, Fax 668 4533
without rest., 🚗 – 📺 🕿 🅿. 🐵 🖭 ⅍
closed 23 to 27 December – **12 rm** ⴲ 40.00/90.00 **st.**

🏨 **Lansdowne Lodge**　　　　　　　　　　　　　FU **e**
6 Lansdowne Terr., Shelbourne Rd D4 🕿 660 5755, Fax 660 5662
without rest., 🚗 – 📺 🕿 🅿. 🐵 *VISA*. ⅍
closed 24 to 26 December – **12 rm** ⴲ 70.00/80.00 **t.**

🏨 **Morehampton Townhouse**　　　　　　　　　EU **c**
46 Morehampton Rd, Donnybrook D4 🕿 660 2106, Fax 660 2566
without rest. – 📺 🕿 🅿. 🐵 *VISA*. ⅍
closed 15 December-13 January – **6 rm** ⴲ 50.00/70.00 **st.**

🏨 **Morehampton Lodge**　　　　　　　　　　　EV **b**
113 Morehampton Rd, Donnybrook D4 🕿 283 7499, Fax 283 7595
without rest. – 📺 🕿 🅿. 🐵 *VISA*
5 rm ⴲ 50.00/75.00 **st.**

🏨 **Belgrave Guest House**　　　　　　　　　　DV **c**
8-10 Belgrave Sq., Rathmines D6 🕿 496 3760, Fax 497 9243
without rest., 🚗 – 📺 🕿 🅿. 🐵 🖭 ⓪ *JCB*. ⅍
closed 21 December-2 January – **24 rm** ⴲ 35.00/60.00 **st.**

🏨 **Uppercross House**　　　　　　　　　　　　DV **d**
26-30 Upper Rathmines Rd, Rathmines D6 🕿 4975486, Fax 4975361
⅙ rm 📺 🕿. 🐵 🖭 *VISA*
Meals (dinner only) 12.50 **st.** and a la carte � 5.95 – **25 rm** ⴲ 39.50/75.00 **st.** –
SB.

🛖 **Anglesea Town House**　　　　　　　　　　FV **x**
63 Anglesea Rd, Ballsbridge D4 🕿 668 3877, Fax 668 3461
without rest. – 📺 🕿. 🐵 🖭 *VISA*. ⅍
closed 23 December-4 January – **7 rm** ⴲ 50.00/90.00 **t.**

🛖 **Clara House**　　　　　　　　　　　　　　　DV **z**
23 Leinster Rd, Rathmines D6 🕿 497 5904, Fax 497 5904
without rest. – 📺 🕿 🅿. 🐵 *VISA*
13 rm ⴲ 36.00/62.00.

⌂ **Grafton House** JY **a**
26-27 South Great Georges St. D2 ☎ 679 2041, Fax 677 9715
without rest. – 📺 ☎. 🎫 VISA. ⌘
closed 22 to 29 December – **15 rm** ⌣ 45.00/80.00 **st.**

⌂ **Glenveagh Town House** FU **u**
31 Northumberland Rd, Ballsbridge D4 ☎ 668 4612, Fax 668 4559
without rest. – 📺 ☎. 🎫 VISA. ⌘
closed 22 to 29 December – **10 rm** ⌣ 50.00/81.00 **st.**

⌂ **St. Aiden's** DV **n**
32 Brighton Rd, Rathgar D6 ☎ 4906178, Fax 4920234
without rest. – ⌘ 📺 ☎ 🅿. 🎫 AE VISA. ⌘
closed 22 to 31 December – **8 rm** ⌣ 33.00/77.00 **st.**

⌂ **Glen** KX **b**
84 Lower Gardiner St. D1 ☎ 855 1374
without rest. – 📺 ☎ 🅿. 🎫 VISA. ⌘
12 rm ⌣ 40.00/58.00 **t.**

XXX **Patrick Guilbaud** KZ **n**
⊛⊛ 46 James' Pl., James' St., off Lower Baggot St. D2 ☎ 676 4192, Fax 661 0052
▤. 🎫 AE ① VISA
closed Sunday, Monday and first week Janaury – **Meals** - French - 22.00/35.00 **st.** and a la carte 34.00/51.00 **st.** 🍷 15.00
Spec. Pan seared Bantry Bay king scallops, watercress and deep fried leeks, Roast squab pigeon, almond and Bunratty mead sauce, Hot rhubarb soufflé.

XXX **The Commons** JZ **e**
⊛ Newman House, 85-86 St. Stephen's Green D2 ☎ 475 2597, Fax 478 0551
« Contemporary collection of James Joyce inspired Irish Art » – 🎫 AE ① VISA
closed Saturday lunch, Sunday, 2 weeks Christmas and Bank Holidays – **Meals** 18.00/32.00-42.00 **t.** 🍷 7.00
Spec. Galantine of foie gras and black pudding, Roast squab, vegetables à la grècque, tarragon oil, Pistachio and chocolate ravioli, ruby orange sauce.

XXX **Ernie's** FV **k**
⊛ Mulberry Gdns., off Morehampton Rd, Donnybrook D4 ☎ 269 3300, Fax 269 3260
« Contemporary Irish Art collection » – ▤. 🎫 AE ① VISA
closed Saturday lunch, Sunday, Monday and 24 December-1 January – **Meals** 13.95/25.00 **t.** and a la carte 26.90/36.35 **t.** 🍷 7.50.

XXX **Viking at Clontarf Castle** CS **a**
Castle Av., Clontarf D3, NE : 3 ½ m. ☎ 833 2271, Fax 833 4549
▤ 🅿. 🎫 AE VISA
closed Sunday dinner, Monday, Good Friday and 24 to 26 December – **Meals** (dinner only and Sunday lunch)/dinner a la carte 12.95/19.40 🍷 5.50.

XXX **Le Coq Hardi** EU **m**
35 Pembroke Rd D4 ☎ 668 9070, Fax 668 9887
🅿. 🎫 AE ① VISA JCB
closed Saturday lunch, Sunday, 2 weeks August, 1 week Christmas and Bank Holidays – **Meals** 18.00/33.00 **t.** and a la carte 🍷 8.00.

XX **Chapter One** JX **r**
⊛ The Dublin Writers Museum, 18-19 Parnell Sq. D1 ☎ 873 2266, Fax 873 2330
▤ 🅿. 🎫 AE ① VISA
closed Monday dinner, Sunday, 25 December-8 January and Bank Holidays – **Meals** 13.50/17.50 and dinner a la carte 19.25/24.75 **t.** 🍷 6.50.

XX **Thornton's** (Thornton) DU **e**
⊛ 1 Portobello Rd D8 ☎ 454 9067, Fax 454 9067
▤. 🎫 AE ① VISA
closed Sunday, Monday, 1 to 14 January and 5 to 12 August – **Meals** (booking essential) (dinner only) a la carte 31.85/40.85 **t.** 🍷 8.50
Spec. Marinated wild Irish salmon with cucumber and Beluga caviar, Magret of duck with gizzards and a girolle sauce, Nougat pyramid with glazed fruit and orange sauce.

XX **Locks** DU **a**
1 Windsor Terr., Portobello ✆ 4543391, Fax 4538352
MC AE Ⓓ VISA
closed Saturday lunch, Sunday, last week July-first week August and 1 week Christmas – **Meals** 13.95/23.50 **t.** and a la carte 🍾 6.50.

XX **Number 10** (at Longfield's H.) KZ **d**
10 Lower Fitzwilliam St. D2 ✆ 676 1367, Fax 676 1542
MC AE Ⓓ VISA
closed lunch Saturday, Sunday and Bank Holidays, 24 to 27 December and 2 January – **Meals** 14.50/27.50 **st.** and a la carte 🍾 6.00.

XX **Zen** DV **t**
89 Upper Rathmines Rd D6 ✆ 4979428
▤. MC AE Ⓓ VISA
closed lunch Monday to Wednesday, Saturday and dinner 24 to 27 December – **Meals** - Chinese (Szechuan) - 8.00 (lunch) and a la carte 11.50/20.00 🍾 5.00.

XX **Les Frères Jacques** HY **x**
74 Dame St. D2 ✆ 679 4555, Fax 679 4725
MC AE Ⓓ VISA
closed Saturday lunch, Sunday, 25 December-1 January and Bank Holidays – **Meals** - French - 13.50/20.00 **t.** and a la carte 🍾 5.50.

XX **L'Ecrivain** KZ **b**
109 Lower Baggot St. D2 ✆ 661 1919, Fax 661 0617
☂ – ▤. MC AE Ⓓ VISA
closed Saturday lunch, Sunday, 25-26 December and Bank Holidays – **Meals** (booking essential) 16.50/25.00 **t.** and dinner a la carte 23.50/31.50 **t.** 🍾 7.00.

XX **La Stampa** JZ **g**
35 Dawson St. D2 ✆ 677 8611, Fax 677 3336
▤ rest. MC AE Ⓓ VISA
closed lunch Saturday and Sunday, Good Friday and 25-26 December – **Meals** 10.50 **t.** (lunch) and dinner a la carte 20.40/26.40 **t.** 🍾 6.00.

XX **Peacock Alley** JY **d**
47 South William St. ✆ 662 0760, Fax 662 0776
MC AE Ⓓ VISA
closed Sunday, Monday and 10 days Christmas – **Meals** (booking essential) 16.95 **t.** (lunch) and dinner a la carte 26.40/36.00 **t.** 🍾 6.00.

XX **Old Dublin** HZ **n**
90-91 Francis St. D8 ✆ 4542028, Fax 4541406
MC AE Ⓓ VISA
closed Saturday lunch, Sunday, 25 December and Bank Holidays – **Meals** - Russian-Scandinavian - 12.50/21.00 **t.** and dinner a la carte 🍾 5.75.

XX Chandni FU **v**
174 Pembroke Rd, Ballsbridge D4 ✆ 668 1458
▤
Meals - Indian rest.

XX **Fitzers Café** FU **a**
RDS, Merrion Rd, Ballsbridge D4 ✆ 667 1301, Fax 667 1299
Ⓟ. MC AE Ⓓ VISA
closed Sunday dinner, 25-26 December, 1 January and Bank Holidays – **Meals** (booking essential) 10.50 **t.** (lunch) and a la carte 16.90/25.65 **t.** 🍾 5.00.

X **Dobbin's** EU **s**
15 Stephen's Lane, off Lower Mount St. D2 ✆ 676 4679, Fax 661 3331
▤ Ⓟ. MC AE Ⓓ VISA
closed Saturday lunch, Monday dinner, Sunday, 1 week Christmas and Bank Holidays – **Meals** - Bistro - 15.50/25.00 **t.** and a la carte.

※ 🍴 **Roly's Bistro**   FU **r**
7 Ballsbridge Terr., Ballsbridge D4 ℰ 668 2611, Fax 660 8535
▤. **MC AE ① VISA**
Meals 10.50 **t.** (lunch) and a la carte 16.75/20.75 **t.** ⌀ 4.75.

※ **Cooke's Café**   JY **c**
14 South William St. D2 ℰ 679 0536, Fax 679 0546
▤. **MC AE ① VISA**
closed 25 December and Bank Holidays – **Meals** 14.95 **t.** and a la carte ⌀ 6.50.

※ **Chili Club**   JZ **r**
1 Anne's Lane, South Anne St. D2 ℰ 677 3721, Fax 493 8284
MC AE ① VISA
closed lunch Sunday and Bank Holidays – **Meals** - Thai - (booking essential) 9.95/17.50 **t.** and a la carte ⌀ 5.20.

at Foxrock SE : 7 ½ m. by N 11 – ⊠ Dublin – 🕿 01 :

※ **Bistro One**
3 Brighton Rd. D18 ℰ 289 7711
MC VISA
closed Sunday, Monday and 24 to 26 December – **Meals** (booking essential) (dinner only) a la carte 13.15/21.15 **t.** ⌀ 4.95.

at Tallaght SW : 7 ½ m. by N 81 – ⊠ Dublin – 🕿 01 :

🏨 **Abberley Court**
Belgard Rd D24 ℰ 459 6000, Fax 462 1000
≒ rm 📺 🕿 ⅃ ⇌ – ⚱ 250. **MC AE ① VISA**. ⅍
closed 25 December – **Meals** 15.00/20.00 **st.** ⌀ 7.00 – **40 rm** ⊃ 79.00/98.00 **st.**

DUBLIN AIRPORT Dublin **405** N 7 – ⊠ Dublin – 🕿 01.

🏨 **Forte Posthouse Dublin Airport**
ℰ 844 4211, Fax 844 6002
≒ rm ▤ rest 📺 🕿 ℗ – ⚱ 130. **MC AE ① VISA**
closed 24 and 25 December – **Bistro : Meals** *(closed Saturday lunch)* 12.00/17.50 – ⊃ 9.95 – **189 rm** 89.00/99.00 **t.** – SB.

DUNDALK (Dun Dealgan) Louth **405** M 5/6 – pop. 25 843 – 🕿 042.

Dublin 51 – Drogheda 22.

🏨 **Carrickdale**
Carrickcarnon, N : 8 m. on N 1 ℰ 71397, Fax 71740
ℐ₆, ≒ₛ, ⅃, ⇌ – 📺 🕿 ℗
47 rm.

DUNDRUM (Dún Droma) Tipperary **405** H 10 – pop. 247 – ⊠ Cashel – 🕿 062.

Dublin 104 – Cork 66 – Limerick 33.

🏨 **Dundrum House**
SE : ¾ m. on R 505 ℰ 71116, Fax 71366
🦢, ℳₐ, ⇌, park, ※ – ⅃ 📺 🕿 ℗ – ⚱ 150. **MC AE ① VISA**. ⅍
Meals 9.00/18.00 and a la carte ⌀ 6.00 – **60 rm** ⊃ 52.00/90.00 – SB.

Besonders angenehme Hotels oder Restaurants sind im Führer rot gekennzeichnet.
Sie können uns helfen, wenn Sie uns die Häuser angeben, in denen Sie sich besonders wohl gefühlt haben.
Jährlich erscheint eine komplett überarbeitete Ausgabe aller Roten Michelin-Führer.

DUNFANAGHY (Dún Fionnachaidh) Donegal 405 I 2 **Ireland G.** – pop. 280 – ✉ Letterkenny – ☎ 074.

Env : Horn Head Scenic Route★, N : 2 ½m.

Exc. : Doe Castle★, SE : 7 m. by N 56 – The Rosses★, SW : 25 m. by N 56 and R 259.

Dublin 172 – Donegal 54 – Londonderry 43.

   🏛 Arnold's
      Main St. ✆ 36208, Fax 36352
      ≼, 🚗, ✕ – 📺 ☎ 🅿. 🔘 🆎 ① *VISA*. ✛
      17 March-1 November – **Meals** 22.00 **t.** (dinner) and a la carte 11.00/21.00 **t.**
      ⌕ 6.00 – **30 rm** ⌑ 33.00/80.00 **t.** – SB.

   🏛 Carrig Rua
      Main St. ✆ 36133, Fax 36277
      ≼ – 📺 ☎ 🅿. 🔘 🆎
      18 March-October – **Meals** (carving lunch)/dinner 20.00 **t.** and a la carte ⌕ 5.00
      – **22 rm** ⌑ 34.00/68.00 **t.** – SB.

DUNGARVAN (Dún Garbháin) Waterford 405 J 11 – pop. 6 920 – ☎ 058.

🛇 Knocknagrannagh ✆ 41605/43310 – 🛇 Gold Coast, Ballinacourty ✆ 42249 – 🛇 Coolcormack ✆ 43216.

Dublin 118 – Cork 44 – Waterford 30.

   🏨 Lawlors
      Meagher St. ✆ 41122, Fax 41000
      🛗 ▤ rest 📺 ☎ – 🔬 250. 🔘 🆎 ① *VISA*. ✛
      closed 25 December – **Meals** 8.75/17.95 **st.** and a la carte – **89 rm** ⌑ 34.00/
      62.00 **t.** – SB.

DUNGLOE (An Clochán Liath) Donegal 405 G 3 – ☎ 075.

Dublin 173 – Londonderry 51 – Sligo 76.

   🏨 Ostan na Rosann
      ✆ 21088, Fax 21365
      ≼, ⇔, 🔲 – 📺 ☎ 🅿. 🔘 🆎 ① *VISA*. ✛
      Easter-October – **Meals** (bar lunch)/dinner 17.00 **st.** and a la carte ⌕ 4.95 –
      48 rm ⌑ 50.00/77.00 **st.** – SB.

DUNKINEELY (Dún Cionnaola) Donegal 405 G 4 – ☎ 073.

Dublin 157 – Londonderry 56 – Sligo 50.

   ✕✕ Castle Murray
      St. Johns Point, SW : 1 ¼ m. by N 56 and St. Johns Point rd turning left at
      T junction ✆ 37022, Fax 37330
      with rm, ≼ – 📺 ☎ 🅿. 🔘 *VISA*
      *closed 3 weeks January-February, Monday and Tuesday November-March and
      24 to 26 December* – **Meals** - French - (dinner only and Sunday lunch)/
      dinner 18.00/26.00 **t.** and a la carte ⌕ 6.00 – **10 rm** ⌑ 40.00/56.00 **st.**

DUN LAOGHAIRE (Dún Laoghaire) Dublin 405 N 8 **Ireland G.** – pop. 55 540 – ☎ 01.

Env : – ≼★★ of Killiney Bay from coast road south of Sorrento Point.

⚓ to Holyhead (Stena Line) 2-4 daily (3 h 30 mn).

🛈 St. Michaels Wharf.

Dublin 9.

Plan on next page

   🏨 Royal Marine   **n**
      Marine Rd ✆ 280 1911, Fax 280 1089
      ≼, 🚗 – 🛗 ▤ rest 📺 ☎ 🅿 – 🔬 500. 🔘 🆎 ① *VISA* 🇯🇨🇧. ✛
      Meals 15.00/19.00 **t.** and a la carte ⌕ 9.00 – ⌑ 10.00 – **104 rm** 180.00 **t.** – SB.

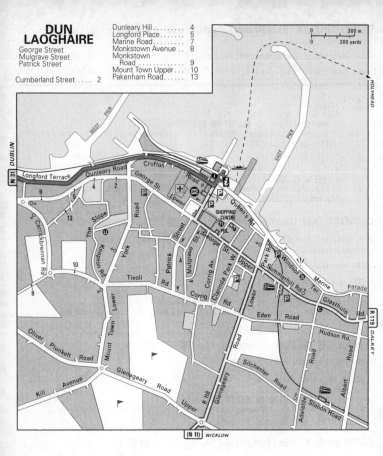

DUN LAOGHAIRE

George Street
Mulgrave Street
Patrick Street

🏠 **Chestnut Lodge**   u
2 Vesey Pl., Monkstown 🔊 280 7860, Fax 280 1466
without rest., « Regency house, antiques » 🐎 – TV ☎. ⓜⓒ VISA. ⅋
5 rm ⚏ 40.00/60.00 **t.**

🏠 **Sandycove House**   a
Newtownsmith, Sandycove 🔊 284 1600, Fax 284 1600
without rest. – TV. ⓜⓒ VISA. ⅋
closed 15 December-2 January – **13 rm** ⚏ 28.50/57.00 **st.**

XXX **Na Mara**   i
1 Harbour Rd 🔊 280 6767, Fax 284 4649
ⓜⓒ AE ⓞ VISA
closed Saturday lunch, Sunday, Good Friday and 25-26 December – **Meals** -
Seafood - 9.95/27.50 **t.** and a la carte ⓘ 6.00.

XX **Morels Bistro**   c
1st floor (above Eagle House), 18 Glasthule Rd 🔊 230 0210, Fax 230 0466
ⓜⓒ AE ⓞ VISA
closed Good Friday and 24 to 27 December – **Meals** (dinner only and Sunday
lunch)/dinner a la carte 19.00/27.75 **st.** ⓘ 6.00.

To visit a town or region : use the Michelin Green Guides.

DUNLAVIN (Dún Luáin) Wicklow 405 L 8 – pop. 720 – ✆ 045.

🏌 Rathsallagh ✆ 403316.

Dublin 31 – Kilkenny 44 – Wexford 61.

🏰 **Rathsallagh House**
SW : 2 m. on Grangecon Rd ✆ 403112, Fax 53343
🐾, ≼, « 18C converted stables, walled garden », ⊑s, 🔲, 🏌, park, ✗ – 📺 ☎
📵 – 🛏 50. 📵 🆎 ① 𝑉𝐼𝑆𝐴 ᴊᴄʙ.
closed 23 to 27 December – **Meals** (dinner only) 35.00 **t.** ♦ 6.00 – **16 rm**
⊇ 65.00/190.00 **t.**, 1 suite – SB.

DUNMANWAY (Dún Mánmhaí) Cork 405 E 12 – pop. 1 404 – ✆ 023.

Dublin 191 – Cork 37 – Killarney 49.

🏠 **Dún Mhuire House**
Kilbarry Rd, W : ½ m. by R 586 taking first right at fork junction ✆ 45162,
Fax 45162
🚂 – 📺 ☎ 📵. 📵 ① 𝑉𝐼𝑆𝐴. ✗
closed 23 to 27 December – **Meals** (closed Sunday to Tuesday September-May)
(booking essential) (dinner only) a la carte 14.00/20.00 **t.** – **6 rm** ⊇ 30.00/
50.00 **t.** – SB.

DUNMORE EAST (Dún Mór) Waterford 405 L 11 **Ireland G.** – pop. 1 038 – ✉
Waterford – ✆ 051.

See : Village★.

Dublin 108 – Waterford 12.

🏠 **Lakefield House**
Dunmore East Rd, Rosduff, NW : 5 m. on R 684 ✆ 382582, Fax 382582
🐾, ≼, ⌇, 🚂, park – ⤙ rest 📺 📵. 📵 𝑉𝐼𝑆𝐴. ✗
mid March-October – **Meals** (by arrangement) 14.00 – **5 rm** ⊇ 23.50/35.00 **st.**
– SB.

✗ **Ship**
Dock Rd ✆ 383141
📵 🆎 𝑉𝐼𝑆𝐴
closed Sunday, Monday and November-April – **Meals** - Seafood - a la
carte 10.20/19.95 **t.** ♦ 5.75.

DUNSHAUGHLIN (Dún Seachlainn) Meath 405 M 7 – pop. 1 275 – ✆ 01.

Dublin 17 – Drogheda 19.

🏠 **Gaulstown House**
NE : 1 ½ m. by Ratoath rd ✆ 825 9147
🐾, « Working farm », 🚂, park – ⤙ 📺 📵. 📵 𝑉𝐼𝑆𝐴. ✗
April-October – **Meals** (by arrangement) 14.00 **st.** – **4 rm** ⊇ 23.00/36.00 **st.** –
SB.

🏠 **Old Workhouse**
Ballinlough ✆ 8259251
🚂 – 📵. 📵 𝑉𝐼𝑆𝐴. ✗
Meals (by arrangement) (communal dining) 18.00 – **4 rm** ⊇ 30.00/50.00 **st.** –
SB.

DURRUS (Dúras) Cork 405 D 13 – pop. 188 – ✆ 027.

Dublin 210 – Cork 56 – Killarney 53.

✗✗ **Blairs Cove**
SW : 1 m. on L 56 ✆ 61127, Fax 61127
« Converted barn », 🚂 – 📵. 📵 🆎 ① 𝑉𝐼𝑆𝐴
closed Sunday, Monday except July and August and November-March – **Meals**
(booking essential) (dinner only) 27.00 **st.**

ENNIS (Inis) Clare 🆘 F 9 **Ireland G.** – pop. 13 730 – ✆ 065.

See : Ennis Friary★ *AC*.

Env : Clare Abbey★, SE : 1 m. by R 469.

Exc. : Quin Franciscan Friary★, SE : 6 ½m. by R 469 – Knappogue Castle★ *AC*, SE : 8 m. by R 469 – Carrofin (Clare Heritage Centre★ *AC*), N : 8 ½m. by N 85 and R 476 – Craggaunowen Centre★ *AC*, SE : 11 m. by R 469 – Kilmacduagh Churches and Round Tower★, NE : 11 m. by N 18 – Scattery Island★, SW : 27 m. by N 68 and boat from Kilrush – Bridge of Ross, Kilkee★, SW : 35 ½m. by N 68 and N 67.

🏌 Drumbiggle Rd ✆ 24074.

🛈 Clare Rd ✆ 28366.

Dublin 142 – Galway 42 – Limerick 22 – Roscommon 92 – Tullamore 93.

🏨   **Auburn Lodge**
    Galway Rd, N : 1 ½ m. on N 18 ✆ 21247, Fax 21202
    🖼 – 📺 ☎ 🅿, 🅼🅲 🄰🄴 ⓪ 🆅🆂🄰. ✗
    Meals (dinner only and Sunday lunch)/dinner 18.50 **st.** and a la carte 🍴 5.00 –
    98 rm 😄 45.00/90.00 **st.** – SB.

↑   **Cill Eoin House**
    Killadysert Cross, Clare Rd, SE : 1 ½ m. at junction of N 18 with R 473
    ✆ 41668, Fax 20224
    without rest., 🖼, ✗ – ✦ 📺 ☎ 🅿
    14 rm.

↑   **Magowna House**
    Inch, Kilmaley, SW : 5 m. by R 474 (Kilmaley rd) ✆ 39009, Fax 39258
    🐾, ≤, 🖼 – ☎ 🅿, 🅼🅲 🄰🄴 ⓪ 🆅🆂🄰
    closed 24 to 26 December – **Meals** 12.95 **st.** 🍴 5.00 – **10 rm** 😄 33.00/52.00 **st.**
    – SB.

    at Barefield NE : 3 ½ m. on N 18 – ✉ Ennis – ✆ 065 :

↑   **Carraig Mhuire**
    Bearnafunshin, NE : 1 ¾ m. on N 18 ✆ 27106, Fax 27375
    🖼 – 🅿, 🅼🅲 🆅🆂🄰. ✗
    closed 20 December-3 January – **Meals** 11.00 **st.** – **5 rm** 😄 16.00/32.00 **s.** –
    SB.

ENNISCORTHY (Inis Córthaidh) Wexford 🆘 M 10 – pop. 4 127 – ✆ 053.

🏌 Knockmarshall ✆ (054) 33191.

Dublin 76 – Kilkenny 46 – Waterford 34 – Wexford 15.

🏛   **Ballinkeele House**
    Ballymurn, SE : 6 ½ m. by unmarked road on Curracloe rd ✆ 38105,
    Fax 38468
    🐾, ≤, « 19C country house, antiques », 🖼, park, ✗ – ✦ rm 🅿, 🅼🅲 🆅🆂🄰
    🅹🅲🅱. ✗
    April-3 November – **Meals** (booking essential) (communal dining) (dinner
    only) 20.00 **st.** – **5 rm** 😄 48.00/80.00 **st.**

ENNISTIMON (Inis Dáomáin) Clare 🆘 E 9 – ✆ 065.

Dublin 158 – Galway 52 – Limerick 39.

↑   **Grovemount House**
    Lahinch Rd, W : ½ m. on N 67 ✆ 71431, Fax 71823
    without rest., 🖼 – ☎ 🅿, 🅼🅲 🆅🆂🄰. ✗
    April-October – **8 rm** 😄 25.00/40.00 **st.**

This Guide is not a comprehensive list of all hotels and restaurants,
nor even of all good hotels and restaurants in Ireland.

Since our aim is to be of service to all motorists,
we must show establishments in all categories and so we have made
a selection of some in each.

FAHAN (Fathain) Donegal 405 J 2 Ireland G. – pop. 309 – ⊠ Inishowen – ☎ 077.

Exc. : Inishowen Peninsula★★ : (Dun Ree Fort★ *AC*), N : 11 m. by R 238.

� North West, Lisfannon ℰ 61027.

Dublin 156 – Londonderry 11 – Sligo 95.

XX **St. John's**
    ℰ 60289
    « Loughside setting », ⌖ – ⁕ **P**. **MO O** **VISA** **JCB**
    closed Good Friday and 25 December – **Meals** (dinner only) a la carte 14.95/
    22.95 **t.** ﹝ 5.90.

FERNS (Fearna) Wexford 405 M 10 Ireland G. – pop. 859 – ⊠ Enniscorthy – ☎ 054.

Exc. : – Mount Leinster★, NW : 17 m.

Dublin 69 – Kilkenny 53 – Waterford 41 – Wexford 22.

⌂ **Clone House**
    S : 2 m. by Boolavogue rd off Monageer rd ℰ 66113, Fax 66113
    ⌖, « Working farm », ⌖, ⌖, park – ⁕ **TV** **P**. ⌖
    April-October – **Meals** (by arrangement) (communal dining) 14.00 **st.** ﹝ 5.00 –
    4 rm ⌷ 25.00/40.00 **st.**

FOXROCK (Carraig an tSionnaigh) Dublin 405 N 7 – see Dublin.

FURBOGH/FURBO (Na Forbacha) Galway 405 E 8 – ☎ 091.

Dublin 42 – Galway 7.

⌂⌂⌂ **Connemara Coast**
    ℰ 592108, Fax 592065
    ⌖, ﹝ᴓ, ⌖, ⌖, ⌖, ⌖ – ⁕ rm **TV** ☎ **P** – ⌖ 500. **MO AE O** **VISA**. ⌖
    closed 25 December – **Meals** (bar lunch)/dinner 21.00 **st.** and a la carte ﹝ 5.95
    – **111 rm** ⌷ 85.00/145.00 **st.**, 1 suite – SB.

GALWAY (Gaillimh) Galway 405 E 8 Ireland G. – pop. 50 855 – ☎ 091.

See : City★★ – Lynch's Castle★ BY – St. Nicholas' Church★ BY – Roman Catholic
Cathedral★ AY – Eyre Square : Bank of Ireland Building (Mace★) BY **D**.

Env : NW : Lough Corrib★★.

Exc. : W : by boat, Aran Islands (Inishmore – Dun Aenghus★★★) BZ – Thoor Bally-
lee★★, SE : 21 m. by N 6 and N 18 BY – Athenry★, E : 14 m. by N 6 and R 348 BY –
Dunguaire Castle, Kinvarra★ *AC*, S : 16 m. by N 6, N 18 and N 67 BY – Knockmoy
Abbey★, NE : 19 m. by N 17 and N 63 BY – Coole Park (Autograph Tree★), SE : 21 m.
by N 6 and N 18 BY – St. Mary's Cathedral, Tuam★, NE : 21 m. by N 17 BY – Loughrea
(St. Brendan's Cathedral★), SE : 22 m. by N 6 BY.

� Galway, Blackrock, Salthill ℰ 23038.

✈ Carnmore Airport : ℰ 752874, NE : 4 m.

🛈 Victoria Pl., Eyre Sq. ℰ 63081.

Dublin 135 – Limerick 64 – Sligo 90.

Plan on next page

⌂⌂⌂ **Glenlo Abbey**
    Bushypark, NW : 3 ¼ m. on N 59 ℰ 526666, Fax 527800
    « Restored part 18C house and church », ﹝ᴓ, ⌖, park – ⌖ 🖿 rest **TV** ☎ ﹠ **P** –
    ⌖ 100. **MO AE O** **VISA**
    French Room : Meals (booking essential) (bar lunch Monday to Saturday)/
    dinner 28.00 **st.** and a la carte – ⌷ 12.00 – **42 rm** 110.00/175.00 **st.**, 3 suites
    – SB.

⌂⌂⌂ **Great Southern**   BY **a**
    Eyre Sq. ℰ 64041, Fax 66704
    ⌖, ⌖ – ⌖ ⁕ rm **TV** ☎ **P** – ⌖ 450. **MO AE O** **VISA** **JCB**. ⌖
    closed 4 days Christmas – **Meals** (carving lunch)/dinner 19.00 **t.** and a la carte
    ﹝ 8.00 – ⌷ 7.50 – **115 rm** 77.00/120.00 **t.**, 1 suite – SB.

GALWAY

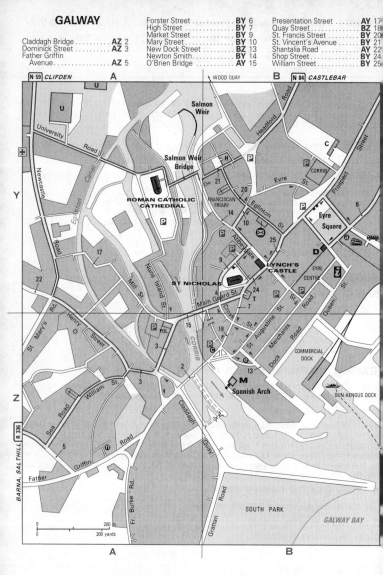

🏨 **Corrib Great Southern**
Dublin Rd, E : 1 ¾ m. on N 6 ℰ 755281, Fax 751390
🔽 – ⧉ ✳ rm ▤ rest 📺 ☎ ♿ ❷ – 🔬 850. ⬛⬤ ⒶⒺ ⓪ 𝘝𝘐𝘚𝘈 𝙅𝘾𝘽. ⅛
closed 25 and 26 December – **Meals** 11.50/18.50 **t.** and dinner a la carte –
176 rm ☲ 66.00/117.00 **t.**, 4 suites – SB.

🏨 **Ardilaun House**
Taylor's Hill, W : 1 ½ m. on R 336 ℰ 521433, Fax 521546
🛁, ⇌, 🏊 – ⧉ ✳ rm 📺 ☎ ❷ – 🔬 450. ⬛⬤ ⒶⒺ ⓪ 𝘝𝘐𝘚𝘈
closed 23 to 26 December – **Meals** 11.00/21.00 **t.** and dinner a la carte –
89 rm ☲ 65.00/105.00 **t.**, 1 suite – SB.

🏨 **Jurys Galway Inn**   BZ **c**
Quay St. ☎ 66444, Fax 68415
🏮 – 🛗 ✻ rm 📺 ☎ – 🔧 40. 🆔 🅰🅴 ① 💳. ✻
closed 24 to 26 December – **Meals** (bar lunch)/dinner 14.50 **t.** and a la carte
🍸 5.25 – ⌑ 6.00 – **128 rm** 60.00 **t.**

🏨 **Brennan's Yard**   BZ **e**
Lower Merchants Rd ☎ 568166, Fax 568262
🏮 📺 ☎. 🆔 🅰🅴 ① 💳. ✻
closed 25 and 26 December – **Meals** (booking essential) (bar lunch)/
dinner 14.50 **t.** and a la carte 🍸 5.00 – **24 rm** ⌑ 60.00/95.00 **st.** – SB.

🏨 **Galway Ryan**
Dublin Rd., E : 1 ¼ m. on N 6 ☎ 753181, Fax 753187
🎱, 🈺, 🏊, 🏮, ✻ – 🅿 – 🔧 60. 🆔 🅰🅴 ① 💳. ✻
closed 25 December – **Meals** (bar lunch)/dinner 15.00 **st.** and a la carte 🍸 7.00
– ⌑ 10.00 – **96 rm** 130.00 **st.** – SB.

🏠 **Adare House**   AZ **n**
9 Father Griffin Pl., Lower Salthill ☎ 582638, Fax 583963
without rest. – 📺 ☎ 🅿. 🆔 💳
closed 24 to 27 December – **11 rm** ⌑ 22.50/60.00 **t.**

✗✗ **Casey's Westwood**
Newcastle, NW : 1 ¾ m. on N 59 ☎ 521442, Fax 521400
🏮 – 🅿. 🆔 🅰🅴 ① 💳. ✻
closed 24 to 28 December – **Meals** 11.50 **t.** (lunch) and dinner a la carte
approx. 17.50 **t.** 🍸 5.95.

at Salthill SW : 2 m. – AZ – ☎ 091 :

🏨 **Jameson's**
Upper Salthill ☎ 528666, Fax 528626
🏮 📺 ☎ 🅿 – 🔧 50. 🆔 🅰🅴 ① 💳
closed 24 to 26 December – **Meals** 9.00/15.00 **st.** and a la carte 🍸 6.00 – **20 rm**
⌑ 48.00/90.00 **st.**

🏨 **Tysons Rockbarton Park**
5-7 Rockbarton Park ☎ 522286, Fax 527692
📺 ☎ 🅿. 🆔 🅰🅴 ① 💳. ✻
closed 1 week Christmas – **Meals** (dinner only) 18.50 **st.** and a la carte 🍸 6.50 –
11 rm ⌑ 39.00/70.00 **st.** – SB.

🏠 **Devondell**
47 Devon Park, Lower Salthill, off Lower Salthill Rd ☎ 523617
without rest. – ✻. ✻
February-October – **4 rm** ⌑ 20.00/40.00 **st.**

GARRYVOE (Garraí Uí Bhuaigh) Cork 🗺 H 12 – ✉ Castlemartyr – ☎ 021.

Dublin 161 – Cork 23 – Waterford 62.

🏨 **Garryvoe**
☎ 646718, Fax 646824
≤, 🏮, ✗ – 📺 ☎ 🅿 – 🔧 300. 🆔 🅰🅴 ① 💳. ✻
closed 25 December – **Meals** 10.00/19.00 **st.** and dinner a la carte 🍸 6.50 –
19 rm ⌑ 35.00/100.00 **st.** – SB.

GLANDORE (Cuan Dor) Cork 🗺 E 13 – ☎ 028.

Dublin 196 – Cork 44 – Killarney 75.

✗✗ **Rectory**
☎ 33072, Fax 33600
≤ – 🅿. 🆔 🅰🅴 ① 💳. ✻
Easter-October – **Meals** *(closed Sunday and Monday except June-October)*
(dinner only) 24.50 **st.**

La Grande-Bretagne et l'Irlande sont maintenant couvertes
par un atlas disponible en trois versions :
broché, relié et à spirale.

GLENBEIGH (Gleann Beithe) Kerry 405 C 11 – ✪ 066.

Dublin 197 – Killarney 21 – Tralee 24.

⌂ **Foxtrot**
Mountain Stage, SW : 3 m. on N 70 ✆ 68417, Fax 68552
without rest., ≤, – ⍰⊁ **P**. *VISA*. ⌘
March-October – **4 rm** ⌷ 21.00/32.00 **st.**

GLENDALOUGH (Gleann dá Loch) Wicklow 405 M 8 – ✪ 0404.

Dublin 28 – Kilkenny 68 – Wexford 63.

🏛 **Glendalough**
✆ 45135, Fax 45142
🚗 – **TV** ☎ **P** – 🏛 150. **MO** **AE** **①** *VISA*. ⌘
closed December and January – **Meals** 9.00/17.00 **t.** and a la carte ⌙ 5.25 –
43 rm ⌷ 48.95/75.90 **st.** – SB.

GLENGARRIFF (An Gleann Garbh) Cork 405 D 12 – ✪ 027.

🛈 ✆ 63084 (July-August).

Dublin 213 – Cork 60 – Killarney 37.

⌂ **Cois Coille**
✆ 63202
⌚ without rest., ≤, 🚗 – ⍰⊁ **P**. ⌘
April-October – **6 rm** ⌷ 22.00/34.00 **st.**

GLEN OF AHERLOW (Gleann Eatharlaí) Tipperary 405 H 10 Ireland G. –
✉ Tipperary – ✪ 062.

See : Glen of Aherlow★.

Exc. : Caher Castle★★ *AC* – Town Square★ – St. Paul's Church★ – Swiss Cottage★
AC, SE : 7 m. by N 24 and R 670 – Clonmel★ (County Museum★, St. Mary's
Church★, Riverside★, Quay★), NE : 16 m. by N 24 – Kilmallock★★ :- Abbey★, Collegiate Church★, Blossom's Gate★, Town Walls★, King's Castle★ – W : 27 ½ m. by
R 664 and R 515.

Dublin 118 – Cahir 6 – Tipperary 9.

🏛 **Aherlow House**
✆ 56153, Fax 56212
⌚, ≤ Galty Mountains, park – **TV** ☎ **P**. **MO** **AE** **①** *VISA*. ⌘
Meals 9.95/18.50 **st.** ⌙ 5.00 – ⌷ 7.50 – **30 rm** 33.00/120.00 **st.** – SB.

GOREY (Guaire) Wexford 405 N 9 Ireland G. – pop. 2 198 – ✪ 055.

Exc. : Ferns★, SW : 11 m. by N 11.

🏌 Courtown, Kiltennel ✆ 25166.

🛈 Town Centre ✆ 21248 (July and August).

Dublin 58 – Waterford 55 – Wexford 38.

🏛 **Marlfield House**
Courtown Rd, E : 1 m. ✆ 21124, Fax 21572
⌚, ≤, « Regency house, conservatory », ⊜s, 🚗, park, ⌘ – **TV** ☎ **P**. **MO** **AE**
① *VISA*. ⌘
closed mid December-February – **Meals** 18.00/32.00 **t.** ⌙ 7.00 – **18 rm**
⌷ 85.00/195.00 **t.**, 1 suite – SB.

GRAIGUENAMANAGH (Gráig na Manach) Kilkenny 405 L 10 – ✪ 0503.

Dublin 77 – Kilkenny 20 – Waterford 25 – Wexford 34.

⌂ **Stablecroft**
Mooneen, N : 2 m. by R 705 off R 703 ✆ 24714, Fax 24714
⌚, ≤, 🚗 – ⍰⊁ **P**. ⌘
restricted opening in winter – **Meals** (by arrangement) (communal dining)
14.00 **s.** – **3 rm** ⌷ 18.00/70.00 **s.**

GREYSTONES (Na Clocha Liatha) Wicklow 405 N 8 – pop. 9 649 – 😊 01.

Dublin 22.

℟ **Hungry Monk**
Southview Church Rd ℰ 287 5759, Fax 287 7183
MC AE ① VISA
closed Monday and 24-26 December – **Meals** (dinner only and Sunday lunch)/
dinner 18.95 **t.** and a la carte ⫪ 6.95.

HOWTH (Binn Èadair) Dublin 405 N 7 Ireland G. – ✉ Dublin – 😊 01.

See : Town★ – The Summit★.

🏌, 🏌, 🏌 Deer Park Hotel, Howth Castle ℰ 832 2624.

Dublin 10.

🏯 **Marine**
Sutton Cross, W : 1 ½ m. ℰ 839 0000, Fax 839 0442
≼, 🖘, 🔲, ☞ – 📺 ☎ 🅿 – 🔏 200. **MC AE ① VISA**. ✻
closed 24 to 26 December – **Meals** 11.50/20.00 **st.** and dinner a la carte ⫪ 4.95
– **26 rm** � 80.00/120.00 **st.** – SB.

🏨 **Howth Lodge**
W : 1 m. ℰ 832 1010, Fax 832 2268
≼, 🖘, 🔲 – 🛗 📺 ☎ & 🅿 – 🔏 200. **MC AE ① VISA**. ✻
closed 23 to 29 December – **Meals** *(closed Sunday dinner)* (bar lunch Monday
to Saturday)/dinner 22.00 ⫪ 4.75 – **46 rm** ⊏ 50.00/130.00 **st.** – SB.

🏨 **Deer Park**
W : ¾ m. ℰ 832 2624, Fax 839 2405
≼, 🏌, 🏌, park – ▤ rest 📺 ☎ & 🅿 – 🔏 100. **MC AE ① VISA JCB**. ✻
closed 24 to 26 December – **Meals** 10.50/17.00 **st.** and dinner a la carte ⫪ 5.00
– **51 rm** ⊏ 62.00/96.00 **st.** – SB.

℟℟ **King Sitric**
Harbour Rd, East Pier ℰ 832 5235, Fax 839 2442
MC AE ① VISA
closed Sunday, 2 weeks January and Bank Holidays – **Meals** - Seafood - (light
lunch Monday to Saturday May-September) (dinner only October-April)/
dinner 26.00 **t.** and a la carte 24.00/30.00 **t.** ⫪ 6.25.

INISHCRONE (Inis Crabhann) Sligo 405 E 5 – 😊 096.

Dublin 160 – Ballina 8 – Galway 79 – Sligo 34.

⋔ **Ceol na Mara**
Main St. ℰ 36351, Fax 36642
≼ – 📺 ☎ 🅿. **MC VISA**. ✻
February-November – **Meals** (by arrangement) 14.00 **s.** – **9 rm** ⊏ 20.00/
40.00 **st.** – SB.

INISHMORE (Inis Mór) Galway 405 CD 8 – see Aran Islands.

INISTIOGE (Inis Tíog) Kilkenny 405 K 10 – 😊 056.

Dublin 82 – Kilkenny 16 – Waterford 19 – Wexford 33.

⋔ **Berryhill**
SE : ¾ m. by R 700 ℰ 58434, Fax 58434
🦢, ≼, « Working farm », ⌇, ☞, park – 🅿. **MC VISA**. ✻
April-November – **Meals** (by arrangement) (communal dining) 25.00 **st.** – **3 rm**
⊏ 38.00/70.00 **st.**

⋔ **Rathsnagadan House**
SE : 4 ½ m. by R 700 ℰ (051) 423641
🦢, ≼, ☞, park – ⤨ rm 🅿. **MC VISA**. ✻
Meals (by arrangement) 18.00 **st.** – **3 rm** ⊏ 25.00/40.00 **st.** – SB.

XX Motte
Plass Newid, NW : ¼ m. on R 700 ℘ 58655
🅿. 🚗🅫 𝚅𝙸𝚂𝙰
closed Sunday except Bank Holidays, Monday, 1 week Spring, 1 weeks Autumn and 1 week Christmas – **Meals** (dinner only) 21.00 **t.** ⅍ 6.00.

INNISHANNON (Inis Eonáin) Cork 🚾🅞🅤 G 12 – pop. 319 – ⓧ 021.

Dublin 169 – Cork 15.

🏨 Innishannon House
S : ¾ m. on R 605 ℘ 775121, Fax 775609
🦢, ≼, « Riverside setting », 🦢, 🥗, park – 📺 ☎ 🅿. 🚗🅫 🅰🅴 ⓪ 𝚅𝙸𝚂𝙰
closed January-February – **Meals** 12.00/26.00 **t.** and a la carte ⅍ 6.50 – **14 rm** ⊠ 65.00/150.00 **st.** – SB.

INVERIN (Indreabhán) Galway 🚾🅞🅤 D8 – ⓧ 091.

Dublin 149 – Galway 17.

⌂ Tigh Chualáin
Kilroe East, on R 336 ℘ 83609
without rest. – 📺 ☎ 🅿
9 rm.

When visiting Great Britain,
use the Michelin Green Guide **"Great Britain".**
– *Detailed descriptions of places of interest*
– *Touring programmes*
– *Maps and street plans*
– *The history of the country*
– *Photographs and drawings of monuments, beauty spots, houses...*

KANTURK (Ceann Toirc) Cork 🚾🅞🅤 F 11 Ireland G. – pop. 1 777 – ⓧ 029.

See : Town★ - Castle★.

🏌 Fairy Hill ℘ 50534.

Dublin 161 – Cork 33 – Killarney 31 – Limerick 44.

🏨 Assolas Country House
E : 3 ¼ m. by R 576 off R 580 ℘ 50015, Fax 50795
🦢, ≼, « Part 17C and 18C country house, gardens, riverside setting », 🦢, park, 🥗 – ☎ 🅿. 🚗🅫 🅰🅴 𝚅𝙸𝚂𝙰. 🥗
April-October – **Meals** (booking essential) (dinner only) 30.00 **st.** ⅍ 7.50 – **9 rm** ⊠ 75.00/160.00 **st.**

🏠 Duhallow Lodge
S : 3 ¼ m. by R 579 on N 72 ℘ 56042, Fax 56152
🛏 rm 📺 ☎ & 🅿 – 🔺 250
22 rm.

KENMARE (Neidín) Kerry 🚾🅞🅤 D 12 Ireland G. – pop. 1 366 – ⓧ 064.

See : Site★.

Exc. : Iveragh Peninsula★★★ (Ring of Kerry★★) – Healy Pass★★ (≼★★), SW : 19 m. by R 571 and R 574 – Mountain Road to Glengarriff (≼★★) S : by N 71 - Slieve Miskish Mountains (≼★★), SW : 30 m. by R 571 - Gougane Barra Forest Park★★, SE : 10 m. – Lauragh (Derreen Gardens★ *AC*), SW : 14 ½m. by R 571 – Allihies (Copper Mines★), SW : 35 ½m. by R 571 and R 575 – Garnish Island (≼★), SW : 42 ½m. by R 571, R 575 and R 572.

🏌 Kenmare ℘ 41291.

🏛 Heritage Centre, The Square ℘ 41233 (April-October).

Dublin 210 – Cork 58 – Killarney 20.

🏨 **Park**
❀
🍴, ≤ Kenmare Bay and hills, « Antiques, paintings », *f₆*, *f₈*, 🦃, 🏊, park, 🍴
– 🔄 📺 ☎ ♿ **P** – 🅰️ 35. **MO AE O VISA**. 🍴
15 April-1 November and 23 December-2 January – **Meals** (dinner only)
39.00 **st.** and a la carte 39.10/59.75 **t.** ⓐ 9.00 – ☕ 14.00 – **47 rm** 110.00/
234.00 **t.**, 2 suites
Spec. Medallions of Sneem black pudding, marinated poussin and chanterelles, Roulade of
sole and prawns, pickled samphire, light Champagne sauce, Summer fruit pudding, lavender
ice cream, red fruit coulis.

🏨 **Sheen Falls Lodge**
❀
SE : 1 ¼ m. by N 71 ℘ 41600, Fax 41386
🍴, « Wooded setting on banks of Sheen River and Kenmare Bay, ≤ Sheen
Falls », ⓐ, 🐎, 🏊, park, 🍴 – 🔄 📺 ♿ **P** – 🅰️ 120. **MO AE O VISA JCB**. 🍴
La Cascade : Meals (bar lunch Monday to Saturday)/dinner 37.50 – ☕ 13.00 –
32 rm 185.00/240.00 **st.**, 8 suites
Spec. Marinated scallops with chilli and leek on a tomato and cucumber essence, Roast loin of
venison on a purée of smoked aubergine, liquorice jus, Grilled turbot fillet, ragout of Puy lentils,
caper and flat parsley cream.

🏨 **Dromquinna Manor**
Blackwater Bridge P.O., W : 3 m. by N 71 on N 70 ℘ 41657, Fax 41791
🍴, « Situated on the banks of Kenmare river », 🦃, 🏊, park, 🍴 – 📺 ☎
P. **MO AE O VISA**
Meals *(closed Sunday dinner)* (dinner only and Sunday lunch)/dinner 18.50
and a la carte ⓐ 5.95 – **28 rm** ☕ 39.50/160.00 **t.** – SB:

🏨 **Sallyport House**
S : ¼ m. on N 71 ℘ 42066, Fax 42067
without rest., ≤, « Antique furnishings », 🏊 – ✸✸ 📺 ☎ **P**. 🍴
Easter-October – **4 rm** ☕ 55.00/70.00.

🏨 **Shelburne Lodge**
Killowen Rd, E : ½ m. on R 569 (Cork Rd) ℘ 41013, Fax 42135
without rest., « Stylishly decorated 18C house », 🏊 – 📺 ☎ **P**. **MO VISA**. 🍴
Easter-September – **Meals** – (see **Packie's** below) – **8 rm** ☕ 40.00/70.00 **t.**

🏨 **Dunkerron**
Sneem Rd, W : 2 ½ m. on N 70 ℘ 41102, Fax 41102
🍴, 🏊, park – ☎ **P**. **MO VISA**. 🍴
April-October – **Meals** (booking essential) (lunch by arrangement) 20.00
and a la carte 17.00/24.00 **st.** – **10 rm** ☕ 40.00/70.00 **st.**

🍴 **Foleys**
Henry St. ℘ 41361, Fax 41799
📺. **MO VISA**. 🍴
Meals (bar lunch)/dinner 14.50 **st.** and a la carte ⓐ 5.75 – **10 rm** ☕ 30.00/
50.00 **st.** – SB.

🏠 **Mylestone House**
Killowen Rd, E : ¼ m. ℘ 41753
without rest., 🏊 – **P**. **MO VISA**. 🍴
March-mid November – **5 rm** ☕ 25.00/36.00 **st.**

🏠 **Ceann Mara**
E : 1 m. on Kilgarvan rd ℘ 41220
🍴, ≤ Kenmare Bay and hills, 🏊 – **P**. 🍴
May-September – **Meals** (by arrangement) 15.00 **s.** – **4 rm** ☕ 23.00/36.00.

🏠 **Ard Na Mara**
Pier Rd ℘ 41399, Fax 41399
without rest., ≤ Kenmare Bay and hills, 🏊 – **P**. 🍴
closed 25 December – **4 rm** ☕ 20.00/31.00 **t.**

🍴🍴 **d'Arcys**
Main St. ℘ 41589, Fax 41589
with rm – **MO VISA**. 🍴
closed last 2 weeks January and 24 to 27 December – **Meals** (dinner only)
17.50 **st.** and a la carte 17.25/25.95 **st.** ⓐ 6.00 – **5 rm** ☕ 20.00/34.00 **st.** – SB.

KENMARE

✂ 🍴 **Lime Tree**
Shelbourne St. ✆ 41225, Fax 41402
« Characterful former schoolhouse » – 🅿. 🇲🇨 𝘝𝘐𝘚𝘈
April-October – **Meals** (dinner only) a la carte 17.70/22.65 **t.** 🍷 6.75.

✂ **Packies**
Henry St. ✆ 41508
🇲🇨 𝘝𝘐𝘚𝘈
closed Sunday and mid November-Easter – **Meals** (dinner only) a la carte 17.00/22.70 **t.** 🍷 5.25.

✂ **An Leath Phingin**
35 Main St. ✆ 41559
🇲🇨 𝘝𝘐𝘚𝘈
closed November – **Meals** (dinner only) a la carte 12.50/16.50 **t.** 🍷 5.50.

KILCUMMIN (Cill Chuimán) Kerry 405 B 11 – ☎ 066.

Dublin 203 – Killarney 34 – Limerick 85 – Tralee 21.

↑ **Strand View House**
Conor Pass Rd ✆ 38131, Fax 39434
without rest., ≤ – 🅿. 🇲🇨 𝘝𝘐𝘚𝘈. 🍴
closed November-February – **4 rm** � 25.00/40.00 **s.**

KILKEE (Cill Chaoi) Clare 405 D 9 – pop. 1 315 – ☎ 065.

Dublin 177 – Galway 77 – Limerick 58.

🏛 **Halpin's**
Erin St. ✆ 56032, Fax 56317
📺 ☎. 🇲🇨 🆎 ⑪ 𝘝𝘐𝘚𝘈. 🍴
15 March-14 November – **Meals** (bar lunch Monday to Saturday)/dinner 18.00
and a la carte 🍷 8.00 – **12 rm** ⊐z 35.00/75.00 **t.** – SB.

KILKENNY (Cill Chainnigh) Kilkenny 405 K 10 Ireland G. – pop. 8 515 – ☎ 056.

See : Town★★ – St. Canice's Cathedral★★ – Kilkenny Castle and Grounds★★ *AC* –
Cityscope★ *AC* – Black Abbey★.

Exc. : Dunmore Cave★ *AC*, N : 7 m. by N 77 and N 78 – Kells Priory★, S : 9 m. by
R 697.

🏌 Glendine ✆ 65400 – 🏌 Geraldine, Callan ✆ 25136 – 🏌 Drumgoole, Castlecomer
✆ 41139.

🛈 Rose Inn St. ✆ 51500.

Dublin 71 – Cork 86 – Killarney 115 – Limerick 69 – Tullamore 52 – Waterford 29.

🏨 **Kilkenny**
College Rd, SW : ¾ m. at junction with N 76 ✆ 62000, Fax 65984
🏋, ⊆s, 🏊, 🌾, 🍴 – 📺 ☎ 🅿 – 🛗 400. 🇲🇨 🆎 ⑪ 𝘝𝘐𝘚𝘈. 🍴
Meals 9.00/17.50 **st.** and a la carte 🍷 4.95 – **80 rm** ⊐z 40.00/95.00 **t.** – SB.

🏨 **Newpark**
Castlecomer Rd, N : 1 m. on N 77 ✆ 22122, Fax 61111
🏋, ⊆s, 🏊, 🌾, park – 🍴 rest 📺 ☎ 🅿 – 🛗 600. 🇲🇨 🆎 ⑪ 𝘝𝘐𝘚𝘈. 🍴
Meals 8.40/18.95 **t.** and dinner a la carte – ⊐z 8.00 – **84 rm** 50.00/81.00 **t.** –
SB.

🏛 **Butler House**
15-16 Patrick St. ✆ 65707, Fax 65626
without rest., 🌾 – 📺 ☎ 🅿 – 🛗 70. 🇲🇨 🆎 ⑪ 𝘝𝘐𝘚𝘈. 🍴
closed 24 to 29 December – **11 rm** ⊐z 35.00/99.00 **t.**, 2 suites.

↑ **Blanchville House**
Dunbell, Maddoxtown, SE : 7 ½ m. by N 10 (eastbound) ✆ 27197, Fax 27636
🐕, ≤, « Georgian country house », 🌾, park – 🍴 rest 🅿. 🇲🇨 𝘝𝘐𝘚𝘈. 🍴
March-October – **Meals** (by arrangement)(communal dining) 20.00 **st.** 🍷 6.00 –
6 rm ⊐z 30.00/60.00 **st.** – SB.

↑ **Shillogher House**
Callan Rd, SW : 1 m. on N 76 *℘* 63249
without rest., 🛏 – ⚒ 🔟 ☎ 🅿. 🐵 *VISA*. ⚒
closed 24 and 25 December – **5 rm** ⚏ 25.00/37.50 **st.**

XX **Lacken House**
Dublin Rd, E : ¾ m. on N 10 *℘* 61085, Fax 62435
with rm, 🛏 – 🍽 rest 🔟 ☎ 🅿. 🐵 🆎 ⓪ *VISA* 🈁. ⚒
closed 1 week Christmas – **Meals** *(closed Sunday and Monday)* (dinner only)
23.00 **st.** and a la carte ⓵ 6.50 – **8 rm** ⚏ 36.00/60.00 **st.** – SB.

X **Ristorante Rinuccini**
1 The Parade *℘* 61575, Fax 51288
🐵 🆎 ⓪ *VISA*
Meals - Italian - a la carte 8.55/18.85 **t.** ⓵ 5.95.

KILL (An Chill) Kildare 🔢 M 8 – pop. 1 518 – ☎ 045.

Dublin 15 – Carlow 36.

🏨 **Ambassador**
on N 7 *℘* 877064, Fax 877515
🔟 ☎ 🅿 – 🛎 220. 🐵 🆎 ⓪ *VISA*. ⚒
Meals (carving lunch Monday to Saturday) 11.50/19.50 **t.** and dinner a la carte
⓵ 5.50 – **36 rm** ⚏ 60.00/90.00 **t.** – SB.

KILLALOE (Cill Dalua) Clare 🔢 G 9 **Ireland G.** – pop. 956 – ☎ 061.

See : Town★ – St. Flannan's Cathedral★.

Env : Graves of the Leinstermen★, N : 4½m. by R 494.

Exc. : Nenagh★ (Heritage Centre★★ *AC*, Castle★), NE : 12 m. by R 496 and N 7 –
Holy Island★ *AC*, N : 8 m. by R 463 and boat from Tuamgraney.

🛈 Lock House *℘* 376866 (1 June-11 September).

Dublin 109 – Ennis 32 – Limerick 13 – Tullamore 58.

🏨 **Kincora Hall**
N : ¾ m. on R 463 *℘* 376000, Fax 376665
🛏 – 🔟 ☎ ♿ 🅿. 🐵 🆎 ⓪ *VISA*. ⚒
closed 25 December – **Meals** (bar lunch Monday to Saturday)/dinner a la
carte 8.40/20.25 **t.** – **25 rm** ⚏ 63.00/80.00 **t.** – SB.

🏨 **Lakeside**
℘ 376122, Fax 376431
≤, 🛁, ⚓s, 🏊, 🎣, 🛏, ✗ – ⚒ rm 🔟 ☎ 🅿 – 🛎 300. 🐵 🆎 ⓪ *VISA*. ⚒
closed 24 and 25 December – **Meals** 10.00/13.75 **st.** and dinner a la carte
⓵ 5.25 – **45 rm** ⚏ 59.00/85.00 **st.** – SB.

at Ogonnelloe N : 6¼ m. on R 463 – ☎ 061 :

↑ **Lantern House**
℘ 923034, Fax 923139
🐾, ≤, 🛏 – 🔟 ☎ 🅿. 🐵 🆎 ⓪ *VISA*. ⚒
15 February-October – **Meals** (by arrangement) 15.00 **t.** ⓵ 4.75 – **6 rm**
⚏ 26.00/40.00 **t.**

When visiting Ireland,
use the Michelin Green Guide **"Ireland".**
– *Detailed descriptions of places of interest*
– *Touring programmes*
– *Maps and street plans*
– *The history of the country*
– *Photographs and drawings of monuments, beauty spots, houses...*

KILLARNEY (Cill Airne) Kerry 🄰🄾🄴 D 11 Ireland G. – pop. 7 275 – ✪ 064.

See : Town★★ – Knockreer Demesne★ – St. Mary's Cathedral★.

Env : Killarney National Park★★★ – Muckross House★★ *AC*, S : 3 ½m. by N 71 – Torc Waterfall★★, S : 5 m. by N 71 – Gap of Dunloe★★, SW : 6 m. by R 582 – Muckross Abbey★, S : 3 ½m. by N 71.

Exc. : Iveragh Peninsula★★★ (Ring of Kerry★★) – Ladies View★★, SW : 12 m. by N 71 – Moll's Gap★, SW : 15 ½m. by N 71.

🛅, 🛅 Mahoney's Point ✆ 31034.

✈ Kerry (Farranfore) Airport : ✆ 066 (Farranfore) 64644, N : 9 ½m. by N 22.

🛈 Town Hall ✆ 31633.

Dublin 189 – Cork 54 – Limerick 69 – Waterford 112.

🏨 **Europe**
Fossa, W : 3 ½ m. on R 562 ✆ 31900, Fax 32118
♨, ≤ lake and mountains, 🕯, ⊆s, 🏊, ⚲, 🎣, park, ✗ – 🛗 📺 ☎ Ⓟ –
🕍 500. 🐼 🄰🄴 ⑥ 𝑉𝐼𝑆𝐴. ✗
14 March-October – **Meals** (light lunch)/dinner 23.00 **st.** and a la carte –
202 rm ⬭ 88.00/144.00 **st.**, 3 suites – SB.

🏨 **Killarney Park**
Kenmare Pl. ✆ 35555, Fax 35266
🕯, 🏊 – 🛗 ▤ rest 📺 ☎ & Ⓟ – 🕍 70. 🐼 🄰🄴 ⑥ 𝑉𝐼𝑆𝐴. ✗
closed 24 to 26 December – **Park : Meals** (dinner only and Sunday lunch)/
dinner 25.00 **st.** and a la carte – **67 rm** ⬭ 100.00/150.00 **st.** – SB.

🏨 **Aghadoe Heights**
NW : 3 ½ m. by N 22 ✆ 31766, Fax 31345
♨, ≤ countryside, lake and Macgillycuddy's Reeks, ⊆s, 🏊, 🎣, ✗ – 📺 ☎ &
Ⓟ – 🕍 100. 🐼 🄰🄴 ⑥ 𝑉𝐼𝑆𝐴. ✗
Meals – (see Fredrick's at the Heights below) – **57 rm** ⬭ 125.00/175.00 **t.**,
3 suites – SB.

🏨 **Great Southern**
East Avenue Rd ✆ 31262, Fax 31642
🕯, ⊆s, 🏊, 🎣, park, ✗ – 🛗 📺 ☎ Ⓟ – 🕍 900. 🐼 🄰🄴 ⑥ 𝑉𝐼𝑆𝐴 𝐽𝐶𝐵
closed early January-mid February – **Dining Room : Meals** (dinner only) 18.00 –
7.75 – **178 rm** 77.00/120.00 **t.**, 3 suites – SB.

🏨 **Dunloe Castle**
Beaufort, W : 6 m. by R 562 ✆ 44111, Fax 44583
♨, ≤ Gap of Dunloe, countryside and mountains, ⊆s, 🏊, 🎣, 🎣, park, ✗ –
🛗 ⇄ rm 📺 ☎ Ⓟ – 🕍 900. 🐼 🄰🄴 ⑥ 𝑉𝐼𝑆𝐴. ✗
May-September – **Meals** (dinner only) 23.00 **st.** – **119 rm** ⬭ 88.00/142.00 **st.**,
1 suite – SB.

🏨 **Muckross Park**
S : 2 ¾ m. on N 71 ✆ 31938, Fax 31965
🎣 – 📺 ☎ Ⓟ – 🕍 40. 🐼 🄰🄴 ⑥ 𝑉𝐼𝑆𝐴. ✗
March-October – **Meals** (bar lunch)/dinner 18.50 **st.** and a la carte – **25 rm**
⬭ 80.00/120.00 **st.**, 2 suites – SB.

🏨 **Randles Court**
Muckross Rd ✆ 35333, Fax 35206
🛗 📺 ☎ Ⓟ. 🐼 🄰🄴 ⑥ 𝑉𝐼𝑆𝐴. ✗
closed mid January-mid March and 22 to 28 December – **Meals** (bar lunch
Monday to Saturday)/dinner 12.00/22.00 **st.** - **37 rm** ⬭ 70.00/110.00 **t.** – SB.

🏨 **Cahernane**
Muckross Rd, S : 1 m. on N 71 ✆ 31895, Fax 34340
♨, ≤, 🎣, ✗ – ☎ Ⓟ 🐼 🄰🄴 ⑥ 𝑉𝐼𝑆𝐴 𝐽𝐶𝐵. ✗
Easter-4 November – **Meals** (bar lunch)/dinner 27.50 **st.** and a la carte 🍷 7.00 –
48 rm ⬭ 85.00/127.50 **st.** – SB.

🏨 **Ross**
Kenmare Pl. ℰ 31855, Fax 31139
🔃 – 💵 🍴 rest 📺 ☎ 🅿. 🆔 🆎 ⓪ *VISA*. ❀
March-October – **Meals** (bar lunch Monday to Saturday)/dinner 17.50 **st.**
and a la carte ⋆ 6.50 – **32 rm** ⊋ 65.00/90.00 **st.** – SB.

🏨 **Royal**
College St. ℰ 31853, Fax 34001
💵 📺 ☎. 🆔 🆎 ⓪ *VISA*
closed 1 week Christmas – **Meals** (bar lunch Monday to Saturday)/dinner
20.00 **t.** and a la carte ⋆ 6.95 – **49 rm** ⊋ 60.00/125.00 **t.** – SB.

🏨 **Torc Great Southern**
Park Rd ℰ 31611, Fax 31824
🔁s, 🔃, 🏊, 🎾 – 📺 ☎ 🅿. 🆔 🆎 ⓪ *VISA*. ❀
28 March-mid October – **Meals** (bar lunch)/dinner 16.00 **t.** ⋆ 8.00 – ⊋ 7.00 –
94 rm 54.00/80.00 – SB.

🏨 **Foley's Townhouse**
23 High St. ℰ 31217, Fax 34683
🍴 rest 📺 ☎ 🅿. 🆔 🆎 *VISA*. ❀
accommodation closed November-March – **Meals** *(closed 23 to 26 December)*
(bar lunch)/dinner 25.00 **st.** and a la carte ⋆ 7.95 – **12 rm** ⊋ 40.00/80.00 **t.**

🏠 **Earls Court**
Woodlawn Junction, Muckross Rd, S : ¾ m. by N 71 ℰ 34009, Fax 34366
without rest. – 🚳 📺 ☎ 🅿. 🆔 *VISA*. ❀
2 March-3 November – **11 rm** ⊋ 35.00/65.00 **st.**

🏠 **Killeen House**
Aghadoe, W : 4 m. by R 562 ℰ 31711, Fax 31811
🌿 – 📺 ☎ 🅿. 🆔 🆎 ⓪ *VISA*
March-October – **Meals** (bar lunch)/dinner 24.50 **st.** ⋆ 6.50 – **15 rm** ⊋ 39.00/
78.00 **t.** – SB.

🏠 **Kathleens Country House**
Tralee Rd, N : 2 m. on N 22 ℰ 32810, Fax 32340
without rest., ≼, 🌿 – 🚳 📺 ☎ 🅿. 🆔 🆎 *VISA*. ❀
5 March-13 November – **17 rm** ⊋ 47.50/75.00 **st.**

🏠 **Fuchsia House**
Muckross Rd, S : ¾ m. on N 71 ℰ 33743, Fax 36588
without rest., 🌿 – 🚳 📺 ☎ 🅿. 🆔 *VISA*. ❀
March-10 November – **10 rm** ⊋ 50.00/70.00 **st.**

🏠 **Victoria House**
Muckross Rd, S : 1 ¼ m. on N 71 ℰ 35430, Fax 35439
without rest. – 📺 ☎ 🅿. 🆔 🆎 ⓪ *VISA*. ❀
closed December – **13 rm** ⊋ 30.00/44.00 **st.**

🏠 **Beaufield House**
Cork Rd, E : 1 m. ℰ 34440, Fax 34663
without rest., 🌿 – 📺 ☎ 🅿. 🆔 🆎 ⓪ *VISA*. ❀
closed 20 to 28 December – **14 rm** ⊋ 27.00/42.00 **t.**

🏠 **Lime Court**
Muckross Rd, S : ¾ m. on N 71 ℰ 34547, Fax 34121
📺 ☎ 🅿. 🆔 *VISA*. ❀
closed 20 to 26 December – **Meals** (dinner only) 15.00 **st.** ⋆ 7.50 – **12 rm**
⊋ 25.00/60.00 **st.** – SB.

⌂ **Gleann Fia Country House**
Deerpark, N : 1 ½ m. by N 22 bypass ℰ 35035, Fax 35000
🐾 without rest., « Riverside setting », 🌿 – 🚳 📺 ☎ 🅿. 🆔 🆎 *VISA*. ❀
closed January and December – **14 rm** ⊋ 25.00/60.00 **st.**

↑ Naughton's Villa
Muckross Rd ℰ 36025
without rest. – 📺 ☎ 🄿. ℅
18 March-4 November – **5 rm** ⌒ 25.00/40.00 **st.**

↑ Sika Lodge
Ballydowney, W : 1 m. on R 562 ℰ 36304, Fax 36746
without rest. – 📺 ☎ 🄿. 🝌 *VISA*. ℅
6 rm ⌒ 30.00/40.00.

↑ Avondale House
Tralee Rd, N : 3 m. on N 22 ℰ 35579
without rest., ≤, 🚗 – 📺 🄿. ℅
closed 1 December-31 January – **5 rm** ⌒ 21.00/32.00 **st.**

↑ Lake Lodge
Muckross Rd, S : ¾ m. on N 71 ℰ 33333, Fax 35109
without rest. – 📺 ☎ 🄿. 🝌 *VISA*. ℅
13 rm ⌒ 22.50/38.00 **st.**

XXX Fredrick's at the Heights (at Aghadoe Heights H.)
NW : 3 ½ m. by N 22 ℰ 31766, Fax 31345
≤ Countryside, lake and Macgillycuddy's Reeks – 🍽 🄿. 🝌 AE ① *VISA*
Meals (booking essential) (buffet lunch Sunday) 19.50/31.50 **t.** and
a la carte 32.50/38.50 **t.** ⌀ 7.50.

XX Gaby's
27 High St. ℰ 32519, Fax 32747
🝌 AE ① *VISA*
*closed lunch Sunday, Monday and November-Easter, 1 week Christmas and
15 February-16 March* – **Meals** - Seafood - a la carte 19.80/29.60 **t.** ⌀ 7.00.

XX West End House
Lower New St. ℰ 32271, Fax 35979
🝌 AE *VISA*
closed Monday and November – **Meals** (light lunch Tuesday to Saturday)
16.90 **st.** (dinner) and a la carte 20.35/26.80 **st.**

X Strawberry Tree
24 Plunkett St. ℰ 32688, Fax 32689
🝌 AE ① *VISA*
closed Sunday, Monday and restricted opening November-February – **Meals**
(dinner only) a la carte 26.25/28.75 **st.** ⌀ 6.75.

KILLEAGH (Cill Ia) Cork 🄰🄾🄴 H 12 – ✆ 024.

Dublin 151 – Cork 23 – Waterford 53.

↑ Ballymakeigh House
N : 1 m. ℰ 95184, Fax 95370
🝌, « Working farm », 🚗, park, 🎾 – 🄿. 🝌 *VISA*. ℅
1 February-1 November – **Meals** (by arrangement) 20.00 **st.** ⌀ 7.00 – **5 rm**
⌒ 30.00/50.00 **st.** – SB.

*When visiting Ireland,
use the Michelin Green Guide* **"Ireland".**

– *Detailed descriptions of places of interest*
– *Touring programmes*
– *Maps and street plans*
– *The history of the country*
– *Photographs and drawings of monuments, beauty spots, houses...*

KILLINEY (Cill Iníon Léinín) Dublin 405 N 8 – ۞ 01.

⛳ Killiney ✆ 851983.

Dublin 8 – Bray 4.

🏰 **Fitzpatrick Castle**
✆ 284 0700, Fax 285 0207
≤, ₤₅, 🚘, 🏊, 🚗, 🍴, squash – 🛗 🗝 rm 📺 ☎ 🅿 – 🛋 400. 🆖 🆎 ⓪ 𝘝𝘐𝘚𝘈
🇯🇨🇧 – **Truffles : Meals** 14.00/19.00 **t.** and a la carte – ⚏ 8.50 – **84 rm** 85.00/125.00 **t.**, 6 suites – SB.

🏰 **Court**
Killiney Bay ✆ 285 1622, Fax 285 2085
≤, 🚗 – 🛗 🗝 rm 🍽 rest 📺 ☎ 🅿 – 🛋 250. 🆖 🆎 ⓪ 𝘝𝘐𝘚𝘈. 🛇
Meals 11.50/21.50 **t.** and a la carte – ⚏ 10.00 – **86 rm** 80.00/115.00 **t.** – SB.

KILLORGLIN (Cill Orglan) Kerry 405 C 11 – pop. 1 229 – ۞ 066.

Dublin 207 – Killarney 12 – Tralee 16.

🏨 **Bianconi**
Annadale Rd ✆ 61146, Fax 61950
🔾 – 📺 ☎. 🆖 🆎 ⓪ 𝘝𝘐𝘚𝘈. 🛇
closed 24 to 28 December – **Meals** (closed Sunday) (bar lunch)/dinner a la carte 18.00/24.00 **t.** ⚆ 6.50 – **15 rm** ⚏ 30.00/55.00 **t.**

🏠 **Westfield House**
Glenbeigh Rd, W : ¾ m. by N 70 ✆ 61909, Fax 61996
🚘s, 🚗, 🍴 – 🗝 rm 📺 ☎ 🅿. 🆖 ⓪ 𝘝𝘐𝘚𝘈. 🛇
Meals (by arrangement) 13.00 **st.** – **10 rm** ⚏ 25.00/36.00 **st.** – SB.

🏠 **Grove Lodge**
Killarney Rd, E : ½ m. on R 562 ✆ 61157, Fax 61157
without rest., « Riverside setting », 🔾, 🚗 – 📺 ☎ 🅿. 🆖 ⓪ 𝘝𝘐𝘚𝘈. 🛇
closed 1 week Christmas – **5 rm** ⚏ 30.00/56.00 **st.**

KILLYBEGS (Na Cealla Beaga) Donegal 405 G 4 Ireland G. – ۞ 073.

Exc. : – Glengesh Pass★★★, SW : 15 m. by N 56 and R 263 – Gweebarra Estuary★, NE : 19 m. by R 262 and R 252.

Dublin 181 – Donegal 17 – Londonderry 64 – Sligo 57.

🏨 **Bay View**
Main St. ✆ 31950, Fax 31856
≤, ₤₅, 🚘s, 🏊 – 🛗 🍽 rest 📺 🗝 🅿 ♿. 🆖 🆎 ⓪ 𝘝𝘐𝘚𝘈. 🛇
Meals 9.50/15.50 **st.** and a la carte ⚆ 5.50 – **36 rm** ⚏ 45.00/75.00 **st.**, 2 suites – SB.

KILTIMAGH (Coillte Mach) Mayo 405 EF 6 – pop. 652 – ۞ 094.

Dublin 138 – Galway 52 – Westport 26.

🏨 **Cill Aodain**
✆ 81761, Fax 81838
📺 ☎. 🆖 𝘝𝘐𝘚𝘈. 🛇
closed 25 December – **Meals** (carving lunch Monday to Saturday)/dinner 18.50 **st.** and lunch a la carte ⚆ 4.75 – **15 rm** ⚏ 35.00/79.50 **st.** – SB.

KINSALE (Cionn Eitigh) Cork 405 G 12 Ireland G. – pop. 1 759 – ۞ 021.

See : Town★★ – St. Multose Church★ – Kinsale Regional Museum★ AC.

Env : Summercove★ (≤★) E : 1 ½m. – Charles Fort★ AC, E : 1¾m.

🛈 Pier Rd ✆ 774417 (March-November).

Dublin 178 – Cork 17.

🏰 **Actons**
Pier Rd ✆ 772135, Fax 772231
≤, ₤₅, 🚘s, 🏊, 🚗 – 🛗 📺 ☎ 🅿 – 🛋 300. 🆖 🆎 ⓪ 𝘝𝘐𝘚𝘈
Meals (bar lunch Monday to Saturday)/dinner 21.00 **t.** and a la carte ⚆ 6.50 – **56 rm** ⚏ 65.00/120.00 **t.** – SB.

🏨 **Blue Haven**
3 Pearse St. ✆ 772209, Fax 774268
📺 ☎. 🖭 🗚 ⑩ 𝘝𝘐𝘚𝘈. ✂
Meals - Seafood - (bar lunch)/dinner 27.00 **t.** and a la carte ⓘ 7.50 – **18 rm**
⊡ 95.00/150.00 **st.** – SB.

🏨 **Old Bank House**
11 Pearse St. ✆ 774075, Fax 774296
without rest. – 📺 ☎. 🖭 🗚 𝘝𝘐𝘚𝘈. ✂
closed 24 to 26 December – **9 rm** ⊡ 80.00/130.00 **st.**

🏨 **Moorings**
Scilly ✆ 772376, Fax 772675
without rest., ≤ Kinsale harbour – 📺 ☎ ℗. 🖭 ⑩ 𝘝𝘐𝘚𝘈. ✂
closed 1 week Christmas – **8 rm** ⊡ 40.00/90.00 **st.**

🏨 **Scilly House Inn**
Scilly ✆ 772413, Fax 774629
without rest., ≤, 🍴 – ☎ ℗. 🖭 🗚 𝘝𝘐𝘚𝘈. ✂
11 April-October – **6 rm** ⊡ 65.00/85.00 **st.**, 1 suite.

⌂ **Quayside House**
Pier Rd ✆ 772188, Fax 772664
without rest. – 📺 ☎. 🖭 𝘝𝘐𝘚𝘈. ✂
6 rm ⊡ 50.00/55.00 **st.**

⌂ **Kilcaw Guesthouse**
E : 1 m. on R 600 ✆ 774155
without rest., 🍴 – ✂ 📺 ☎ ℗. 🖭 🗚 𝘝𝘐𝘚𝘈
closed December – **7 rm** ⊡ 30.00/50.00 **t.**

⌂ **Murphys Farm House**
NE : 1 ¼ m. by R 600 ✆ 772229, Fax 774176
without rest., 🍴 – ℗. ✂
March-October – **3 rm** ⊡ 17.00/34.00 **st.**

XX **Annelie's**
18-19 Lower O'Connell St. ✆ 773074, Fax 773075
▤. 🖭 𝘝𝘐𝘚𝘈
closed Monday and 22 December-7 January – **Meals** (dinner only and Sunday lunch)/dinner a la carte 27.00/40.00 **t.** ⓘ 5.95.

XX **Chez Jean Marc**
Lower O'Connell St. ✆ 774625, Fax 774680
🖭 🗚 ⑩ 𝘝𝘐𝘚𝘈
closed Monday except June-August, 15 February-15 March and 24-26 December – **Meals** (dinner only) a la carte 10.00/20.25 **t.**

XX **Vintage**
Main St. ✆ 772502, Fax 774828
▤. 🖭 🗚 ⑩ 𝘝𝘐𝘚𝘈 𝗝𝗖𝗕
closed Sunday and Monday in low season, 25 December and 15 January-28 February – **Meals** (dinner only) a la carte 26.50/40.00 **t.**

X **Max's**
Main St. ✆ 772443
🖭 𝘝𝘐𝘚𝘈
March-October – **Meals** 12.00 **t.** and a la carte.

at Ballinclashet E : 5 m. by R 600 – ✉ Kinsale – ✿ 021 :

XX **Oystercatcher**
✆ 770822, Fax 770822
℗. 🖭 🗚 𝘝𝘐𝘚𝘈
closed mid January-Easter – **Meals** *(closed Sunday and Monday)* (lunch by arrangement)/dinner 28.95 **t.** ⓘ 7.75.

| **Prices** | *For full details of the prices quoted in the guide, consult the introduction.* |

KNOCK (An Cnoc) Mayo 🅐🅓🅑 F 6 Ireland G. – pop. 440 – 🅐 094.

See : Basilica of our Lady, Queen of Ireland★.

✈ Knock (Connaught) Airport : ☎ 67222, NE : 9 m. by N 17.

🅱 Knock Airport ☎ 67247 (June-September).

Dublin 132 – Galway 46 – Westport 32.

LAHINCH (An Leacht) Clare 🅐🅓🅑 D 9 Ireland G. – pop. 550 – 🅐 065.

Env : Cliffs of Moher★★★.

🏌, 🏌 Lahinch ☎ 81003 – 🏌 Spanish Point, Miltown Malbay ☎ 84198.

Dublin 162 – Galway 49 – Limerick 41.

🏨 **Aberdeen Arms**
  ☎ 81100, Fax 81228
  ⇌s, ※ – ▤ rest 📺 ☎ 🅿 – 🛆 200. 🆎 🆎 🅞 💳 ※
  Meals a la carte 9.50/20.00 **st.** ¼ 4.50 – **55 rm** ⌑ 57.00/90.00 **st.** – SB.

LARAGH (Láithreach) Wicklow 🅐🅓🅑 N 8 – pop. 248 – ✉ Wicklow – 🅐 0404.

Dublin 26 – Kilkenny 70 – Wexford 61.

🏠 **Laragh Trekking Centre**
  Glendalough East, NW : 1 ½ m. on Sallygap rd ☎ 45282, Fax 45204
  ⬡ without rest., ≼, ⬡, 🚗 – ⁂ 📺 ☎ 🅿. 🆎 💳 ※
  closed 1 week Christmas – **6 rm** ⌑ 32.00/40.00 **st.**

LEENANE (An Líonán) Galway 🅐🅓🅑 C 7 Ireland G. – ✉ Clifden – 🅐 095.

See : Killary Harbour★.

Env : Joyce Country★★ – Aasleagh Falls★, NE : 2 ½m.

Exc. : Lough Nafooey★★, SE : 8 ½m. by R 336 – Doo Lough Pass★, NW : 9 m. by N 59 and R 335.

Dublin 173 – Ballina 56 – Galway 41.

🏛 **Delphi Lodge**
  NW : 8 ¼ m. by N 59 on Louisburgh rd ☎ 42211, Fax 42296
  ⬡, ≼, « Georgian sporting lodge, loughside setting », ⬡, park – ☎ 🅿 –
  🛆 30. 🆎 💳 ※
  closed 18 December-10 January – **Meals** (residents only) (communal dining)
  (dinner only) 25.00 **st.** – **11 rm** ⌑ 54.00/110.00 **st.**

🏠 **Portfinn Lodge**
  ☎ 42265, Fax 42315
  ≼ – ☎ 🅿. 🆎 🅞 💳
  April-October – **Meals** (by arrangement) 18.50 **t.** ¼ 5.50 – **8 rm** ⌑ 38.00 **t.** – SB.

LETTERFRACK (Leitir Fraic) Galway 🅐🅓🅑 C 7 – 🅐 0195.

Dublin 189 – Ballina 69 – Galway 57.

🏨 **Rosleague Manor**
  W : 1 ½ m. on N 59 ☎ 41101, Fax 41168
  ⬡, ≼ Ballynakill harbour and Tully mountain, ⇌s, 🚗, park, ※ – ⁂ rest ☎ 🅿.
  🆎 🆎 💳
  Easter-October – **Meals** (bar lunch)/dinner 26.00 **t.** and a la carte ¼ 7.00 –
  20 rm ⌑ 65.00/160.00 **t.** – SB.

LETTERKENNY (Leitir Ceanainn) Donegal 🅐🅓🅑 I 3 Ireland G. – pop. 7 166 – 🅐 074.

Exc. : Glenveagh National Park★★ (Gardens★★), NW : 12 m. by R 250, R 251 and R 254 – Grianan of Aileach★★ (≼★) NE : 17 ½m. by N 13 – Church Hill (Colmcille Heritage Centre★ *AC*, Glebe House and Gallery★ *AC*) NW : 10 m. by R 250.

🏌 Barnhill ☎ 21150 – 🏌 Dunfanaghy ☎ 36335.

Dublin 150 – Londonderry 21 – Sligo 72.

🏠 **Castlegrove House**
Ramelton Rd, NE : 4 ½ m. by N 13 off R 245 *ℰ* 51118, Fax 51384
🍸, ≼, « Late 17C country house », 🐾, 🍴, park – 🚫 ☎ **℗**. **⑩** **AE** **①** **VISA**.
🍴
closed 22 to 26 December and 9 January-1 February – **Meals** *(closed Sunday
September-May)* (dinner only) 24.50 **t.** and a la carte � 6.00 – **8 rm** ⌷ 35.00/
150.00 **t.** – SB.

🏠 **Gleneany House**
Port Rd *ℰ* 26088, Fax 26090
☰ rest **TV** ☎ **℗**. **⑩** **AE** **VISA**. 🍴
Meals 5.50/14.95 **t.** and dinner a la carte � 4.50 – **22 rm** ⌷ 28.00/56.00.

LIMERICK **(Luimneach)** Limerick 🔲🔲🔲 G 9 Ireland G. – pop. 52 083 – 🅔 061.

See : City★★ - St Mary's Cathedral★★ Y – Limerick Museum★★ Z – King John's
Castle★ *AC* Y – John Square★ Z **20** – St. John's Cathedral★ Z.

Env : Hunt Museum, Limerick University★ *AC*, E : 2 m. by N 7 Y – Cratloe Wood
(≼★) NW : 5 m. by N 18 Z.

Exc. : Lough Gur Interpretive Centre★ *AC*, S : 11 m. by R 512 and R 514 Z – Clare
Glens★, E : 13 m. by N 7 and R 503 Y – Monasteranenagh Abbey★, S : 13 m. by
N 20 Z.

✈ Shannon Airport : *ℰ* 061 (Shannon) 471444, W : 16 m. by N 18 Z – **Terminal :**
Limerick Railway Station.

🛈 Arthur's Quay *ℰ* 317522 Y.

Dublin 120 – Cork 58.

Plan opposite

🏨 **Castletroy Park**
Dublin Rd, E : 2 ¼ m. on N 7 *ℰ* 335566, Fax 331117
Ⅰ₆, ⓢ, 🏊, 🍴 – ❙ 🚫 rm **TV** ☎ 🐾 **℗** – 🔏 450. **⑩** **AE** **①** **VISA** **JCB**. 🍴
closed 26 and 27 December – **McLaughlin's : Meals** *(closed Sunday dinner)*
(dinner only and Sunday lunch)/dinner 26.00 **t.** and a la carte – ⌷ 9.00 –
105 rm 120.00/165.00 **st.**, 2 suites – SB.

🏨 **Limerick Inn**
Ennis Rd, NW : 4 m. on N 18 *ℰ* 326666, Fax 326281
Ⅰ₆, ⓢ, 🏊, 🍴 – ❙ ☰ rest **TV** ☎ ⅁ **℗** – 🔏 600. **⑩** **AE** **①** **VISA** **JCB**. 🍴
closed 24 and 25 December – **Meals** 12.50/24.50 **st.** and dinner a la carte
⍻ 6.00 – ⌷ 8.00 – **149 rm** 94.00/110.00 **t.**, 4 suites – SB.

🏨 **Jurys**   Y z
Ennis Rd *ℰ* 327777, Fax 326400
Ⅰ₆, ⓢ, 🏊, 🍴, 🍴 – ☰ rest **TV** ☎ **℗** – 🔏 200. **⑩** **AE** **①** **VISA**. 🍴
closed 25 to 27 December – **Copper Room : Meals** 10.50/22.00 **t.** and a la carte
– ⌷ 8.00 – **93 rm** 86.00/106.00 **t.**, 1 suite – SB.

🏨 **Limerick Ryan**
Ennis Rd, NW : 1 ¼ m. on N 18 *ℰ* 453922, Fax 326333
🍴 – ❙ 🚫 rm ☰ rest **TV** ☎ ⅁ **℗** – 🔏 120. **⑩** **AE** **①** **VISA**. 🍴
Meals 12.50/20.00 **t.** and dinner a la carte ⍻ 5.95 – ⌷ 9.00 – **179 rm** 75.00/
100.00 **t.**, 2 suites – SB.

🏠 **Clifton House**
Ennis Rd, NW : 1 ¼ m. on N 18 *ℰ* 451166, Fax 451224
without rest., 🍴 – **TV** ☎ **℗**. **⑩** **VISA**. 🍴
closed 20 December-3 January – **16 rm** ⌷ 28.00/40.00 **t.**

🏠 **Clonmacken House**
Clonmacken Rd, off Ennis Rd, NW : 2 m. by N 18 *ℰ* 327007, Fax 327785
without rest., 🍴 – **TV** ☎ **℗**. **⑩** **VISA**. 🍴
closed 1 week Christmas – **10 rm** ⌷ 25.00/40.00 **st.**

🍴🍴 **Quenelle's**   Z r
Upper Henry St. *ℰ* 411111, Fax 400111
⑩ **AE** **VISA**
closed Sunday, Good Friday and 24-25 December – **Meals** (dinner only) 25.00 **t.**
⍻ 5.50.

LIMERICK

GREEN TOURIST GUIDES

Picturesque scenery, buildings
Attractive routes
Touring programmes
Plans of towns and buildings.

129

LISDOONVARNA (Lios Dúin Bhearna) Clare 👁️👁️👁️ E 8 Ireland G. – pop. 842 – 🕸 065.

Env : The Burren★★ (Cliffs of Moher★★★, Scenic Routes★★, Aillwee Cave★ *AC* (Waterfall★), Corcomroe Abbey★, Kilfenora Crosses★).

Dublin 167 – Galway 39 – Limerick 47.

🏰 **Ballinalacken Castle**
NW : 3 m. by N 67 (Doolin rd) on R 477 ℘ 74025, Fax 74025
🗬, ≤, park – ➳ rest 📺 ☎ 🅿. 🐶 *VISA*. 🛠
April-4 October – **Meals** (light lunch)/dinner a la carte approx. 19.50 **st.** ▯ 6.00 –
13 rm ⊇ 40.00/65.00 **st.**

🏠 **Sheedy's Spa View**
Sulphir Hill ℘ 74026, Fax 74555
🛏, 🛠 – ☎ 🅿. 🐶 🆎 ① *VISA*. 🛠
15 April-November – **Meals** – (see Orchid below) – **11 rm** ⊇ 40.00/60.00 **t.**

🏠 **Woodhaven**
Doolin Coast Rd, W : 1 m. by N 67 (Doolin rd) off R 477 ℘ 74017
without rest., 🛏 – 🅿. 🛠
4 rm ⊇ 21.00/32.00.

XX **Orchid** (at Sheedy's Spa View H.)
Sulphir Hill ℘ 74026, Fax 74555
🅿. 🐶 🆎 ① *VISA*
15 April-November – **Meals** (dinner only) a la carte 17.95/29.50 **t.** ▯ 9.50.

LISTOWEL (Lios Tuathail) Kerry 👁️👁️👁️ D 10 – 🕸 068.

X **Allo's**
41 Church St. ℘ 22880
🐶 🆎 *VISA*
closed Sunday, Good Friday and 25 December – **Meals** (booking essential) a la
carte 8.80/20.00 **t.** ▯ 5.00.

MACROOM (Maigh Chromtha) Cork 👁️👁️👁️ F 12 – pop. 2 303 – 🕸 026.

🏌 Lackaduve ℘ 41072.

Dublin 186 – Cork 25 – Killarney 30.

🏰 **Castle**
Main St. ℘ 41074, Fax 41505
🗬, squash – 📺 ☎ 🅿 – 🕍 60. 🐶 🆎 ① *VISA*. 🛠
Meals 9.50/15.00 **t.** and a la carte ▯ 7.50 – **26 rm** ⊇ 35.00/60.00 **st.** – SB.

🏠 **Bower**
Gortanaddan, Kilnamartyra, W : 8 m. by N 22 ℘ 40192
🗬, 🛏 – 🅿
5 rm.

MALAHIDE (Mullach Íde) Dublin 👁️👁️👁️ N 7 Ireland G. – pop. 12 088 – 🕸 01.

See : Castle★.

🏌, 🏌 Beechwood, The Grange ℘ 846 1611.

Dublin 9 – Drogheda 24.

🏰 **Grand**
℘ 845 0000, Fax 845 0987
≤ – 🛗 ➳ rm 📺 ☎ 🅿 – 🕍 750. 🐶 🆎 ① *VISA*. 🛠
closed 25 and 26 December – **Meals** 12.00/22.00 **t.** and a la carte ▯ 6.20 –
100 rm ⊇ 90.00/140.00 **t.** – SB.

🏠 **Liscara**
Malahide Rd, Kinsealy, S : 3 m. on Dublin rd ℘ 848 3751, Fax 848 3751
without rest – ➳ 🅿
February-October – **6 rm** ⊇ 25.00/36.00.

130

MALLOW (Mala) Cork 405 F 11 Ireland G. – pop. 6 238 – ✆ 022.

See : Town★ – St. James' Church★.

Exc. : Doneraile Wildlife Park★ *AC*, NE : 6 m. by N 20 and R 581 – Buttevant Friary★, N : 7 m. by N 20.

⛳18 Balleyellis ✆ 21145.

Dublin 149 – Cork 21 – Killarney 40 – Limerick 41.

Longueville House
W : 3 ½ m. by N 72 ✆ 47156, Fax 47459
≫, ≤, « Part Georgian mansion in extensive grounds, working farm », ≫, 🌳
– ⇔ TV ☎ P – 🎓 25. MC AE D VISA. ✗
closed 22 December-early March – **Presidents : Meals** (booking essential) (bar lunch Monday to Saturday)/dinner 29.00 – **20 rm** ☕ 59.00/164.00 **t.** – SB.

Springfort Hall
N : 4 ¾ m. by N 20 on R 581 ✆ 21278, Fax 21557
≫, 🌳, park – TV ☎ P. MC AE D VISA. ✗
closed 24 December-3 January – **Meals** *(closed Sunday)* (dinner only) a la carte 19.00/25.00 **st.** 🍷 6.00 – **24 rm** ☕ 42.50/67.50 **st.** – SB.

Central
Main St. ✆ 21527, Fax 21527
TV ☎ P – 🎓 350
20 rm.

In this guide
a symbol or a character, printed in red or **black**, *in* **bold** *or light type, does not have the same meaning.*
Pay particular attention to the explanatory pages.

MAYNOOTH (Maigh Nuad) Kildare 405 M 7 Ireland G. – pop. 6 027 – ✆ 01.

Env : Castletown House★★ *AC*, SE : 4 m. by R 405.

Dublin 15.

Moyglare Manor
Moyglare, N : 2 m. ✆ 628 6351, Fax 628 5405
≫, ≤, « Georgian country house, antique furnishings », 🌳, park – ☎ P – 🎓 35. MC AE D VISA. ✗
closed 24 to 29 December – **Meals** *(closed Saturday lunch)* 17.50/28.00 **t.** and a la carte 🍷 8.50 – **17 rm** ☕ 95.00/150.00 **t.**

Moyglare Glebe
Moyglare, N : 1 ¾ m. ✆ 629 0689, Fax 628 5405
≫, ≤, 🏊, 🎾 – TV ☎ P. MC AE D VISA. ✗
Meals (booking essential) (residents only) (dinner only) 25.00 **t.** 🍷 7.95 – **7 rm** ☕ 65.00/90.00 **t.**

MIDLETON (Mainistir na Corann) Cork 405 H 12 – pop. 2 990 – ✆ 021.

⛳18 East Cork, Gortacue ✆ 631687.

ℹ Jameson Heritage Centre ✆ 613702 (April-September).

Dublin 161 – Cork 12 – Waterford 61.

Midleton Park
Old Cork Rd ✆ 631767, Fax 631605
🌳 – ▤ rest TV ☎ ♿ P – 🎓 400. MC AE D VISA. ✗
closed 24 to 26 December – **Meals** 10.95/18.95 **st.** and a la carte 🍷 4.75 – **39 rm** ☕ 60.00/80.00 **st.**, 1 suite – SB.

Bailick Cottage
S : ½ m. by Broderick St. ✆ 631244
without rest., 🌳 – P
6 rm.

MONAGHAN (Muineachán) Monaghan 405 L 5 – © 047.

Dublin 83 – Belfast 43 – Drogheda 54 – Dundalk 22 – Londonderry 75.

🏨 **Hillgrove**
Old Armagh Rd, SE : ¾ m. by N 2 📞 81288, Fax 84951
📶 🍴 rest 📺 ☎ & 🅿 – 🔺 800. 🅜🅒 🅐🅔 ① VISA JCB. 🕸
Meals (carving lunch)/dinner 17.50 **t.** and a la carte ⌄ 5.95 – **44 rm** ⫿ 45.00/
90.00 **st.** – SB.

🏨 **Four Seasons**
Coolshannagh, N : 1 m. on N 2 📞 81888, Fax 83131
🆚, 🔳, 🌿 – 📺 ☎ 🅿. 🅜🅒 🅐🅔 ① VISA. 🕸
closed 25 December – **Meals** (carving lunch) 10.50/20.00 **st.** and dinner
a la carte ⌄ 5.20 – **40 rm** ⫿ 36.00/95.00 **st.** – SB.

MOYCULLEN (Maigh Cuilinn) Galway 405 E 7 – pop. 545 – © 091.

Dublin 139 – Galway 7.

🏠 **Knockferry Lodge**
Knockferry (on Lough Corrib), NE : 6 ½ m. by Knockferry rd 📞 80122,
Fax 80328
🐬, ≤, 🎣, 🌿 – ⛵ rest 🅿. 🅜🅒 🅐🅔 ① VISA. 🕸
April-October – **Meals** (dinner only) 16.00 **st.** – **10 rm** ⫿ 27.00/42.00 **t.** – SB.

↟ **Moycullen House**
SW : 1 m. on Spiddle rd 📞 555566, Fax 555566
🐬, 🌿 – ⛵ rm 🅿. 🅜🅒 🅐🅔 VISA. 🕸
March-October – **Meals** (communal dining) (by arrangement) 20.00 – **5 rm**
⫿ 40.00/60.00 **st.**

🍽🍽 **Drimcong House**
NW : 1 m. on N 59 📞 555115, Fax 555836
« 17C estate house », 🌿 – 🅿. 🅜🅒 🅐🅔 ① VISA
closed Sunday, Monday and Christmas-March – **Meals** (booking essential)
(dinner only) 22.00 **st.** ⌄ 5.50.

MULLINAVAT (Muileann an Bhata) Kilkenny 405 K 10 – pop. 283 – © 051.

Dublin 88 – Kilkenny 21 – Waterford 8.

🏠 **Rising Sun**
Main St. 📞 898173, Fax 898173
📺 ☎ 🅿. 🅜🅒 VISA
closed 23 December-1 January – **Meals** (bar lunch Monday to Friday)/dinner
a la carte 10.50/15.00 **st.** ⌄ 5.00 – **10 rm** ⫿ 28.00/44.00 **st.** – SB.

MULLINGAR (An Muileann gCearr) Westmeath 405 JK 7 Ireland G. – pop. 8 003 –
© 044.

Env : Belvedere House and Gardens★ *AC*, S : 3 ½m. by N 52.

Exc. : Multyfarnham Franciscan Friary★, N : 8 m. by N 4 – Tullynally Castle★ *AC*,
N : 13 m. by N 4 and R 394 – Fore Abbey★, NE : 17 m. by R 394.

🏌 Belvedere 📞 48366/48629.

🛈 Dublin Road 📞 48650.

Dublin 49 – Drogheda 36.

🏨 **Greville Arms**
Pearse St. 📞 48563, Fax 48052
📶 rest 📺 ☎ 🅿 – 🔺 100. 🅜🅒 🅐🅔 ① VISA. 🕸
closed 25 December – **Meals** 8.95 **st.** (lunch) and dinner a la carte 9.50/
23.40 **st.** ⌄ 6.95 – **40 rm** ⫿ 37.00/80.00 **st.** – SB.

↟ **Hilltop Country House**
Rathconnell, NE : 2 ½ m. by R 52 📞 48958, Fax 48013
without rest., 🌿 – 📺 🅿. 🕸
closed 2 weeks Christmas – **5 rm** ⫿ 22.00/34.00 **st.** – SB.

NENAGH (An tAonach) Tipperary 405 H 9 – ❸ 067.

🏠 **St. David's Country House**
Puckane, NW : 7 ½ m. by N 52 and R 493 turning left after church in Puckane
🖉 24145, Fax 24388
🕭, ≤, « Loughside setting », 🍃, 🌳, park – ⊱ rm ☎ 🅿. 🐵 🆎 𝘝𝘐𝘚𝘈. 🎜
closed 15 January-15 March – **Meals** (booking essential) (dinner only) 28.00 **st.**
🍸 10.00 – **10 rm** � 80.00/150.00 **st.**

NEWBRIDGE (An Droichead Nua) Kildare 405 L 8 Ireland G. – pop. 11 778 – ❸ 045.

See : Town★.

Env : Tully★★★ (Japanese Gardens★★★ *AC*, Irish National Stud★★ *AC*) SW : 6 m. by
N 7 – Kildare★ (Cathedral★★) SW : 5 ½m. by N 7.

🏌 Curragh 🖉 41238/41714.

🎫 Main St. 🖉 33835 (July-August).

Dublin 28 – Kilkenny 57 – Tullamore 36.

🏨 **Keadeen**
Ballymany, SW : 1 m. 🖉 431666, Fax 434402
🌳 – 📺 ☎ 🅿 – 🔬 350. 🐵 🆎 ⓞ 𝘝𝘐𝘚𝘈. 🎜
Meals 12.50/22.50 **st.** and dinner a la carte 🍸 5.50 – **32 rm** ⊱ 70.00/
170.00 **st.**, 1 suite – SB.

NEWMARKET-ON-FERGUS (Cora Chaitlín) Clare 405 F 7 – pop. 1 583 – ❸ 061.

Dublin 136 – Ennis 8 – Limerick 15.

🏰 **Dromoland Castle**
NW : 1 ½ m. on N 18 🖉 368144, Fax 363355
🕭, ≤, « Converted castle », 🏌, 🍃, 🌳, park, 🍴 – 📺 ☎ 🅿 – 🔬 450. 🐵 🆎
ⓞ 𝘝𝘐𝘚𝘈. 🎜
Meals 16.50/34.00 **t.** and a la carte 🍸 8.00 – ⊱ 12.50 – **67 rm** 210.00 **st.**,
6 suites – SB.

🏨 **Clare Inn**
NW : 2 m. on N 18 🖉 368161, Fax 368622
🏋, ≋s, ⬚, 🏌, 🍴 – 📺 ☎ 🅿 – 🔬 400. 🐵 🆎 ⓞ 𝘝𝘐𝘚𝘈. 🎜
Meals 9.95/20.00 **s.** 🍸 5.00 – **121 rm** ⊱ 52.00/87.50 **s.** – SB.

🏠 **Carrygerry Country House**
SW : 8 m. by N 18 🖉 472339, Fax 472123
🕭, park – ⊱ rm 📺 ☎ 🅿. 🐵 🆎 ⓞ 𝘝𝘐𝘚𝘈. 🎜
Meals (bar lunch Monday to Saturday)/dinner 21.50 **t.** 🍸 6.00 – **14 rm**
⊱ 48.50/85.00 **t.** – SB.

NEWPORT (Baile Uí Fhiacháin) Mayo 405 D 6 Ireland G. – pop. 512 – ❸ 098.

Env : Burrishoole Abbey★, NW : 2 m. by N 59 – Furnace Lough★, NW : 3 m. by N 59.

Dublin 164 – Ballina 37 – Galway 60.

🏠 **Newport House**
🖉 41222, Fax 41613
🕭, « Country house atmosphere, antiques », 🍃, 🌳, park – ⊱ rest ☎ 🅿.
🐵 🆎 ⓞ 𝘝𝘐𝘚𝘈. 🎜
19 March-September – **Meals** (dinner only) 30.00 **st.** 🍸 8.00 – **18 rm** ⊱ 69.00/
138.00 **st.**

---

*Besonders angenehme Hotels oder Restaurants
sind im Führer rot gekennzeichnet.*

*Sie können uns helfen, wenn Sie uns die Häuser angeben,
in denen Sie sich besonders wohl gefühlt haben.*

*Jährlich erscheint eine komplett überarbeitete Ausgabe
aller Roten Michelin-Führer.*

NEW ROSS (Ros Mhic Thriúin) Wexford 405 L 10 **Ireland G.** – pop. 5 018 – ✉ Newbawn – 🕆 051.

See : St. Mary's Church★.

Exc. : Kennedy Arboretum, Campile★ *AC*, S : 7 ½m. by R 733 – Dunbrody Abbey★, S : 8 m. by R 733 – Inistiage★, NW : 10 m. by N 25 and R 700 – Graiguenamanagh★ (Duiske Abbey★) N : 11 m. by N 25 and R705.

🏌 Tinneranny, New Ross ℘ 21433.

🛈 Town Centre ℘ 21857 (mid June-August).

Dublin 88 – Kilkenny 27 – Waterford 15 – Wexford 23.

🏠 **Cedar Lodge**
Carrigbyrne, E : 8 m. on N 25 ℘ 428386, Fax 428222
🍴 – 📺 ☎ 🅿. 🏧 VISA. ⌗
closed 1 December-1 February – **Meals** (lunch booking essential)/dinner 23.00 **st.** ⋀ 9.95 – **28 rm** ⇄ 60.00/90.00 **st.** – SB.

⌂ **Riversdale House**
Lower William St. ℘ 422515, Fax 422800
without rest., 🍴 – ⛝ 📺 🅿. ⌗
March-October – **4 rm** ⇄ 21.00/32.00 **st.**

OGONNELLOE (Tuath Ó gConaíle) Clare 405 G 9 – see Killaloe.

OMEATH (Ó Méith) Louth 405 N 5 – pop. 249 – 🕆 042.

Dublin 63 – Dundalk 10.

🏨 **Omeath Park**
NW : ½ m. on B 79 ℘ 75116, Fax 75116
🐾, ≤, 🍴, park – 📺 ☎ 🅿. 🏧 ⓞ VISA. ⌗
closed 25 December – **Meals** (bar lunch Monday to Saturday)/dinner a la carte 9.00/18.75 **st.** ⋀ 5.75 – **13 rm** ⇄ 35.00/55.00 **st.** – SB.

🏠 **Granvue House**
℘ 75109, Fax 75415
≤ – 📺 ☎ 🅿. 🏧 VISA. ⌗
closed 23 December-6 January – **Meals** (bar lunch Monday to Saturday)/ dinner 15.00 **t.** ⋀ 5.00 – **8 rm** ⇄ 25.00/44.00 **t.** – SB.

ORANMORE (Órán Mór) Galway 405 F 8 – 🕆 091.

🏌 Athenry, Palmerstown ℘ 94466.

Dublin 131 – Galway 7.

🏠 **Mooring's**
Main St. ℘ 790462, Fax 790462
📺 ☎ 🅿 – ⛏ 30. 🏧 🅰🄴 VISA. ⌗
Meals (dinner only) a la carte 13.90/21.40 **t.** ⋀ 6.60 – **6 rm** ⇄ 30.00/50.00 **st.**

OUGHTERARD (Uachtar Ard) Galway 405 E 7 **Ireland G.** – pop. 711 – 🕆 091.

See : Town★.

Env : Lough Corrib★★ (Shore road – NW – ≤★★) – Aughnanure Castle★ *AC*, SE : 2 m. by N 59.

🏌 Gortreevagh ℘ 82131.

🛈 Main St. ℘ 82808.

Dublin 149 – Galway 17.

🏨 **Connemara Gateway**
SE : ¾ m. on N 59 ℘ 552328, Fax 552332
≘s, 🏊, 🍴, 🏑 – 🍽 rest 📺 ☎ 🅿. 🏧 ⓞ VISA. ⌗
closed 3 January-12 February and 30 November-28 December – **Meals** (bar lunch)/dinner 20.00 **st.** and a la carte ⋀ 5.75 – **61 rm** ⇄ 78.50/110.00 **st.**, 1 suite – SB.

🏛 **Currarevagh House**
NW : 4 m. ☎ 552312, Fax 552731
🐟, ≤, « Country house atmosphere », 🐾, 🚄, park, ✗ – ✗ rest 🅿. 🎤
28 March-17 October – **Meals** (booking essential) (dinner only) 19.50 **t.** ⅄ 4.90
– **15 rm** ⌁ 45.00/94.00 **t.**

🏛 **Ross Lake House**
Rosscahill, SE : 4 ½ m. by N 59 ☎ 550109, Fax 550184
🐟, 🚄, ✗ – ☎ 🅿. 🐵 🆎 ⓪ 𝗩𝗜𝗦𝗔. 🎤
15 March-October – **Meals** (dinner only) 19.00 **t.** ⅄ 5.90 – **13 rm** ⌁ 40.00/
80.00 **t.** – SB.

🏛 **Boat Inn**
☎ 552196, Fax 55694
📺 ☎. 🐵 🆎 𝗩𝗜𝗦𝗔. 🎤
closed 25 December – **Meals** a la carte 7.15/18.65 **st.** – **11 rm** ⌁ 28.00/
46.00 **st.** – SB.

🏠 **Cnoc na Curra**
Pier Rd ☎ 82225, Fax 82225
🐟, without rest., ≤, 🐾, 🚄 – ✗ 🅿. 𝗩𝗜𝗦𝗔. 🎤
15 May-15 September – **4 rm** ⌁ 18.50/40.00 **st.**

PARKNASILLA (Páirc na Saileach) Kerry **405** C 12 **Ireland G.** – ✪ 064.

Env : Sneem★, NW : 2 ½m. by N 70.

Exc. : Iveragh Peninsula★★★ (Ring of Kerry★★) – Staigue Fort★, W : 13 m. by N 70.

Dublin 224 – Cork 72 – Killarney 34.

🏰 **Great Southern**
☎ 45122, Fax 45323
🐟, ≤ Kenmare River, bay and mountains, ⚑s, 🏊, 🎾, 🐾, 🚄, park, ✗ – 🛗 📺
☎ ₺ 🅿 – 🔬 80. 🐵 🆎 ⓪ 𝗩𝗜𝗦𝗔. 🎤
closed 2 January-14 February – **Meals** (bar lunch)/dinner 25.00 **st.** and
a la carte ⅄ 8.00 – **83 rm** ⌁ 97.00/180.00 **st.**, 1 suite – SB.

PORTLAOISE (Port Laoise) Laois **405** K 8 **Ireland G.** – pop. 8 360 – ✪ 0502.

Env : Rock of Dunamase★ (≤★), E : 4 m. by N 80 – Emo Court★ *AC*, NE : 7 m. by N 7.

Exc. : Stradbally★, E : 6 ½m. by N 80 – Timahoe Round Tower★, SE : 8 m. by R 426.

🏌 The Heath ☎ 46533.

🚩 James Fintan Lawlor Av. ☎ 21178 (May-December).

Dublin 54 – Kilkenny 31 – Limerick 67.

🏛 **Killeshin**
Dublin Rd, E : 1 m. on N 7 ☎ 21663, Fax 21976
✗ rm 📺 ☎ 🅿. 🐵 🆎 ⓪ 𝗩𝗜𝗦𝗔
Meals 9.90/18.15 **st.** and a la carte ⅄ 5.00 – **44 rm** ⌁ 45.00/65.00 **t.** – SB.

🏠 **Aspen**
Dunamase, E : 4 ½ m. by N 80 ☎ 25405, Fax 25442
without rest., ≤, 🚄 – ✗ 🅿. 🎤
April-October – **4 rm** ⌁ 22.50/35.00.

PORTMAGEE (An Caladh) Kerry **405** A 12 – ✪ 066.

⚓ **Moorings**
☎ 77108, Fax 77220
≤ – ☎ 🅿. 🐵 𝗩𝗜𝗦𝗔. 🎤
March-October – **Meals** *(closed mid October-Easter)* (bar lunch)/dinner
18.00 **t.** and a la carte ⅄ 5.50 – **9 rm** ⌁ 23.00/36.00 **st.** – SB.

In this guide

*a symbol or a character, printed in red or black, in **bold** or light type,
does not have the same meaning.*

Pay particular attention to the explanatory pages.

PORTMARNOCK (Port Mearnóg) Dublin 〔405〕 N 7 – pop. 9 173 – ✪ 01.

Dublin 5 – Drogheda 28.

🏨 Portmarnock H. and Golf Links
  𝒫 846 0611, Fax 846 2442
  ≼, ⌡₁₈, 🐎 – 📺 ☎ 🅿 – 🏊 750. 🆖 AE ⓞ VISA . 🦌
  Meals (dinner only) 30.00 **st.** ⫶ 9.00 – **103 rm** ⫼ 120.00/190.00 **st.** – SB.

RATHMELTON (Ráth Mealtain) Donegal 〔405〕 J 2 – ✪ 074.

Dublin 154 – Donegal 37 – Londonerry 27 – Sligo 76.

⌂ Ardeen
  𝒫 51243
  🛏 without rest., 🐎, 🦌 – 🅿. 🆖 AE VISA
  Easter-October – **4 rm** ⫼ 18.50/37.00.

RATHMULLAN (Ráth Maoláin) Donegal 〔405〕 J 2 **Ireland G.** – pop. 536 – ✉ Letterkenny – ✪ 074.

Exc. : Knockalla Viewpoint★★, N : 8 m. by R 247 – Rathmelton★, SW : 7 m. by R 247.

🏌₉ Otway, Saltpans 𝒫 58319.

Dublin 165 – Londonderry 36 – Sligo 87.

🏨 Rathmullan House
  N : ½ m. on R 247 𝒫 58188, Fax 58200
  🛏, ≼ Lough Swilly and hills, « Part 19C country house, gardens », ≈s, ◳, ↘,
  park, 🦌 – ⇥✗ rest 📺 ☎ 🅿. 🆖 AE ⓞ VISA . 🦌
  18 March-October – **Meals** (bar lunch Monday to Saturday)/dinner 25.00 **t.**
  ⫶ 5.50 – **20 rm** ⫼ 40.00/125.00 **t.** – SB.

🏨 Fort Royal
  N : 1 m. by R 247 𝒫 58100, Fax 58103
  🛏, ≼ Lough Swilly and hills, 🐎, park, 🦌, squash – ⇥✗ rest 📺 ☎ 🅿. 🆖 AE
  ⓞ VISA
  April-October – **Meals** (bar lunch Monday to Saturday)/dinner 23.00 **st.** ⫶ 7.50 –
  15 rm ⫼ 76.00/110.00 **st.** – SB.

RATHNEW (Ráth Naoi) Wicklow 〔405〕 N 8 – see Wicklow.

RECESS (Sraith Salach) Galway 〔405〕 C 7 **Ireland G.** – ✪ 095.

Exc. : Lough Nafooey★★, NE : by N 59 on R 345 – Lough Corrib★★, SE : by R 336 on N 59.

Dublin 173 – Ballina 72 – Galway 36.

🏨 Lough Inagh Lodge
  NW : 4 ¾ m. by N 59 on R 344 𝒫 34706, Fax 34708
  🛏, ≼ Lough Inagh and The Twelve Bens, ↘ – 📺 ☎ 🅿. 🆖 AE ⓞ VISA
  28 March-27 October – **Meals** (bar lunch)/dinner 25.30 ⫶ 6.50 – **12 rm**
  ⫼ 88.00/154.00 – SB.

REDCROSS (Chrois Dhearg, An) Wicklow 〔405〕 N 9 – ✉ Wicklow – ✪ 0404.

Dublin 39 – Kilkenny 66 – Wexford 47.

⌂ Saraville
  𝒫 41745
  🅿. 🦌
  17 March-September – **Meals** (by arrangement) (communal dining) 13.00 –
  4 rm ⫼ 18.00/32.00 – SB.

Plan Guide **Le Tunnel sous la Manche**

  〔260〕 *Version française avec les curiosités touristiques en Angleterre*

  〔261〕 *Version anglaise avec les curiosités touristiques sur le continent*

RINVYLE/RENVYLE (Rinn Mhaoile) Galway **405** C 7 – ☎ 095.

Dublin 193 – Ballina 73 – Galway 61.

   🏫   Renvyle House
        ℰ 43511, Fax 43515
        ॐ, ⩽ Atlantic Ocean, 🏊, ₁₉, ⚓, 🚥, park, ⋇ – 📺 ☎ 🅿. 🐱🐵 AE ① VISA JCB.
        ⋇
        closed January and February – **Meals** (light lunch Monday to Saturday)/
        dinner 23.00 **t.** ╻ 8.50 – **64 rm** � 80.00/160.00 **t.**, 1 suite – SB.

RIVERSTOWN (Baile idir Dhá Abhainn) Sligo **405** G 5 – pop. 274 – ☎ 071.

Dublin 123 – Sligo 13.

   🏠   Coopershill
        ℰ 65108, Fax 65466
        ॐ, ⩽, « Georgian country house », ⚓, 🚥, park, ⋇ – ⋡ rm ☎ 🅿. 🐱🐵 AE ①
        VISA JCB. ⋇
        April-October – **Meals** (residents only) (dinner only) 24.00 **st.** ╻ 4.75 – **8 rm**
        ⊻ 60.00/100.00 **st.**

ROSAPENNA (Rosapenna) Donegal **405** I 2 Ireland G. – ☎ 074.

Env : N : Rosguill Peninsula Atlantic Drive★.

🏌 Downings ℰ 55301.

Dublin 216 – Donegal 52 – Londonderry 47.

   🏨   Rosapenna Golf
        Downings ℰ 55301, Fax 55128
        ⩽, ₁₈, ⋇ – 📺 ☎ 🅿. 🐱🐵 AE ① VISA
        15 March-25 October – **Meals** (dinner only) 23.00 **t.** and a la carte ╻ 5.00 –
        46 rm ⊻ 57.50/110.00 **t.** – SB.

ROSCOMMON (Ros Comáin) Roscommon **405** H 7 Ireland G. – pop. 1 314 –
☎ 0903.

See : Castle★.

Exc. : Castlestrange Stone★, SW : 7 m. by N 63 and R 362 – Famine Museum★,
Strokestown Park House★ *AC*, N : 12 m. by N 61 and R 368 – Castlerea : Clonalis
House★ *AC*, NW : 19 m. by N 60.

🏌 Moate Park ℰ 26382.

🛈 ℰ 26342 (20 June-4 September).

Dublin 94 – Galway 57 – Limerick 94.

   🏫   Abbey
        on N 63 ℰ 26240, Fax 26021
        ॐ, 🚥 – 📺 ☎ 🅿 – 🔬 200. 🐱🐵 AE ① VISA JCB. ⋇
        closed 25 December – **Meals** 11.50/22.50 **st.** and dinner a la carte – **25 rm**
        ⊻ 50.00/120.00 – SB.

ROSSLARE (Ros Láir) Wexford **405** M 11 – pop. 847 – ☎ 053.

₁₈, ₁₉ Rosslare Strand ℰ 32113.

🛈 Rosslare Terminal ℰ 33622.

Dublin 104 – Waterford 50 – Wexford 12.

   🏨   Kelly's Resort
        ℰ 32114, Fax 32222
        ⩽, ₁₆, ⇌ₛ, 🏊, 🚥, ⋇, squash – 🛗 ☰ rest 📺 ☎ 🐾 🅿. 🐱🐵 AE VISA. ⋇
        March-November – **Meals** 13.75/23.05 **st.** ╻ 6.00 – **99 rm** ⊻ 63.00/120.00 **t.** –
        SB.

🏠 **Cedars**
Strand Rd *✆* 32124, Fax 32243
🍴 – 🍽 rest 📺 ☎ 🅿. 🌐 *VISA*. 🌿
April-October, Christmas and New Year – **Meals** (bar lunch)/dinner 16.95 **t.**
and a la carte ⓘ 6.50 – **34 rm** ⌖ 55.00/90.00 **st.** – SB.

ROSSLARE HARBOUR (**Calafort Ros Láir**) Wexford 🗺 N 11 **Ireland G.** –
pop. 968 – 🕿 053.

Env : Lady's Island★, SW : 6 m. by N 25 and R 736 – Tacumshane Windmill★, SW :
6 m. by N 25 and R 736.

⚓ to France (Cherbourg, Le Havre and Roscoff) (Irish Ferries) – to Fishguard
(Stena Line) 2 daily (3 h 30 mn) – to Pembroke (Irish Ferries) 2 daily (4 h 15 mn).

🛈 Kilrane *✆* 33232 (May-mid September).

Dublin 105 – Waterford 51 – Wexford 13.

🏠 **Great Southern**
✆ 33233, Fax 33543
Fδ, ⓢ, 🗔, ⚒ – 🕴 📺 ☎ ⅋ 🅿 – 🛆 150. 🌐 🆎 ⓪ *VISA*. 🌿
April-December – **Meals** (bar lunch Monday to Saturday)/dinner 17.00 **st.**
and a la carte ⓘ 6.00 – ⌖ 7.00 – **100 rm** 54.00/88.00 **t.** – SB.

🏠 **Rosslare**
✆ 33110, Fax 33386
≼, « Nautical memorabilia », ⓢ, ⓘ₈, squash – 📺 ☎ 🅿. 🌐 🆎 ⓪ *VISA*. 🌿
closed 25 December – **Meals** 4.95/18.00 **st.** and a la carte ⓘ 4.95 – **25 rm**
⌖ 29.50/78.50 **st.** – SB.

🏠 **Tuskar House**
St. Martins Rd *✆* 33363, Fax 33363
≼, *🍴* – 📺 ☎ 🅿. 🌐 🆎 *VISA*. 🌿
Meals 9.95/14.95 **st.** and a la carte ⓘ 4.95 – **30 rm** ⌖ 39.00/66.00 **st.** – SB.

🏠 **Devereux**
Wexford Rd *✆* 33216, Fax 33301
≼ – 📺 ☎ 🅿. 🌐 🆎 *VISA* JCB
closed 25 December – **Meals** (bar lunch)/dinner a la carte 13.95/21.45 **st.**
ⓘ 5.75 – **24 rm** ⌖ 30.00/61.60 **t.** – SB.

at Tagoat W : 2 ½ m. on N 25 – ✉ Rosslare – 🕿 053 :

🏠 **Churchtown House**
N : ½ m. on Rosslare rd *✆* 32555, Fax 32555
🌭, *🍴* – *✖* rm 📺 ⅋ 🅿. 🌐 *VISA*. 🌿
16 March-4 November – **Meals** (booking essential) (residents only) 16.00 **st.**
ⓘ 7.50 – **11 rm** ⌖ 28.50/59.00 **st.** – SB.

ROSSNOWLAGH (**Ros Neamhlach**) Donegal 🗺 H 4 – 🕿 072.

Dublin 153 – Donegal 14 – Sligo 31.

🏠 **Sand House**
✆ 51777, Fax 52100
🌭, ≼ bay, beach and mountains, ⚓, ⚒ – ☎ 🅿. 🌐 🆎 ⓪ *VISA*. 🌿
Easter-mid October – **Meals** (bar lunch Monday to Friday)/dinner 22.50 **t.**
and a la carte ⓘ 8.50 – **45 rm** ⌖ 50.00/120.00 **t.** – SB.

ROUNDSTONE (**Cloch na Rón**) Galway 🗺 C 7 – pop. 281 – 🕿 095.

Dublin 193 – Galway 47.

🏠 **Eldon's**
✆ 35933, Fax 35921
≼, *🍴* – 📺 ☎. 🌐 🆎 ⓪ *VISA*. 🌿
closed 5 January-25 March – **Meals** 7.50/18.50 **t.** ⓘ 5.50 – **19 rm** ⌖ 40.00/
80.00 **st.** – SB.

SALTHILL (**Bóthar na Trá**) Galway 🗺 E 8 – see Galway.

SHANAGARRY (An Seangharraí) Cork 405 H 12 Ireland G. – pop. 242 – ✉ Midleton – 😊 021.

Env : Ballycotton★, SE : 2 ½m. by R 629 – Cloyne Cathedral★, NW : 4 m. by R 629.

Exc. : Rostellan Wood★, W : 9 m. by R 629 and R 631 on R 630.

Dublin 163 – Cork 25 – Waterford 64.

🏛 **Ballymaloe House**
NW : 1 ¾ m. on L 35 ℘ 652531, Fax 652021
⑤, ≼, « Part 16C, part Georgian country house », ⬛, 🎋, park, ⬚ – ⇖ rest
☎ 🅿. 🐴 🆎 ⓪ 𝘝𝘐𝘚𝘈. ⬚
closed 24 to 26 December – **Meals** (buffet Sunday) 17.00/31.50 **t.** – **32 rm**
☲ 80.00/140.00 **t.** – SB.

SHANNON (Sionainn) Clare 405 F 9 – pop. 7 920 – 😊 061.

🏌 Shannon ,Airport ℘ 471020.

✈ Shannon Airport : ℘ 471444.

🛈 Shannon Airport ℘ 471644.

Dublin 136 – Ennis 16 – Limerick 15.

🏛 **Oak Wood Arms**
on N 19 ℘ 361500, Fax 361414
🚗 ⇖ rm 🔲 📺 ☎ 🅿 – 🔬 200. 🐴 🆎 ⓪ 𝘝𝘐𝘚𝘈. ⬚
closed 24 and 25 December – **Meals** (carving lunch)/dinner 19.45 **t.**
and a la carte ⓘ 5.95 – **73 rm** ☲ 70.00/96.00 **st.**, 2 suites.

at Shannon Airport SW : 2 ½ m. on N 19 – ✉ Shannon – 😊 061 :

🏛 **Great Southern**
℘ 471122, Fax 471982
📶 ⇖ rm 🔲 rest 📺 ☎ 🅿 – 🔬 200. 🐴 🆎 ⓪ 𝘝𝘐𝘚𝘈. ⬚
closed 24 to 28 December – **Meals** (carving lunch)/dinner 16.00 **st.**
and a la carte ⓘ 6.00 – ☲ 7.50 – **113 rm** 68.00/96.00 **st.**, 2 suites – SB.

SHANNON AIRPORT Clare 405 F 9 – see Shannon.

SKERRIES (Na Sceirí) Dublin 405 N 7 – pop. 7 032 – 😊 01.

🏌 Skerries ℘ 849 1204.

🛈 Community Office ℘ 849 0888.

Dublin 19 – Drogheda 15.

XX **Red Bank**
7 Church St. ℘ 849 1005, Fax 849 1598
🐴 🆎 ⓪ 𝘝𝘐𝘚𝘈
closed Sunday dinner and Monday – **Meals** - Seafood - (dinner only and Sunday
lunch)/dinner 21.00 **t.** and a la carte ⓘ 5.75.

SKIBBEREEN (An Sciobairán) Cork 405 E 13 – 😊 028.

Dublin 205 – Cork 51 – Killarney 64.

🏛 **Liss Ard Lake Lodge**
SE : 2 ¾ m. by R 596 on Tragumna rd ℘ 22365, Fax 22839
⑤, ≼, « Minimalistic interior, themed feature gardens », 🎋, 🎋, park, ⬚ –
⇖ 📺 ☎ 🅿 – 🔬 25. 🐴 🆎 ⓪ 𝘝𝘐𝘚𝘈. ⬚
Meals (booking essential) (dinner only) 32.00 **t.** ⓘ 14.00 – **10 rm** ☲ 100.00/
260.00 **t.** – SB.

*Great Britain and Ireland is now covered
by an Atlas at a scale of 1 inch to 4.75 miles.*

Three easy to use versions: Paperback, Spiralbound and Hardback.

SKULL/SCHULL (An Scoil) Cork 405 D 13 – pop. 579 – ✪ 028.

Dublin 226 – Cork 65 – Killarney 64.

🏠 **Corthna Lodge Country House**
W : ¾ m. by R 592 *ℰ* 28517, Fax 28517
⤫ without rest., ≼, 🚗 – ☎ 🅿. ⌧
April-October – **6 rm** ⌑ 25.00/40.00.

✗✗ **Restaurant in Blue**
W : 2 ½ m. on R 592 *ℰ* 28305
🅿. 🆎 🆎 ⑩ 𝗩𝗜𝗦𝗔
closed Bank Holidays and Mondays in summer and restricted opening in winter
– **Meals** (booking essential) (dinner only) 24.00 **t.** ⌑ 7.25.

SLIEVEROE (Sliabh Rua) Waterford – see Waterford.

SLIGO (Sligeach) Sligo 405 G 5 Ireland G. – pop. 17 302 – ✪ 071.

See : Town★★ – Abbey★.

Env : SE : Lough Gill★★ – Carrowmore Megalithic Cemetery★ *AC*, SW : 3 m. –
Knocknarea★ (≼★★★) SW : 6 m. by R 292.

Exc. : Parke's Castle★★ *AC*, E : 9 m. by R 286 – Glencar Waterfall★, NE : 9 m. by N 16
– Creevelea Abbey, Dromahair★, SE : 11 ½m. by N 4 and R 287 – Creevykeel Court
Cairn★, N : 16 m. by N 15.

🏌 Rosses Point *ℰ* 77134/77186.

✈ Sligo Airport, Strandhill : *ℰ* 68280.

🛈 Temple St. *ℰ* 61201.

Dublin 133 – Belfast 126 – Dundalk 106 – Londonderry 86.

🏨 **Sligo Park**
Pearse Rd, S : 1 m. on N 4 *ℰ* 60291, Fax 69556
🛌, ≘s, 🔲, 🚗, ✗ – 📺 ☎ 🅿 – 🏛 100. 🆎 🆎 ⑩ 𝗩𝗜𝗦𝗔. ⌧
Meals (bar lunch Saturday) 9.50/17.95 **st.** and dinner a la carte ⌑ 5.50 – **89 rm**
⌑ 57.00/99.00 **st.** – SB.

🏠 **Benwiskin Lodge**
Shannon Eighter, N : 2 m. by N 15 *ℰ* 41088
without rest., 🚗 – ⤫ 📺 🅿. 🆎 𝗩𝗜𝗦𝗔. ⌧
closed 24 to 27 December – **5 rm** ⌑ 16.00/32.00 **t.**

🏠 **Tree Tops**
Cleveragh Rd, S : ¼ m. by Dublin rd *ℰ* 60160, Fax 62301
without rest., 🚗 – ⤫ 📺 ☎ 🅿. 🆎 𝗩𝗜𝗦𝗔. ⌧
closed 15 December-15 January – **5 rm** ⌑ 22.00/33.00 **st.**

SPIDDAL (An Spidéal) Galway 405 E 8 – ✪ 091.

Dublin 143 – Galway 11.

🏠 **Bridge House**
Main St. *ℰ* 83118, Fax 83435
🚗 – 📺 ☎ 🅿. 🆎 🆎 𝗩𝗜𝗦𝗔. ⌧
closed 22 December-1 March – **Meals** 10.50/25.00 **st.** and a la carte ⌑ 6.95 –
12 rm ⌑ 35.00/90.00 **t.**

🏠 **Ardmor Country House**
W : ½ m. on R 336 *ℰ* 553145, Fax 553596
without rest., ≼, 🚗 – ⤫ 🅿. 🆎 𝗩𝗜𝗦𝗔. ⌧
7 rm ⌑ 25.00/32.00.

140

STRAFFAN (Teach Srafáin) Kildare 405 M 8 – pop. 341 – ✪ 01.

🇮🇸 Naas, Kerdiffstown ℰ (0145) 97509.

Dublin 15 – Mullingar 47.

🏨 **Kildare H. & Country Club**
ℰ 627 3333, Fax 627 3312
⟨⟩, ≼, 🛁, « Part early 19C country house on banks of the River Liffey », ℔,
≘ₛ, 🛏, 🇮🇸, ⟨⟩, ✿, park, ✕indoor/outdoor, squash – 🔩 📺 ☎ 🄿 – ⅍ 130. 🆎
🆎 ① 🆅🅸🆂🅰. ✕
Byerley Turk : Meals (dinner only and Sunday lunch)/dinner 39.00 **t.**
and a la carte 39.00/55.00
Legends (in K Club) : **Meals** a la carte 19.25/26.25 – 🖵 14.00 – **38 rm** 260.00/
320.00 **t.**, 7 suites – SB.

🏨 **Barberstown Castle**
N : ½ m. ℰ 628 8157, Fax 627 7027
« Part Elizabethan, part Victorian house with 13C castle keep », ✿ – 📺 ☎ 🄿.
🆎 🆎 ① 🆅🅸🆂🅰. ✕
closed 23 to 27 December – **Meals** (dinner only and Sunday lunch)/dinner
25.00 **t.** and a la carte – **26 rm** 🖵 65.00/175.00 **t.** – SB.

⌂ **Barberstown House**
N : ½ m. on R 403 ℰ 627 4007
without rest., « Georgian house », ✿ – ⟵✕ 📺 🄿. 🆎 🆅🅸🆂🅰. ✕
March-September – **5 rm** 🖵 30.00/45.00.

SWORDS (Sord) Dublin 405 N 7 – pop. 17 705 – ✪ 01.

🇮🇸 Balcarrick, Corballis, Donabate ℰ 843 6228.

Dublin 8 – Drogheda 22.

🏨 **Travelodge** (Granada)
Miltons Field, S : ½ m. on N 1 ℰ 840 9233
Reservations (Freephone) 0800 850950 (UK), 1800 709709 (Republic of
Ireland) – 📺 ⅗ 🄿
40 rm.

TAGOAT (Teach Gót) Wexford 405 M 11 – see Rosslare Harbour.

TAHILLA (Tathuile) Kerry 405 C 12 Ireland G. – ✪ 064.

Exc. : Iveragh Peninsula★★★ (Ring of Kerry★★).

Dublin 222 – Cork 70 – Killarney 32.

🏨 **Tahilla Cove**
ℰ 45204, Fax 45104
⟨⟩, ≼ Tahilla Cove and mountains, « Waterside setting », 🇮🇸, ✿, park – 📺 ☎
🄿. 🆎 🆎 🆎 ① 🆅🅸🆂🅰
April-mid October – **Meals** (bar lunch)/dinner 17.50 **st.** – **9 rm** 🖵 51.00/
72.00 **st.** – SB.

TALLAGHT (Tamhlacht) Dublin 405 N 8 – see Dublin.

TEMPLEGLANTINE (Teampall an Ghleanntáin) Limerick 405 E 10 Ireland G. –
✪ 069.

Exc. : Newcastle West★, NE : 4 ½m. by N 21.

🇮🇸 Newcastle West, Ardagh ℰ 76500.

Dublin 154 – Killarney 36 – Limerick 33.

🏨 **Devon Inn**
on N 21 ℰ 84122, Fax 84122
📺 ☎ 🄿 – ⅍ 60. 🆎 🆎 ① 🆅🅸🆂🅰. ✕
closed 24 and 25 December – **Meals** 9.00/15.00 **st.** and dinner a la carte ♨ 5.25
– **37 rm** 🖵 35.00/100.00 **st.** – SB.

TERMONFECKIN Louth 405 N 6 – see Drogheda.

TERRYGLASS (Tír Dhá Ghlas) Tipperary 👁️5️⃣ H 8 – ✉️ Nenagh – ☎️ 067.

Dublin 114 – Galway 51 – Limerick 43.

↑ **Riverrun House**
   𝒫 22125, Fax 22187
   ᘒ, ≋, ✗ – ☎ 🅿. 🆖 🆑 𝘝𝘐𝘚𝘈
   Meals (by arrangement) – **6 rm** 🖵 27.50/45.00 **st.**

↑ **Tír na Fiúise**
   SE : 1 ½ m. 𝒫 22041, Fax 22041
   ᘒ without rest., « Working farm », ≋, park – ⚡🅿. 🆖 𝘝𝘐𝘚𝘈. ✗
   April-30 October – **4 rm** 🖵 25.00/40.00 **s.**

THOMASTOWN (Baile Mhic Andáin) Kilkenny 👁️5️⃣ K 10 Ireland G. – pop. 1 487 – ✉️ Kilkenny – ☎️ 056.

See : Ladywell Water Garden★ *AC.*

Env : Jerpoint Abbey★★, SW : 1 ½m. by N9.

🏌️ Mount Juliet 𝒫 24725.

Dublin 77 – Kilkenny 11 – Waterford 30 – Wexford 38.

🏨 **Mount Juliet**
   NW : 1 ½ m. 𝒫 24455, Fax 24522
   ᘒ, « 18C manor and sporting estate, ≤ River Nore and park », ℔, ≘s, ▦, 🏌️,
   ⚲, ≋, ✗ – ⚡ rest 📺 ☎ 🅿 – 🔏 40. 🆖 🆑 ① 𝘝𝘐𝘚𝘈. ✗
   Meals (dinner only and Sunday lunch)/dinner 38.00 **st.**

      🏨 **Hunters Yard at Mount Juliet**, NW : 1 ½ m. 𝒫 24455, Fax 24522, « Con-
      verted 18C stables », ℔, ≘s, ▦, 🏌️, ⚲, ≋, park, ✗ – 📺 ☎ 🅿 – 🔏 40. 🆖
      🆑 ① 𝘝𝘐𝘚𝘈. ✗
      February-October – **Meals** a la carte 15.00/30.00 **st.** – 🖵 12.50 – **30 rm**
      155.00/295.00 **st.**, 2 suites – 🖵 12.50 – **13 rm** 140.00 **st.**, 8 suites.

TOORMORE (An Tuar Mór) Cork 👁️5️⃣ D 13 – ✉️ Goleen – ☎️ 028.

Dublin 221 – Cork 68 – Killarney 65.

↑ **Fortview House**
   Gurtyowen, NE : 1 ½ m. on Durrus rd (R 591) 𝒫 35324
   ᘒ – ⚡ rest 🅿. ✗
   March-October – **Meals** (by arrangement) 14.00 **st.** – **5 rm** 🖵 17.00/40.00 **st.**

TOWER Cork 👁️5️⃣ G 12 – see Blarney.

TRALEE (Trá Lí) Kerry 👁️5️⃣ C 11 Ireland G. – pop. 17 225 – ☎️ 066.

Env : Blennerville Windmill★★ *AC*, SW : 2 m. by N 86 – Ardfert Cathedral★, NW : 5 ½ m. by R 551.

Exc. : Banna Strand★★, NW : 8 m. by R 551 – Crag Cave★★ *AC*, W : 13 m. by N 21 – Rattoo Round Tower★, N : 12 m. by R 556.

🅱 Ashe Memorial Hall, Denny St. 𝒫 21288.

Dublin 185 – Killarney 20 – Limerick 64.

🏨 **Grand**
   Denny St. 𝒫 21499, Fax 22877
   ⚡ rm 🍽 rest 📺 ☎ – 🔏 250. 🆖 🆑 𝘝𝘐𝘚𝘈. ✗
   Meals 10.00/15.00 **st.** and a la carte 🍷 6.00 – **44 rm** 🖵 40.00/72.00 **s.** – SB.

🏨 **Ballyseede Castle**
   SE : 3 ¼ m. by N 22 𝒫 25799, Fax 25287
   ᘒ, ≋, park – 📺 ☎ 🅿. 🆖 ① 𝘝𝘐𝘚𝘈. ✗
   Meals *(closed dinner November-February)* (bar lunch October-April)/dinner 18.00 **t.** and a la carte 🍷 6.75 – 🖵 7.50 – **14 rm** (dinner included) 75.00/160.00 **t.**

🏠 **Brook Manor Lodge**
Fenit Rd, Spa, NW : 2 ¼ m. by R 551 on R 558 ℰ 20509, Fax 27552
without rest., 🌲 – ⚡ 📺 ☎ 🅿. 🆖🅾 𝗩𝗜𝗦𝗔. 🛇
March-October – **7 rm** 🖃 27.00/52.00 **t.**

🏠 **Barnakyle**
Clogherbrien, NW : 1 ½ m. on R 551 ℰ 25048, Fax 25048
without rest., 🌲 – ⚡ 📺 ☎ 🅿. 🆖🅾 𝗩𝗜𝗦𝗔. 🛇
closed 21 to 31 December – **4 rm** 🖃 22.00/32.00 **st.**

🏠 **Kilteely House**
Ballyard, S : 1 m. via Princes St. ℰ 23376, Fax 25766
🔊, 🌲 – ⚡ rest ☎ 🅿. 🆖🅾 𝗩𝗜𝗦𝗔. 🛇
Meals (by arrangement) 14.00 **st.** 🍸 6.00 – **11 rm** 🖃 28.00/56.00 **st.**

🏠 Knockanish House
The Spa, NW : 3 m. by R 551 on R 558 ℰ 36268
without rest., 🌲 – 🅿
6 rm.

TRIM (Baile Átha Troim) Meath 🄰🄾🄾 L 7 Ireland G. – pop. 1 784 – 🕾 046.

See : Trim Castle★★ – Town★.

Env : Bective Abbey★, NE : 4 m. by R 161.

Dublin 27 – Drogheda 26 – Tullamore 43.

🏠 **Crannmór**
Dunderry Rd, N : 1 ¼ m. ℰ 31635
🔊 without rest., 🌲 – ⚡ 🅿. 🆖🅾 𝗩𝗜𝗦𝗔. 🛇
April-September – **4 rm** 🖃 21.00/32.00.

TULLAMORE (Tulach Mhór) Offaly 🄰🄾🄾 J 8 – pop. 8 622 – 🕾 0506.

Dublin 65 – Kilkenny 52 – Limerick 80.

🏠 **Sea Dew House**
Clonminch Rd, SE : ¼ m. on N 80 ℰ 52054, Fax 52054
without rest., 🌲 – ⚡ 📺 ☎ 🅿. 🆖🅾 𝗩𝗜𝗦𝗔. 🛇
closed 22 December-2 January – **10 rm** 🖃 30.00/50.00 **st.**

🏠 **Pine Lodge**
Screggan, SW : 4 ½ m. by N 52 on Mountbolus rd ℰ 51927, Fax 51927
🔊, 🖃, 🔲, 🌲 – ⚡ 🅿. 🛇
closed 15 December-15 February – **Meals** (by arrangement) 18.00 **st.** – **4 rm**
🖃 27.00/44.00 **st.** – SB.

VIRGINIA (Achadh an Iúir) Cavan 🄰🄾🄾 K 6 – pop. 720 – 🕾 049.

Dublin 51 – Drogheda 39 – Enniskillen 60.

🏠 **Sharkey's**
Main St. ℰ 47561, Fax 47761
🌲 – 📺 ☎ 🅿. 🆖🅾 𝗩𝗜𝗦𝗔. 🛇
Meals (carving lunch Monday to Saturday) 11.50/18.00 **t.** and a la carte 🍸 5.00
– **10 rm** 🖃 34.00/70.00 **t.** – SB.

WATERFORD (Port Láirge) Waterford 🄰🄾🄾 K 11 Ireland G. – pop. 40 328 – 🕾 051.

See : Town★ – City Walls★ – City Hall and Theatre Royal★.

Env : Waterford Crystal★, SW : 1 ½m. by N 25.

Exc. : Tramore★, S : 9 m. by R 675 – Duncannon★, E : 12 m. by R 683, ferry from
Passage East and R 374 (south) – Dunmore East★, SE : 12 m. by R 684 – Tintern
Abbey★, E : 13 m. by R 683, ferry from Passage East, R 733 and R 734 (south).

🏌 Newrath ℰ 76748.

✈ Waterford Airport, Killowen : ℰ 75589.

🇿 41 The Quay ℰ 75788.

Dublin 96 – Cork 73 – Limerick 77.

Waterford Castle
The Island, Ballinakill, E : 2 ½ m. by R 683, Ballinakill Rd and private ferry
℘ 878203, Fax 879316
🌿, ≤, « Part 15C and 19C castle, river island setting », ◪, ▯₈, ◡, 🎠, park,
✗ – ❙❖❖ rest 📺 ☎ 🅿 🅼🅢 🄰🄴 ⓪ 𝑽𝑰𝑺𝑨 . ✗
Meals (bar lunch)/dinner 33.00 **t.** – ☑ 11.00 – **14 rm** 150.00/220.00 **st.**,
5 suites – SB.

Granville
Meagher Quay ℘ 855111, Fax 870307
❙❙ ❖❖ rm ▤ rest 📺 ☎ – 🕍 180. 🅼🅢 🄰🄴 ⓪ 𝑽𝑰𝑺𝑨 . ✗
closed 25 and 26 December – **Meals** 7.50/14.00 **st.** and dinner a la carte ⌀ 5.15
– **Bells : Meals** *(closed Sunday and Bank Holidays)* (dinner only) a la carte
20.75/21.75 – **74 rm** ☑ 57.50/130.00 **st.** – SB.

Jurys
Ferrybank ℘ 832111, Fax 832863
≤ City, ℔, ≘, ◪, 🎠, park, ✗ – ❙❙ ❖❖ rm 📺 ☎ 🅿 – 🕍 700. 🅼🅢 🄰🄴 ⓪ 𝑽𝑰𝑺𝑨
✗
closed 24 to 28 December – **Meals** 14.00/15.00 **t.** and a la carte ⌀ 5.50 –
☑ 8.50 – **97 rm** 76.00/96.00 **t.**, 1 suite – SB.

Bridge
The Quay ℘ 77222, Fax 77229
❙❙ 📺 ☎ – 🕍 250. 🅼🅢 🄰🄴 ⓪ 𝑽𝑰𝑺𝑨 . ✗
closed 25 December – **Meals** (bar lunch)/dinner 17.95 and a la carte ⌀ 5.25 –
90 rm ☑ 56.00/92.00 **t.** – SB.

Dooley's
The Quay ℘ 873531, Fax 870262
❖❖ rm 📺 ☎. 🅼🅢 🄰🄴 ⓪ 𝑽𝑰𝑺𝑨 . ✗
closed 25 to 27 December – **Meals** (bar lunch Monday to Saturday)/dinner
13.95 **t.** and a la carte ⌀ 6.90 – **115 rm** ☑ 45.00/80.00 **t.** – SB.

Coach House
Butlerstown Castle, Butlerstown, SW : 5 ¼ m. by N 25 ℘ 384656,
Fax 384751
🌿, ≤, ≘, 🎠 – 📺 ☎ 🅿. 🅼🅢 🄰🄴 ⓪ 𝑽𝑰𝑺𝑨 . ✗
closed 3 weeks Christmas and New Year – **Meals** *(closed Sunday and Monday)*
(booking essential) (dinner only) 15.50 **st.** ⌀ 6.00 – **7 rm** ☑ 36.50/53.00 **st.** –
SB.

Foxmount Farm
SE : 4 ½ m. by R 683, off Cheekpoint rd ℘ 874308, Fax 854906
🌿, ≤, « Working farm », 🎠, park, ✗ – 🅿. ✗
April-October – **Meals** (by arrangement) 16.00 **st.** – **6 rm** ☑ 30.00/45.00 **st.** –
SB.

Dwyer's
8 Mary St. ℘ 877478, Fax 871183
🅼🅢 🄰🄴 ⓪ 𝑽𝑰𝑺𝑨
closed Sunday, Bank Holidays and 1 week Christmas – **Meals** (dinner only)
14.00 **t.** and a la carte ⌀ 6.10.

Prendiville's
Cork Rd, SW : ¾ m. on N 25 ℘ 378851, Fax 374062
🅿. 🅼🅢 🄰🄴 ⓪ 𝑽𝑰𝑺𝑨
closed Saturday lunch, Sunday and 24 to 27 December – **Meals** 13.50/15.00 **t.**
and dinner a la carte ⌀ 6.25.

Wine Vault
High St. ℘ 853444, Fax 853777
« Converted bonded warehouse » – ▤. 🅼🅢 🄰🄴 𝑽𝑰𝑺𝑨
closed Bank Holiday lunch, Sunday, Good Friday and 25-26 December –
Meals 12.95 **st.** (dinner) and a la carte 16.40/24.40 **st.** ⌀ 6.95.

at Slieveroe NE : 2 ¼ m. by N 25 – ⊠ Waterford – 🕃 051 :

🏠 Diamond Hill
    𝒫 832855, Fax 32254
    🛒 – 🍴 rest 📺 ☎ 🅿. 🐵 🖭 𝘝𝘐𝘚𝘈
    Meals (by arrangement) 12.00 **st.** ⅄ 7.00 – **10 rm** ⊊ 25.00/44.00 **st.** – SB.

at Cheekpoint E : 7 m. by R 683 – ⊠ Waterford – 🕃 051 :

🏠 Three Rivers
    𝒫 382520, Fax 382542
    🍴 without rest., ≤ – 🍴 ☎ 🅿. 🐵 🖭 ⓪ 𝘝𝘐𝘚𝘈. 🎟
    14 rm ⊊ 28.00/56.00 **st.**

WATERVILLE (An Coireán) Kerry 🔢 B 12 **Ireland G.** – pop. 463 – 🕃 066.

Exc. : Iveragh Peninsula★★★ (Ring of Kerry★★) – Skellig Islands★★, W : 8 m. by N 70, R 567 and ferry from Ballinskelligs – Derrynane National Historic Park★★ *AC*, S : 9 m. by N 70 – Leacanabuaile Fort (≤★★), N : 13 m. by N 70 – Cahergall Fort★, N : 12 m. by N 70.

📇 Ring of Kerry 𝒫 74102/74545.

Dublin 238 – Killarney 48.

🏨 Butler Arms
    𝒫 74144, Fax 74520
    ≤, 🎣, 🛒, 🎿 – 📺 ☎ 🅿. 🐵 🖭 𝘝𝘐𝘚𝘈. 🎟
    mid April-mid October – **Meals** (bar lunch)/dinner 24.50 **t.** and a la carte ⅄ 5.95
    – **30 rm** ⊊ 55.00/130.00 **t.** – SB.

🏨 Waterville House and Golf Links
    𝒫 74244, Fax 74567
    without rest., ≤, ⩘s, ⬦, 📇, 🎣, 🛒 – 📺 ☎ 🅿. 🐵 🖭 𝘝𝘐𝘚𝘈. 🎟
    April-October – **6 rm** ⊊ 55.00/105.00 **t.**, 4 suites.

🏠 Golf Links View
    Murreigh, N : 1 m. on N 70 𝒫 74623, Fax 74623
    without rest. – 📺 🅿. 🐵 𝘝𝘐𝘚𝘈. 🎟
    March-October – **4 rm** ⊊ 20.00/32.00 **st.**

🏠 Klondyke House
    New Line Rd, N : ½ m. on N 70 𝒫 74119, Fax 74666
    without rest., ≤ – 🅿. 🐵 𝘝𝘐𝘚𝘈. 🎟
    6 rm ⊊ 18.00/32.00 **st.**

WESTPORT (Cathair na Mart) Mayo 🔢 D 6 **Ireland G.** – pop. 3 688 – 🕃 098.

See : Town★★ (Centre★) – Westport House★★ *AC*.

Exc. : SW : Murrisk Peninsula★★ – Silver Strand★★, SW : 21 m. by R 335 – Ballintubber Abbey★, SE : 13 m. by R 330 – Croagh Patrick★, W : 6 m. by R 335 – Bunlahinch Clapper Bridge★, W : 16 m. by R 335.

📇 Carowholly 𝒫 25113/27070.

🏛 The Mall 𝒫 25711.

Dublin 163 – Galway 50 – Sligo 65.

🏨 Westport Woods
    Louisburgh Rd, W : ½ m. 𝒫 25811, Fax 26212
    🛒, 🎿 – 📺 ☎ 🅿. 🐵 🖭 ⓪ 𝘝𝘐𝘚𝘈. 🎟
    closed 3 weeks January – **Meals** (bar lunch Monday to Saturday)/dinner
    15.00 **st.** and a la carte ⅄ 4.95 – ⊊ 7.00 – **95 rm** 58.00/136.00 **st.** – SB.

🏠 Wilmaur
    Rosbeg, W : 2 m. by R 335 𝒫 25784, Fax 26224
    🍴 without rest., ≤, 🛒 – 🅿
    April-October – **5 rm** ⊊ 27.50/33.00 **st.**

WEXFORD (Loch Garman) Wexford █0█ M 10 **Ireland** G. – pop. 15 393 – ⚙ 053.

See : Town★ – Main Street★ – Franciscan Friary★.

Env : Irish Agricultural Museum, Johnstown Castle★★ *AC*, SW : 4 ½m. – Irish National Heritage Park, Ferrycarrig★ *AC*, NW : 2 ½m. by N 11 – Curracloe★, NE : 5 m. by R 741 and R 743.

Exc. : Tacumshane Windmill★, S : 11 m. by N 25 – Lady's Island★, S : 11 m. by N 25 – Kilmore Quay★, SW : 15 m. by N 25 and R 739 (Saltee Islands★ - access by boat) – Enniscorthy Castle★ (County Museum★ *AC*) N : 15 m. by N 11.

▣ Mulgannon ✆ 42238.

🅩 Crescent Quay ✆ 23111 (1 March-4 November).

Dublin 88 – Kilkenny 49 – Waterford 38.

🏨 **Ferrycarrig**
Ferrycarrig Bridge, NW : 2 ¾ m. on N 11 ✆ 20999, Fax 20982
🍴, ≤, ⌖, ⌖s, 🛥 – ❙❚ rm 📺 ☎ 🅿 – 🔬 400. 🅼🅾 🅰🅴 ⑪ 𝗩𝗜𝗦𝗔. ✼
Meals (bar lunch)/dinner 23.50 **t.** ₪ 5.25 – **38 rm** ⌹ 55.00/90.00 **st.**, 1 suite – SB.

🏨 **Talbot**
Trinity St. ✆ 22566, Fax 23377
⌖, ⌖s, 🏊, squash – ❙❚ 📺 ☎ ♿ 🅿. 🅼🅾 🅰🅴 ⑪ 𝗩𝗜𝗦𝗔. ✼
Meals (carving lunch)/dinner 18.50 **st.** and a la carte ₪ 6.50 – **99 rm** ⌹ 55.00/98.00 **st.** – SB.

🏨 **Whitford House**
New Line Rd, W : 2 ¼ m. on R 733 ✆ 43444, Fax 46399
🏊, 🛥, ⌖ – 📺 ☎ 🅿. 🅼🅾 𝗩𝗜𝗦𝗔. ✼
closed 23 December-13 January – **Meals** (bar lunch)/dinner 19.50 **t.** ₪ 8.00 – **23 rm** ⌹ 27.00/70.00 **t.** – SB.

🏨 **White's**
George St. ✆ 22311, Fax 45000
⌖, ⌖s – ❙❚ 📺 ☎ 🅿 – 🔬 200. 🅼🅾 🅰🅴 ⑪ 𝗩𝗜𝗦𝗔. ✼
closed 25 December – **Meals** 18.00 **st.** (dinner) and a la carte 9.35/24.50 **st.** ₪ 5.75 – **81 rm** ⌹ 54.50/83.00 **st.**, 1 suite – SB.

🏠 **Newbay Country House**
W : 4 m. by N 25 and Clonard rd ✆ 42779, Fax 46318
🍴, ≤, 🛥, park – 🅿. 🅼🅾 𝗩𝗜𝗦𝗔. ✼
Meals *(closed Sunday and Monday)* (by arrangement) (residents only) (communal dining) (dinner only) 25.00 **st.** ₪ 6.00 – **6 rm** ⌹ 43.00/70.00 **st.**

🏠 **Slaney Manor**
Ferrycarrig, W : 3 m. on N 25 ✆ 20051, Fax 20510
🍴, 🛥, park – ❙❚ ⌖ 📺 ☎ 🅿. 🅼🅾 ⑪ 𝗩𝗜𝗦𝗔. ✼
closed December and January – **Meals** (residents only) (bar lunch)/dinner 15.00 **st.** ₪ 5.00 – **8 rm** ⌹ 38.00/70.00 **st.** – SB.

🏠 **Ardruadh Manor**
Spawell Rd ✆ 23194, Fax 23194
🍴 without rest., « Gothic style Victorian house », 🛥 – 📺 🅿. 🅼🅾 𝗩𝗜𝗦𝗔. ✼
closed 23 December-5 January – **5 rm** ⌹ 28.00/44.00 **st.**

🏠 **Farmers Kitchen**
Rosslare Rd, Drinagh, S : 2 ½ m. ✆ 43295, Fax 45827
🛥, squash – 📺 ☎ 🅿. 🅼🅾 🅰🅴 𝗩𝗜𝗦𝗔. ✼
closed Good Friday and 25 December – **Meals** (bar lunch Monday to Saturday)/dinner 15.00 **t.** and a la carte ₪ 4.75 – **11 rm** ⌹ 28.00/48.00 **t.** – SB.

🏠 **Rathaspeck Manor**
Rathaspeck, SW : 4 m. by R 733 off N 25 ✆ 42661
🍴, « Georgian country house », ▣, 🛥, ⌖ – 📺 🅿. ✼
May-6 November – **Meals** (by arrangement) (residents only) (dinner only) 14.00 **st.** ₪ 4.00 – **7 rm** ⌹ 23.00/40.00 **st.**